HOME MADE

FARINE
DE BLÉ
MÉNAGÈRE
250
2000
1500
le
lait
Tout
Simplement
demi écrémé

## USEFUL TIPS

All recipes serve 4, unless indicated otherwise.

I bake in a convection (fan-forced) oven. Baking times may be longer or shorter in other ovens. Baking times in this book are therefore provided as suggestions only. It is best to rely on your own experience with your own oven. I typically use extra-large free-range eggs. I always use free-range or, even better, organic meat, but that seems like a no-brainer to me.

TEXT, DESIGN, AND ILLUSTRATIONS: Yvette Van Boven
PHOTOGRAPHY: Oof Verschuren
EDITING: Hennie Franssen-Seebregts
TRANSLATION: Olivier De Vriese, www.dutch-translator.co.uk

First published in 2010 by Fontaine uitgevers bv, 's-Graveland, www.fontaineuitgevers.nl

Published in 2011 by Stewart, Tabori & Chang
An imprint of ABRAMS

Cataloging-in-Publication Data has been applied for and may be obtained from the Library of Congress.

ISBN: 978-1-58479-946-7

The text of this book was composed in Yvette and Adobe Garamond.

Printed and bound in New Zealand
10 9 8 7 6 5 4 3 2 1

Stewart, Tabori & Chang books are available at special discounts when purchased in quantity for premiums and promotions as well as fundraising or educational use. Special editions can also be created to specification. For details, contact specialsales@abramsbooks.com or the address below.

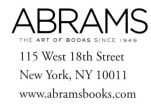

ABRAMS
THE ART OF BOOKS SINCE 1949
115 West 18th Street
New York, NY 10011
www.abramsbooks.com

To my mother Mariëtte, who encouraged me to cook
To her sister Emilie, who encouraged me to make a book
To their children, my sister Sophie, & my cousin Joris,
who encouraged me to do both.

I am no stranger to writing cookbooks. I wrote my first one when I was four years old. From then on I continued to indulge my almost morbid passion for collecting recipes and cookbooks, preferably illustrated.

It is actually odd that I ended up doing nothing with them until later, but strangely enough the idea never occurred to me. After some wanderings I did end up in the kitchen eventually. I can most often be found in my own kitchen, but I currently also work in a professional kitchen, which is completely mine. Okay, it also belongs to my cousin Joris, since I run a restaurant and catering business with him. So it turned out all right.

I have been writing and drawing recipes for numerous periodicals, websites, and newspapers for years and at some point also started doing so for our restaurant. I primarily draw inspiration from my memories, for example from my youth, which I spent in Ireland.

My mother and the women in our street made a lot of things with their own hands, out of necessity or by tradition, and my sister and I did the same. We made soda bread, biscuits, shortbread, jelly, and stew for our toy restaurant, which we built in our room or in the garden. We made ice creams, cheeses, yogurt, butterfly cakes, and ginger ale for our dolls or friends.

Fresh memories were created during summers with the Colombet family in their orchard in Provence where Oof, my husband, has been part of the family from a young age. Each time these visits resulted in a slew of family recipes. George and Jacqueline taught me to make liqueurs, nut wine, jams, and all manner of dishes from their vegetable gardens. With Norbert we built campfires each summer and we walked along the Durance, in search of fennel to grill fish over the open fire. The Colombet family took us to the *courses camarguaises*, innocent races between bulls and husky men, called *rasateurs*, and to *charettes*, fabulous traditional parades in the surrounding villages. Afterwards, we received recipes for bull meat, bohémien, and chi chi stews and we drank cold beer, pastis, and cool red wine.

Travel to Italy, our life in Paris, and working with the chefs in our restaurant, Aan de Amstel, in Amsterdam, resulted in so many memories that my collection eventually started to burst at the seams.

I had to start writing out, sorting, photographing, drawing, editing, and cataloguing the recipes. All this work resulted in this book—a book in which I aim to show you that preparing your own food is simple. I chose recipes that I am certain are easy to make; recipes that will not let you down because you do not own the right appliances. Sometimes you don't even need anything, just a little patience. I have learned to be creative and to cook with what I have available. That is what I wanted this book to be about. Do not let yourself get discouraged if there are no blueberries, just look at what is available; perhaps it is raspberry season and the fruit grows in your own backyard free of charge.

I have used things that I thought you will have in your house—an oven, a range, maybe also a food processor or hand blender, but in any case a knife and a colander, etc.

I hope that this book will encourage you to collect jam jars or beautiful bottles with matching corks, as you won't need more than those for preserving. My recipes represent a starting point to help you on your way, but I hope you will make up your own versions and create fresh memories. Be sure to invite me. Who knows, I could write another book about it.

Yvette Van Boven

Foreword

10

## RUE
## DU FAUBOURG
## SAINT MARTIN

# PATISSERIE

A L'EPID'OR

CROISSANTS

GATEAUX SECS

PAINS
FRANÇAIS

PAINS
de
GRUAU

We start the morning with strong coffee. After which we dash out the door most of the time. Without breakfast.
But if we have a day off, we fill the table. Or the floor, or the bed.
Since we are off, we prepare something we have been looking forward to for a week.
Or we allow ourselves to be seduced by our Parisian baker's window when we are out walking the dog.
Or we bake delicious bread the previous evening.

# MAKING JAM

BREAKFAST STARTS WITH HOMEMADE JAM, WHICH IS MADE IN A FLASH. YOU REALLY DON'T HAVE TO MAKE A GAZILLION JARS; SOME THREE JARS ARE ENOUGH. I WILL RUSH YOU THROUGH IT IN EIGHT STEPS. I MADE A NUMBER OF JARS LAST SUMMER WITH GEORGE WITH FRUIT FROM HIS GARDEN.

PICK THE FRUIT YOURSELF (WHATEVER IS GROWING AT THE TIME) OR PICK UP LEFTOVER FRUIT AT THE MARKET, AT THE END OF THE DAY. IF YOU ARE UNABLE TO GET FRESH FRUIT, FROZEN FRUIT ALSO WORKS WELL.

>> >> ALWAYS USE YOUR LEFTOVER FRUIT FOR JAM, AS YOU WILL WANT TO EAT YOUR GORGEOUS FRESH FRUIT.

COLLECT A MAXIMUM OF 6–7 LB OF FRUIT EACH TIME.

WASH CAREFULLY UNDER COLD RUNNING WATER.
REMOVE ANY TWIGS, LEAVES, AND STALKS.

WEIGH AND ADD APPROXIMATELY THE SAME QUANTITY OF JELLING SUGAR (OR USE GRANULATED SUGAR AND PECTIN – ADD PECTIN ACCORDING TO INSTRUCTIONS ON THE PACKAGE). CUT LARGER FRUIT INTO SMALLER CHUNKS OR CRUSH SMALL FRUIT COARSELY. THIS RELEASES THE ALL-IMPORTANT PECTIN, WHICH IS WHAT ENSURES THAT THE JAM SETS MORE EASILY. YOU CAN ALSO ADD IT SEPARATELY: PECTIN IS PRIMARILY FOUND IN APPLES AND LEMON.

BRING THE JAM TO A BOIL. ABOUT 15–30 MINUTES OF COOKING (DEPENDING ON THE TYPE OF FRUIT) IS OFTEN ENOUGH. IF YOU COOK IT FOR TOO LONG YOU WILL MAKE THE JAM MORE LIQUID.
DO THE REFRIGERATOR TEST
PLACE A TEASPOON OF JAM BRIEFLY IN THE REFRIGERATOR AND CHECK WHETHER IT HAS SET SUFFICIENTLY AFTER 5 MINUTES. YOU CAN ALSO PUREE THE JAM, BUT KEEPING IT A LITTLE CHUNKY IS ALSO AN OPTION, WHATEVER TAKES YOUR FANCY.

PLAN AHEAD FOR ENOUGH CLEAN JARS. BOIL THEM FOR 10 MINUTES IN A LARGE PAN. NEVER DRY THE JARS, BUT DRAIN THEM ON A CLEAN TOWEL. IT IS IMPORTANT THAT NO INVISIBLE MOLDS ARE LEFT BEHIND IN THE JARS, WHICH WOULD THEN LEAD TO MOLD IN THE JAM. ALSO MAKE SURE THAT THE LIDS ARE STILL INTACT, IF YOU HAVE USED THE LIDS PREVIOUSLY.

FILL THE JARS TO THE RIM USING A LARGE SPOON: (I OFTEN USE A JUG). WARNING! THE JAM WILL BE VERY HOT, SO USE GLOVES TO BE ON THE SAFE SIDE.

SCREW ON THE LIDS AND TURN THE JARS UPSIDE DOWN, ALLOWING THE HOT AIR IN THE JARS TO CREATE A VACUUM AND THE JAM TO HAVE A SHELF LIFE OF AT LEAST ONE YEAR!

AND THEN, OF COURSE, ALL THOSE STICKY UTENSILS HAVE TO BE WASHED IMMEDIATELY . . .

George

# GOOSEBERRY JAM WITH ORANGE

2 lb gooseberries (green or red)
juice and zest of 2 large oranges
4½ cups jelling sugar or use granulated sugar and pectin (add pectin according to instructions on the package)
4 clean jam jars

Wash the gooseberries, remove stems and crowns and heat, just covered with water, until soft. Add orange zest and juice and return to a boil. Add all of the sugar. Stir using a wooden spoon (a metal spoon will get too hot!) until the sugar is dissolved. Test whether the jam is setting properly: Allow a drop of jam to fall on a saucer and place in the refrigerator for 1 minute. If it has thickened nicely, the jam is ready. Quickly fill the jars and apply the lids. Tighten the lids securely and turn the jars upside down, in order for the vacuum to be created. The jam will have a shelf life of one year. After opening, store in a cool place.

# LET'S GET GOING . . .

NOW THAT YOU HAVE BEEN THROUGH THE BASICS OF MAKING JAM, YOU WILL PROBABLY WANT TO ACTUALLY MAKE SOME. I WILL START WITH A SIMPLE RED FRUIT JAM AND WILL THEN PROVIDE SOME RECIPES FOR JAMS YOU WILL NOT TYPICALLY SEE IN THE STORES (OTHERWISE YOU MIGHT AS WELL BUY THEM, OF COURSE).

## BASIC RASPBERRY JAM

*For approx. 8 x 1 cup jars*
10 cups raspberries or other red fruit
4½ cups jelling sugar or use granulated sugar and pectin (add pectin according to instructions on the package)
juice of ½ lemon

Add all ingredients to a large thick-bottomed pot. Stir well and slowly bring to a boil. Using a wooden spoon (a metal one gets too hot), crush a portion of the fruit against the side of the pot, in order to release the pectin. This is necessary for the jam to set. Allow to simmer for approx. 15 minutes. Scoop a spoonful of jam onto a saucer and briefly place in the refrigerator to test whether it sets. If not, continue to cook until it does. Using a slotted spoon, scoop the foam from the jam in the pan.
In the meantime, boil the jam jars and lids in another pot for 10 minutes. Remove them from the water using tongs and drain on a clean towel. Scoop the jam into the jars, allow to set briefly, then stir the mixture in each jar using a clean spoon, in order to spread the fruit. Tighten the lids and turn the jars upside down to cool.

## BLACKBERRY, RASPBERRY, AND BASIL JAM

*For approx. 10 x 1 cup jars*
10 cups blackberries
5 cups raspberries
⅔ cup grapefruit or orange juice
⅔ cup lime or lemon juice
7 cups jelling sugar or use granulated sugar and pectin (add pectin according to instructions on the package)
1 bunch basil

Allow the mixture, except for the basil, to cook for approx. 20 minutes. Briefly puree the jam using a hand blender and check whether it has thickened sufficiently (refrigerator test). Remove the jam from the heat, add the basil leaves, and puree the jam again. Fill the clean jars.

COVER THE LID WITH A PIECE OF FABRIC AND GIVE IT AWAY AS A PRESENT.

## PEAR AND STAR ANISE JAM

*For approx. 12 x 1 cup jars*
6½ lb peeled cubed pears
9 cups jelling sugar or use granulated sugar and pectin (add pectin according to instructions on the package)
2 handfuls of star anise
5 cups mixed raisins

Cook all ingredients for at least 1 hour on low heat until the jam is reduced and turns an attractive brown. Remove the star anise. Very briefly puree the jam using a hand blender but don't make it too smooth!

## APRICOT-ALMOND JAM

*For approx. 8 x 1 cup jars*
2½ lb apricots
4½ cups jelling sugar or use granulated sugar and pectin (add pectin according to instructions on the package)
¾ cup blanched almond halves
few drops of almond extract, as needed

Halve the apricots, remove the stones, and if necessary cut the halves into smaller chunks. Fold in the sugar and simmer for approx. 30 minutes. Do the refrigerator test to check whether the jam is thick enough. Coarsely chop the almonds and add them to the jam with the almond extract. Pour into clean jars and tighten the lids. Turn upside down to cool.

# CONFIT DE VIN

*This is actually not a jam but a jelly. After having made it once, you will be sold. Serve with a cheeseboard, for example. We also eat the confit on toast with aged cheese.*

*The type of wine you choose matters: This recipe calls for white wine, but red wine is also fine. Adjust your spices and use those that are warmer and fuller in flavor: Cloves, mandarin peel, and star anise, for example.*

*You can also vary the types of wine: A sauvignon blanc will result in a different jelly from a muscat.*

*For approx. 4 x 1 cup jars*
2 vanilla beans
1½ bottles white wine
4½ cups jelling sugar or use granulated sugar and pectin (add pectin according to instructions on the package)
6 cardamom pods
juice of 1 lemon
zest of ½ lemon
zest of ½ orange

Cut open the vanilla beans, scrape out the seeds, and combine with all other ingredients in a large pot (seeds and pods). Bring to a boil and allow to simmer for approx. 30 minutes. Check if the jelly sets properly by pouring a teaspoon onto a saucer and briefly placing it in the refrigerator. If it is nice and stiff it can be poured into clean jars. First remove the cardamom pods and vanilla beans. Tighten the lids on the jars and turn the jars upside down, allowing them to cool.

# ELDERBERRY APPLE JAM WITH BAY

*For approx. 8 x 1 cup jars*
5½ lb ripe elderberries
2 cups chopped apples
juice of 1 lemon
6 bay leaves (preferably fresh)
11 cups jelling sugar or use granulated sugar and pectin (add pectin according to instructions on the package)

Stem the berries and wash. Bring the berries to a boil in enough water to cover the bottom of a large pot. Immediately pour into a sieve and push through using a wooden spoon. Discard the peels and seeds. Return the resulting pulp together with the apple chunks, lemon juice, bay leaves to a boil and add the sugar. Allow the jam to reduce for 30 minutes. Do the refrigerator test and fill clean jars. Tighten the lids and turn upside down to cool.

# RHUBARB JAM WITH GINGER

*For approx. 8 x 1 cup jars*
2 lb rhubarb, washed and cut in lengths of approx. 1 inch
4½ cups jelling sugar or use granulated sugar and pectin (add pectin according to instructions on the package)
2½ cups water

some slices of fresh ginger
juice of 1 orange and 1 lemon
4 oz preserved ginger in syrup, in chunks

Bring all of the ingredients, except the preserved ginger to a boil. Allow to simmer for approx. 15 minutes, stirring occasionally. Add the preserved ginger and cook until clear. Do the refrigerator test, skim the foam from the surface, and pour the jam into clean jars.

# ORANGE MARMALADE WITH LAVENDER

*For approx. 8 x 1 cup jars*
2 lb oranges
1 lemon
8 cups water
9 cups jelling sugar or use granulated sugar and pectin (add pectin according to instructions on the package)
2 tbsp dried lavender flowers

Peel the oranges and lemon. Carefully cut in half and squeeze out the juice. Cut the peel into thin strips. Place the peel, juice, and water in a heavy pot and bring to a boil. Allow to gently simmer for approx. 90 minutes (or longer). Stir in the sugar until dissolved. Add the lavender and allow the mixture to cook for approx. 10 minutes. Do the refrigerator test. Leave the marmalade to stand for 30 minutes, then pour into the clean jars.

*Note: These days dried lavender can be easily bought or you can pluck it from your own garden or window box and leave it to dry for a few days.*

17

# BREAD WITHOUT WORKING THE DOUGH

BAKING YOUR OWN BREAD SEEMS DIFFICULT, BUT AFTER A MINOR INVESTIGATION HERE AT HOME AND ON THE INTERNET I CAME UP WITH A RECIPE FOR BREAD IN WHICH YOU DON'T EVEN HAVE TO WORK THE DOUGH. WELL, ONLY TEN TIMES, WHICH IS NEXT TO NOTHING. THE RESULT IS AMAZING! THE ONLY THING YOU NEED IS A LITTLE BIT OF PATIENCE. > PREPARE THE DOUGH IN THE EVENING AND BAKE THE NEXT DAY. THE BREAD IS BAKED IN A HEAVY HEAT-RESISTANT POT. PROFESSIONAL OVENS ARE FITTED WITH STEAM GENERATORS, WHICH IS WHY PROFESSIONALLY BAKED BREAD HAS SUCH A GREAT CRUST. WE HAVE ACHIEVED THE SAME EFFECT BY MAKING THE OVEN SMALLER AND BAKING THE BREAD IN A HEAVY POT. THE HOT MOIST AIR REMAINS, AND THE BREAD COMES OUT OF THE OVEN PERFECTLY. I WILL EXPLAIN IN A FEW STEPS (RECIPE ON NEXT PAGE):

COMBINE ALL INGREDIENTS . . .

IN A BOWL, AND IMMEDIATELY FORM . . .

INTO A BALL.

COVER WITH PLASTIC WRAP AND SET ASIDE FOR 8 TO 18 HOURS.

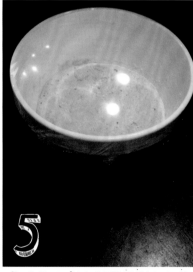

AFTER SOME 12 HOURS THIS IS WHAT IT LOOKS LIKE AT OUR HOUSE!

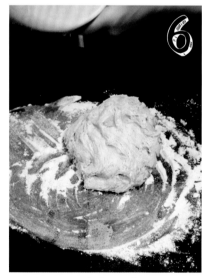

DUST THE COUNTERTOP WITH FLOUR AND REMOVE THE BALL FROM THE BOWL.

PUNCH DOWN THE DOUGH EXACTLY 10 TIMES

MOLD INTO A NICE BALL OR OVAL SHAPE

PLACE THE BALL ON A PLATE ON A LARGE SHEET OF PARCHMENT PAPER.

LOOSELY COVER WITH PLASTIC WRAP AND LEAVE TO STAND FOR 2 MORE HOURS.

SPRINKLE WITH A LITTLE FLOUR AND SCORE THE TOP.

PLACE A HEAVY POT IN THE OVEN AND PREHEAT THE OVEN WITH THE POT TO 375°F/GAS 5.
CAREFULLY LIFT THE PARCHMENT PAPER WITH THE DOUGH ON IT, PLACE IT IN THE POT, AND COVER IMMEDIATELY.

LOWER THE TEMPERATURE TO 340°F/GAS 4 AND BAKE THE BREAD FOR 30 MINUTES. REMOVE THE LID FROM THE POT AND BAKE FOR ANOTHER 20 MINUTES, APPROXIMATELY.

CONGRATS! THE BREAD TURNED OUT WELL! THAT WAS NO TROUBLE AT ALL!

# BREAD WITHOUT WORKING THE DOUGH – WELL, ALMOST

*I promised you the recipe, so here are the quantities:*

2¾ cups all-purpose flour (I used rye here)
¼ tsp yeast
2 tsp salt
1 cup water
approx. ½ cup beer
1 tbsp vinegar

See previous pages for preparation.

# LET'S GET GOING . . .

22

## COUNTRY BREAD WITH HAZELNUTS & ROASTED CUMIN

3⅓ cups whole-wheat flour
1 cup lukewarm water
dab of butter (2 tbsp)
pinch of salt
1 package yeast (2¼ tsp)
½ cup unsalted hazelnuts
4 tbsp roasted cumin seeds, plus 1 tbsp for garnish

Make the dough from the first five ingredients. Punch down for 10 minutes on a countertop dusted with flour. Allow to rise for 1 hour in a warm place covered with plastic wrap. Punch down the dough again and also fold in the nuts and cumin seeds. Shape the dough into a long ball. Grease a cake pan and place the ball in it.

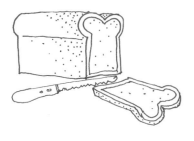

Allow to rise again for 30 minutes and in the meantime preheat the oven to 350°F/Gas 4. Wet the surface of the dough with some water and sprinkle with the remaining cumin seeds. Using a sharp knife, score the bread and bake for approx. 30 minutes. The bread is baked as soon as it makes a hollow sound when tapped. Allow the bread to cool for 5 minutes on a rack before slicing.

## TURKISH POGACA

*These are brioche-like buns, but much easier to make. You can also turn it into a large flatbread, but I often make pointed balls with it.*
*For approx. 8 buns*

2 packages yeast (5½ tsp)
5 tbsp lukewarm water
3⅓ cups all-purpose flour
pinch of salt
2 sticks butter at room temperature
2 eggs, plus 1 extra

Dissolve the yeast in the warm water and leave to stand for 10 minutes. Add the flour and salt to a large bowl and fold in the butter. Make a "well" in the flour and pour in the yeast and water. Add 2 eggs and punch down the mixture into a pliable ball. Place in a greased bowl, cover with plastic wrap, and allow to rise for 1 hour. Punch down again and divide the dough into 8 equal portions. Roll into balls and press the dough on either side between thumb and index finger to create "eye-shaped" buns. Using a sharp knife, score the top of the dough. Lay on a greased baking sheet and leave to stand for approx. 30 minutes. In the meantime preheat the oven to 400°F/Gas 6. Carefully brush the buns with beaten egg. Bake until done and golden brown, approx. 20 minutes.

## HOMEMADE FOCACCIA WITH OLIVES AND ROSEMARY

3⅓ cups all-purpose flour
1¼ cups lukewarm water
pinch of salt
2 packages yeast (5½ tsp)
1½ cups mixed olives, cut into rounds
small bunch of rosemary, needles removed from twigs and cut in half
olive oil
2 tbsp coarse sea salt (optional)

Thoroughly work in the flour, water, pinch of salt, and yeast in a bowl or food processor, at least 10 minutes, creating a smooth and pliable dough.

Fold in half of the olives and chopped rosemary. Allow the dough to rise for 1 hour in a greased bowl covered with plastic wrap. Thoroughly grease a baking pan using plenty of olive oil, punch down the dough again, and roll into a slab that more or less fits into the baking pan. Press the dough into the corners of the pan using your fingers. Do not worry about any unevenness. Cover with olives and rosemary leaves and drizzle generously with olive oil. Press everything in place using your fingers. Lastly, sprinkle some coarse sea salt on the bread and allow to rise for another 30 minutes or so. In the meantime preheat the oven to 350°F/Gas 4. Bake the focaccia until golden brown, approx. 30 minutes.

## SAFFRON BREAD WITH PISTACHIO NUTS

few strands saffron
1 package yeast (2¼ tsp)
1¼ cups lukewarm water
3⅓ cups all-purpose flour
pinch of salt
dab of butter (2 tbsp)
½ cup roasted and peeled pistachio nuts

Leave the saffron and the yeast to soak in water for 10 minutes. Combine flour, salt, and butter in a large bowl. Create a well in the middle and add the yeast, water, and pistachio nuts. Punch down thoroughly. Dust flour onto the countertop and spread the dough on it. Punch down for another 10 minutes until pliable. Add some water if it is too dry. Add some flour if it is too wet. Place the dough in a greased bowl, cover with plastic wrap, and allow to rise for another hour. Punch down the dough again and

place in the greased pan in which you plan on baking the bread. Leave to rise for another 30 minutes. Bake the bread in an oven preheated to 350°F/Gas 4. The bread is ready as soon as it sounds hollow when tapped. Great with a drink served with sausage and olives.

## THREE-COLORED PLAITED BREAD

3⅓ cups all-purpose flour
1¼ cups lukewarm water
2 tbsp olive oil
1 package yeast (2¼ tsp)
pinch of salt
2 tbsp homemade! pesto
8 sun-dried tomatoes in oil, finely chopped
2 cloves garlic, crushed

Make the dough from the first five ingredients. Thoroughly punch down for 10 minutes. Allow to rise for 1 hour in a warm place.
Punch down the dough again and divide it into three equal parts. Work the pesto through the first part. Work the finely chopped sun-dried tomatoes through the second part. Work the garlic through the last part. Roll all parts into equal "sausages" and braid them. Pinch the ends and brush the braid with a little beaten egg. Place the braid on a cookie sheet and allow

to rise for at least 30 minutes. In the meantime preheat the oven to 350°F/ Gas 4. Bake the braid until done, approx. 35 minutes. The bread must sound hollow when tapped.

## RED CHERRY AND THYME BREAD

*I sometimes make bread as follows: Partially replace the water in the recipe with red cherry juice from a can of preserved cherries in syrup.*
*Also work a handful of cherries and a little thyme through the dough.*
*The result is not a very sweet bread, but of a pretty pinkish red color and great with fresh fillings such as cottage cheese and scallions.*

9 oz can cherries in light syrup and a little water
3⅓ cups all-purpose flour
2 packages yeast (5½ tsp)
pinch of salt
small bunch of thyme, leaves stripped from the twigs

HEY THAT ISN'T A PLAIT!

YUP, IT SURE IS!

Pour the cherries through a strainer and collect the liquid in a measuring cup. Top up the fruit juice with water to 1 cup. Combine the flour, yeast, salt, and thyme in a bowl. Add the cherry syrup. Punch down the mixture into a pliable dough for at least 10 minutes. Allow to rise, covered, in a warm place for 1 hour. Punch down the dough again and fold in the cherries. Create a nice ball. Place the ball on a cookie sheet and allow to rise for at least another 30 minutes. Bake the bread until done in the lower third of an oven preheated to 350°F/Gas 4 for approx. 30 minutes. Carefully tap on the bread to hear whether it is cooked: It has to sound hollow; if it sounds dull, briefly return to the oven.

# WINTER SQUASH BUNS

*These buns are of course best while still warm, tied in a dish towel. Serve during a picnic with small portions of thyme butter, wrapped separately in waxed paper.*

7 oz winter squash, peeled, in cubes
1 tsp chile powder
1 tsp ground paprika
1 tsp grated nutmeg
pinch of salt and freshly ground pepper
2 tbsp butter
1 package yeast (2¼ tsp)
2 cups all-purpose flour
8 oz aged cheese, grated (reserve a little for the garnish)
⅔ cup milk
1 handful of pumpkin seeds to garnish, briefly roasted in a pan

Preheat the oven to 350°F/Gas 4. Grease a baking sheet with olive oil and arrange the winter squash on it. Sprinkle with the chile and ground paprika, nutmeg, salt, and pepper. Bake the squash until done, approx. 30 minutes. Leave to cool. Puree in a food processor and blend in the butter, yeast, flour, and cheese. Carefully add the milk; maybe you won't need all of it, maybe a little more, depending on the squash's moisture content. Continue to work into a pliable dough. Grease a bowl with some oil and place the dough ball in it. Cover with plastic wrap. Allow to rise for 1 hour in a warm draft-free place. Thoroughly punch down the dough again and divide into approx. 16 equal portions. Shape into balls and place on a greased cookie sheet. Loosely cover with plastic wrap and allow to rise for approx. 30 minutes. Preheat the oven to 350°F/Gas 4, brush the buns with a little water, and sprinkle with the pumpkin seeds and reserved cheese. Bake the buns until done and golden brown, approx. 30 minutes. Serve with thyme butter.

# THYME BUTTER

handful of thyme, thoroughly washed and the leaves stripped from the twigs
approx. 2 sticks butter at room temperature
1 tbsp salt flakes
freshly ground pepper

Place all ingredients in a bowl and thoroughly stir. Wrap in a sheet of plastic wrap and shape into a sausage. Place in the refrigerator for approx. 3 hours to firm. Cut the butter roll into slices and if necessary wrap individually to take out for a picnic. Store in the refrigerator.

# WHOLE-WHEAT MUESLI BALLS

3⅓ cups whole-wheat flour
1¼ cups lukewarm water
1 tsp salt
1 package yeast (2¼ tsp)
approx. ½ cup raisins or chopped dried fruit
approx. ½ cup nuts, pumpkin seeds, sunflower seeds
a mixture of crushed oat flakes and bran to garnish

Make the dough from the first four ingredients. Punch down for 10 minutes on a floured surface. Allow to rise for 1 hour in a warm place covered with plastic wrap. Punch down again and fold in the raisins or chopped dried fruit, and nuts and seeds. Divide the dough into approx. 12 balls, place on a greased cookie sheet, and cover with plastic wrap. Leave to rise for 30 minutes. Preheat the oven to 350°F/Gas 4. Wet the top of each and sprinkle with oat flakes and bran. Bake until golden brown, approx. 25 minutes.

# SMALL BUNS WITH WALNUTS AND FENNEL SEEDS IN SMALL FLOWER POTS

2 cups all-purpose flour
⅓ cup sugar
2 tsp baking powder
pinch of salt
approx. 1 stick cold butter, cubed, plus extra
2 egg yolks
approx. ⅔ cup buttermilk
⅓ cup raisins, blanched
approx. ½ cup walnuts, coarsely chopped
1 tbsp fennel seeds
1 egg, beaten with 1 tbsp. water
12 small unglazed clay flower pots

Preheat the oven to 350°F/Gas 4. Grease the flower pots with butter, dust with flour, and shake off the extra flour. Blend the flour, sugar, baking powder, and salt with the butter in a food processor until the mixture looks like coarse sand. Fold in the egg yolks and buttermilk. Remove the mixture from the food processor and blend in the raisins, walnuts, and fennel seeds. Gently punch down the dough with floured hands into a smooth ball. Then roll the ball into a long sausage. Cut the sausage in half, then cut these two pieces in half and continue cutting until you have 12 equal pieces. Quickly roll each piece into a small ball and place each ball in its own clay flower pot. Spread beaten egg on top of each ball. Bake until done and golden brown, approx. 20 minutes. Serve hot with salted butter and, if desired, with soft goat cheese.

# TASTY MINI-MUFFINS

*For 35 small muffins*

⅛ cups self-rising flour
approx. ½ stick butter
1 egg yolk
¾ cup milk
4 sun-dried tomatoes, finely chopped
½ bunch chives, finely chopped
1 tsp ground paprika
salt and freshly ground pepper

Preheat the oven to 350°F/Gas 4. Combine all ingredients in a blender into a nice batter. Fit an icing bag with a tip approx. ½ inch in diameter. If you do not own one, you can also create balls using two tablespoons. Fill paper mini muffin cups with the batter. Place cups in the cavities in a mini muffin tin; if you do not own one, use two paper cups for strength. Bake until golden brown in hot oven for 22–25 minutes.

THOSE CACTUSES ARE VERY STRANGE INDEED...

# SPINACH AND GOAT CHEESE BUTTER BUNS WITH PISTACHIO NUTS

*For six 5-oz bread molds*

1 egg
approx. ⅔ cup milk
2⅓ cups all-purpose flour
1 package yeast (2¼ tsp)
pinch of salt
approx. 2 sticks cold butter, cubed
approx. ¾ cup pistachio nuts
5 oz goat cheese
7 oz spinach

Beat the egg with the milk. In the food processor combine the flour, yeast, salt, and cold butter into coarse crumbs. Add the milk-egg mixture slowly, since you might not need all the milk, or perhaps you will need a little more. Also fold in half of the pistachio nuts. Do not beat for too long; the dough must be well blended, but not too smooth. Cover with plastic wrap and place in the refrigerator for at least 4 hours or overnight. Allow the dough to reach room temperature and thoroughly punch down for a few minutes. Divide into 6 equal balls. Grease the bread molds and place the balls in them. Sauté the spinach in a wok, squeeze out the moisture, distribute over the buns. Crumble the goat cheese over the top, as well as the remaining pistachio nuts. Allow to rise again for 90 minutes. Preheat the oven to 350°F/Gas 4 and bake until golden brown, approx. 30 minutes.

25

*Joris*

# GINGER COFFEE

YESSS → JUST MAKE COFFEE THE
OLD-FASHIONED WAY, BY HAND!

COMBINE THE
GROUND COFFEE
WITH 1 TBSP
GROUND
GINGER

POUR HOT
WATER
ONTO IT →
FOR A
STRONG
CUP!

NICE, EH? A CHANGE OF PACE! AND IF YOU DON'T LIKE
GINGER, USE CARDAMOM, CLOVES, OR ALLSPICE.
→OR EVEN MIXED SPICES OR CINNAMON!

# IRISH BROWN SODA BREAD

*For this bread you do not need yeast, and it is ready in about 30 minutes. A good recipe for a Sunday morning! While the bread is baking, boil the eggs and squeeze some oranges. Still warm from the oven and with slightly salted melted butter on top, I can easily eat an entire loaf . . .*

3⅓ cups whole-wheat flour
3⅓ cups bread flour
1 tsp salt
2 tsp baking soda
approx. 4 cups buttermilk

Preheat the oven to 400°F/Gas 6. Sieve the dry ingredients into a bowl. Add nearly all of the buttermilk to the mixture. If necessary add more buttermilk or more flour. Rapidly punch down the mixture into a smooth dough, since the acid in the buttermilk will work immediately. Working it too long will result in stiff and unleavened bread. Quickly shape into a large ball and score a large cross in the middle using a knife. Immediately bake the bread in the middle of the hot oven for approx. 30 minutes. The soda bread is ready when it sounds hollow when tapped on the bottom. If you wrap the bread in a dish towel immediately after baking, the crust will soften.

**TIP** Make white bread by replacing the whole-wheat flour with bread flour. You will probably need a little more buttermilk.

**TIP** Add a generous handful of raisins to the dough. The Irish call this bread "spotted dick."

# BISCUITS

*For 8–10 easy peasy biscuits (scones)*

3 cups all-purpose flour
2 teaspoons baking powder
⅓ cup confectioners' sugar
pinch of salt
1 stick cold butter, cubed
⅔ cup milk or buttermilk, plus more for the tops

Preheat the oven to 400°F/Gas 6—i.e., hot! Combine all ingredients, except for the milk, in a food processor or large bowl. Work the mixture briefly but thoroughly, until the butter and the flour turn into coarse grains. In Ireland they do it with two knives, in order not to warm the butter with their hands, but I really don't think this is practical. Doing it fast is best, chop, chop . . .
Add the milk and work the mixture into a smooth ball. Perhaps you will need less milk, or perhaps more. Dust the countertop with flour. Roll the ball of dough into a ¾-inch-thick slab. Cut out the biscuits, using a cutter or drinking glass. Punch down the remaining dough into a ¾-inch-thick slab and continue until all the dough is used up. Brush milk over the biscuits and place on a greased cookie sheet or on a sheet of parchment paper in the hot oven. Bake until done and golden brown, approx. 15 minutes, depending on size. Serve with jam, slightly salted butter, or unsweetened whipped cream.

*Biscuits with raspberry jam; recipe on page 16.*

# HOMEMADE MUESLI

*Making crunchy muesli is easier than you think. This recipe is for a large jar—i.e., 4 cups content. Store the muesli in a sealed jar and it will have a shelf life of about two to three months.*
*As soon as you have mastered this recipe, you can add your own favorite ingredients, since this recipe is only a start.*

4 cups regular granola (I make it up myself: In organic stores you can buy all kinds of grains, bran, crushed oat flakes, and nuts that you can blend into your own mixture)
1⅔ cups unsalted mixed nuts, walnuts, sliced almonds, pecan nuts, etc., the large nuts chopped coarsely, not too finely!
3 tbsp sunflower oil
6 tbsp honey
approx. ½ cup organic apple juice
pinch of salt
approx. ½ cup raisins

Preheat the oven to 350°F/Gas 4. Cover a cookie sheet with parchment paper and coat with a little sunflower oil.
Mix the granola and the nuts in a bowl. Beat the honey and the oil, the apple juice, and the salt, and fold into the granola.
Spread the muesli as thinly as possible on the cookie sheet and place in the oven.
Bake for approx. 25 minutes until the mixture is golden brown. Thoroughly stir the muesli every 6–7 minutes. Allow to fully cool and only then fold in the raisins.

In the restaurant we serve this with organic sheep's yogurt and lots of fresh fruit.

# CROQUE MONSIEUR

*Serves 4*

*For the béchamel*
4 teaspoons butter
approx 2 tbsp all-purpose flour
1 cup thick cream
Salt and freshly ground pepper
1 egg

*And also*
8 slices tasty bread
8 slices cured ham
8 oz Swiss cheese or Emmentaler, grated
ground paprika

Preheat the oven to 350°F/Gas 4.

First make the béchamel sauce: Melt the butter in a thick-bottomed pot. Stir in the flour and cook briefly. Stir carefully, then blend in the cream and cook until the mixture thickens. Simmer briefly while stirring. Remove from the heat, season with salt and pepper, and beat in the egg. Cover the bread slices with a thick layer of béchamel. Place them on a greased baking sheet. Cover with the ham and generously sprinkle with the grated cheese.

Place in the oven and cook for 10 minutes or until the cheese bubbles. Sprinkle with ground paprika and serve.

# WELSH RAREBIT

*Serves 4*

8 slices firm bread (preferably sourdough), toasted
4 cups grated aged cheese
5 tbsp beer
3 tbsp butter
2 tbsp spicy mustard
3⅓ cups bread crumbs
parsley to garnish

Arrange the bread slices on a cookie sheet covered with parchment paper, neatly fitting them in. Mix cheese, beer, butter, and mustard in a saucepan on low heat. Fold in the bread crumbs and blend into a thick sauce. Pour this sauce over the toast slices on the cookie sheet. Heat the broiler to its highest setting. Broil until the cheese bubbles and has light brown patches. This will happen quite quickly. Serve with a little parsley sprinkled on top.

# TOASTED CAMEMBERT SANDWICH WITH APRICOT JAM

*Serves 4*

4 slices light sourdough bread
dab of butter
4 slices Camembert
2 tbsp apricot jam

Spread the butter on the bread slices. Turn half of the slices the buttered side down and cover with the Camembert and a dab of apricot jam. Cover each with a slice of bread. Cook the sandwiches in a griddle pan or in a regular skillet. Make sure the Camembert does not run from all sides!

*Left above: Toasted camembert sandwich with apricot jam. Left below: Welsh rarebit and croque monsieur.*

# OEUF COCOTTE

*This is really nothing more than a small bowl from the oven with an egg in it that cooks in the sauce. There are endless variations, so delicious and ready in a jiffy. As a starting point, for one serving you will require:*

dab of butter
salt and freshly ground pepper
1 tbsp thick cream
1–2 tbsp filling (see below)
1 egg
chopped chives or parsley or other topping (grated cheese, for example)

Preheat the oven to 350°F/Gas 4. Grease a small ovenproof bowl with butter. Sprinkle with pepper and salt. Fill the bottom with cream and cover with filling, which can be ham, salmon, or a pre-cooked vegetable. Break the egg on it. You could also add some spices on it. Place the bowl with the egg in a gratin dish, or another shallow dish, place in the oven and pour (preferably boiling) water into the dish to halfway up the egg bowls.

Bake the egg for 10–15 minutes, or to taste. The egg white must be solid; the yolk is up to you. This is the basic recipe. Now you can make variations. On the page opposite you will see a number of variations, but you can probably think of more. Sometimes it is good to add leftovers from the previous day. Always reserve a little filling to garnish the egg. Serve your oeuf cocotte with croutons.

*Right: Various cocottes for inspiration. (Some cocottes are double.)*

## SOFT GOAT CHEESE

Replace the thick cream with goat cheese, as fresh and soft as possible. Garnish with chives.

## RATATOUILLE

Make ratatouille with 1 eggplant, 1 zucchini, and 2 tomatoes, all cubed. Pan fry for approx. 30 minutes in a generous splash of good-quality olive oil, season with salt and pepper, and possibly also some garlic. Cover the bottom of the bowl with the ratatouille and thick cream.

## CURED HAM, CURRY CREAM, AND EMMENTALER

Stir a teaspoon of curry powder through the thick cream with some salt and pepper. Cover with strips of ham, reserving some to garnish. Break the egg on top and sprinkle with a generous amount of grated Emmentaler.

## FRIED MUSHROOMS, SCALLIONS, AND PARSLEY

Pan fry some tasty mushrooms with a sliced scallion and some flat-leaf parsley in a skillet. Season with salt and pepper. Reserve some parsley to garnish.

# EGGS BENEDICT

*This dish is for the fairly experienced cook. You will need some skill, but since it tastes so good, you will make it more often and you will automatically become an expert!*

*For the hollandaise sauce*
2 egg yolks
2 tbsp water
2 tbsp white wine vinegar or lemon juice
2 sticks butter, in small pats

*And also*
8 eggs, preferably freshly laid
dash of vinegar
8 English muffins or other thick round toasted buns
8 slices fried ham, or cured side of pork, or smoked salmon (I used smoked trout here)
a few leaves of chives or parsley, chopped

First make the hollandaise sauce: Bring a large pot of water to a boil. Beat the egg yolks with the 2 tbsp water and vinegar in a metal bowl that fits into this large pot, but doesn't touch the water (in other words a double boiler). Using a whisk or hand blender begin to beat the eggs. Never stop whisking, as the eggs will set on the bottom of the bowl and you will have to start again. Lower the heat and allow the water to simmer.

After a few minutes the egg mixture will thicken considerably into a firm foam (after beating for 5 to 10 minutes). While whisking, add the butter pats, one by one. Only add the next pat of butter when the previous one has melted. It sounds like quite a fuss, but you will become quicker and it gets easier. A mayonnaise-like sauce should be the result. If it is too thick, you can dilute it by adding a few drops of hot water.

Remove the bowl from the pan, cover with lid or plate, and proceed to poach the eggs.

Again bring a pan with water and a splash of vinegar to a boil. Break an egg into a small strainer and allow the excess egg white to run through. Gently shake the strainer. Keep the water near boiling and stir a "well" into it, using a spoon. Slide the egg into the water. Allow to poach for 2 to 3 minutes and remove from the pan using a slotted spoon.

Save on a warm plate covered with aluminum foil. Continue until all eggs are poached. Once you have some practice, you can try two eggs at the same time.

Halve the muffins and toast them in the toaster or oven. Cover them with some pan fried or cured ham, or salmon (or spinach!). Place a poached egg on each muffin and generously cover with hollandaise sauce. Sprinkle with chives or parsley.

# SMOOTHIES

*All smoothie recipes are for approx. 4 glasses*

## MORNING SMOOTHIE

3 bananas

2 pints strawberries or other red fruit

2 tbsp milk

2 tsp vanilla sugar

juice of 1 lemon

Puree mixture using a hand blender.

## FOR INCREASED ENERGY

2 bananas

1⅔ cups raspberries (frozen is okay)

2 tbsp honey

6 ice cubes

Puree mixture using a food processor or blender; strain.

## AFTER A NIGHT ON THE TOWN

approx. ¾ cup raspberries

1 mango, peeled and cubed

2 blanched celery ribs, clean and in chunks

1 pear, peeled and cubed

juice of 1 lime

2 cups buttermilk

Puree mixture using a hand blender; strain if necessary because of the seeds.

## MELON & LIME SMOOTHIE

1 honeydew melon or cantaloupe, clean and in chunks

1 cup thick yogurt (Greek)

juice and zest of 2 limes

honey to taste, if desired

Puree mixture using a hand blender.

## MIXED BERRIES YOGURT SHAKE

approx. ¾ cup mixed berries (from the freezer)

2 tbsp confectioners' sugar (to taste)

1¼ cups yogurt

1¼ cups buttermilk

Puree mixture using a food processor or blender; strain if necessary because of the seeds.

## STRAWBERRIES, CURRANT & BALSAMIC SHAKE

1⅔ cups strawberries, in chunks

1 cup fresh currants, cleaned

2 tbsp ginger syrup (to taste)

1 tbsp balsamic vinegar

½ cups buttermilk

Puree mixture using a food processor or blender; strain.

## CUCUMBER & AVOCADO SMOOTHIE

2 cucumbers, peeled and in chunks

1 avocado, peeled and pitted

1 small bunch mint sprigs

a few chive sprigs

2 cups low-fat yogurt

salt and freshly ground pepper

Puree mixture using a hand blender.

## SPICY CARROT & MANGO LASSI

3 mangos, peeled and in chunks

1 carrot, grated

1 cup low-fat yogurt

10 ice cubes

⅔ cup skim milk

2 tbsp honey

1 tsp cinnamon and 1 tsp ground cardamom

Puree mixture using a hand blender.

## WATERMELON SOUP!

juice of 2 limes

1 tbsp brown sugar

1 inch ginger, peeled and finely chopped

¼ seedless watermelon, flesh only

⅔ cup orange juice

some mint leaves

Puree mixture using a hand blender.

My cousin Joris and I run a breakfast and lunch restaurant as well as a catering business in Amsterdam. It is called Aan de Amstel, which is in fact where it is located. Since we feel that Dutch people do not eat proper lunches, and often only just a cheese sandwich and an apple, we try to treat our guests to something different. It works out quite well, and most of the time we are packed for lunch. We serve our guests salads, pies, and soups that are as unexpected as possible. I have given you the recipes for a number of delicious dishes, but since our menu changes on a weekly basis, it was quite difficult to make a selection.

*Sophie*

GOOD
FOOD
SERVED
HERE!

→ APPELTAART MET 'N
VLEUG COGNAC

→ GEMBER-CHOCOLADEFUDGE

GELDEN MET KANEELROOM EN

SHAKE VAN DE
PAASDAGEN:

MANGO &
SINAASAPPEL 3,-

*Kelly*

# FRITTATA
# WITH MINT, SPINACH & PECORINO

approx. ¼ cup olive oil

1 lb spinach, washed

1 tbsp lemon juice

salt and freshly ground pepper

8 eggs

⅔ cup thick cream

1 small bunch of mint sprigs, washed and finely chopped

approx. ½ cup grated pecorino cheese

Preheat the oven to 340°F/Gas 3.

Heat a tablespoon of olive oil in a wok and fry the spinach with the water still clinging to it for a few minutes, until cooked. Add the lemon juice, stir, and season with salt and pepper. Beat the eggs with the cream, grind some pepper and salt, and fold in the mint. Grease a (preferably square) brownie baking tray or six small pans with 2 tablespoons of olive oil and cut a sheet of parchment paper to the fit the bottom. Grease. Spread the spinach on the bottom of the pan and cover with the egg mixture. Shake the pan slightly in order for the egg to even out and blend with the spinach. Generously sprinkle with pecorino and reserve a little to garnish. Bake the frittata in the middle of the hot oven for approx. 15 minutes. It is ready when the top starts turning light brown and feels firm. Leave to cool and cut in diamond or block shapes. Garnish with the reserved pecorino. Serve with a small green salad.

# OTHER FILLINGS

- Grilled winter squash, goat cheese, and sage.
- Stewed kale, pancetta, and olive oil.
- Eggplant with oregano and cheese (e.g., Taleggio, Port Salut).
- Parma ham and blanched green asparagus.
- Artichoke hearts, slices of boiled potatoes, and aged goat cheese.
- Truffle paste, slices of prosciutto (Coppa di Parma).
- Roasted zucchini and eggplant, with basil.
- Strips of salmon (raw or smoked), cilantro, and lime zest.

# TABOULEH WITH POMEGRANATE

*Eat as a main meal with white wine or a delicious rosé.*

2¼ cups coarse bulghur (available from Arab delicatessens or organic supermarkets)
11 cups fresh fava beans
2 cups green beans
4 large bunches of herbs:

       parsley (preferably flat-leaf)

       basil

       lots of mint, dill, or tarragon

2 pomegranates
juice of 2 lemons
⅔ cup high-quality olive oil
salt and freshly ground pepper

Bring 2½ cups water to a boil; add the salt and bulghur. Cook on low heat for 2 minutes and remove from heat to allow the bulghur to further simmer. Stir occasionally to loosen any grains. The grains must be nice and *al dente*. If they are still too hard, add a little boiling water; if they are too wet, put the pan back on the heat and stir until all the water has evaporated. Shell the fava beans and blanch briefly in salted water. Rinse them in cold water. Pod the fava beans again to remove the gray "skin" from the bean by making a cut in the side and squeezing out the green bean.
Blanch the green beans, rinse in cool water, and cut into three pieces.
Coarsely chop all the herbs. Cut the pomegranates into sections and fill a large bowl halfway with water. Remove the seeds from the peel under water. The bitter white pith will float and the arils (seeds) will sink. Remove the white pith from the water and drain the arils.
Once the bulghur is fluffy and fully cooled, fold in all the ingredients.
Season the salad with lemon juice, olive oil, and salt and pepper.
You can easily prepare this salad in advance. It can only get better.

# FALL SALAD WITH HAZELNUTS AND FRIED MUSHROOMS & YOGURT-NUT DRESSING

4 small artichokes, or 1 can artichoke hearts, quartered

½ lemon

4 oz mixed salad leaves

2½ oz spinach leaves

2 tbsp olive oil

2⅔ cups mixed forest mushrooms, cut up or torn

salt and freshly ground pepper

2 tbsp white wine vinegar

1 tbsp honey

2 scallions, sliced

1 tbsp hazelnuts

1 tbsp walnuts

2 teaspoons pine nuts

*For the dressing*

1 tbsp honey

½ cup white wine vinegar

½ cup yogurt

⅓ cup walnut oil or as much as needed

salt and freshly ground pepper

Cut off the tips of the fresh artichokes. Peel away the hard outer leaves. Using a sharp knife, trim away the base and stem. Rub with lemon. Cook in boiling water until done, approx. 25 minutes. Scoop from the pot and rinse in cool water. Quarter. Mix the salad with the spinach leaves and arrange over four plates. Cover with the artichoke hearts. Heat the olive oil in a skillet. Briefly pan fry the mushrooms, sprinkle with salt and pepper, and add the vinegar.

Pour a tablespoon of honey over the mixture and briefly sauté. Fold in the scallions. Spread the mushrooms over the salad. Wipe the skillet clean and swiftly toast the nuts. Sprinkle them over the salads.

Make the dressing by dissolving the honey in the vinegar and folding in the yogurt. Lastly, add the walnut oil, and beat into a nice thick dressing. Season with salt and pepper and pour over the salads.

Serve immediately with tasty bread.

# MINI FOCACCIAS WITH GOAT CHEESE, BELL PEPPER, AND JALAPEÑO

*For the focaccia*
3⅓ cups all-purpose flour
1 package dried yeast (2¼ tsp)
pinch of salt
3 tbsp olive oil
1¼ cups lukewarm water
1 tbsp coarse sea salt
3 sprigs rosemary

*For the goat cheese mix*
1 red bell pepper
4 cups soft goat cheese
a few sprigs of fresh mint and small mint leaves to garnish
4 tbsp (or more, to taste) sliced jalapeño peppers (from a jar)

First, make the dough by working all ingredients except the sea salt and rosemary into a pliable dough in a bowl. Continue to work the dough on a floured surface for approx. 10 minutes. This is necessary as all this will help the dough rise better.
Pour a dash of olive oil into a bowl and rotate the bowl so that all sides are coated with oil. Place the dough ball in the bowl and cover with plastic wrap. Put in a warm place. Allow to rise for 1 hour or until the volume has doubled.
Light one gas burner on your range and place the bell pepper on it. Allow the skin to turn black. Turn the bell pepper over every once in a while so that all sides are scorched. Place in a plastic bag and set aside for about 30 minutes. Remove the bell pepper from the bag and rub off the skin under running water. Quarter and remove the seeds. Place the bell pepper with the goat cheese, mint leaves, and jalapeño peppers in a food processor and blitz.
Remove the dough from the bowl and punch down again. Grease a baking sheet with olive oil and roll out the dough into a flat square "pizza." Use your hands to push it out further. This untidy "imprecise" aspect is part of the deal. Place the dough on the baking sheet and using your fingertips make a lot of "dents" in the dough. Sprinkle the bread with coarse salt and rosemary. Leave to stand for a half hour and bake for approx. 25 minutes, or until golden yellow, in an oven preheated to 350°F/Gas 4.
Allow the bread to slightly cool off. Cut into small 1½-inch squares and coat with the goat cheese mixture. Garnish each with a mint leaf.

# SALAD WITH LAMB WRAPS FILLED WITH GOAT CHEESE, DATES, AND SWEET-AND-SOUR CILANTRO DRESSING

53

*For the dressing*

1 small bunch of cilantro sprigs, washed and finely chopped

½ red onion, sliced

1 generous tbsp honey

1 tsp. curry powder

1 small red pepper, seeds removed and finely chopped

¼ cup red wine vinegar

⅔ cup high-quality olive oil

*For the salad*

1⅔ cups goat cheese

4 oz or 8 slices of lamb gammon or cured ham

⅔ cup dates, pitted and cut into strips

3 cups arugula

olive oil for frying

2 tbsp pine nuts, briefly roasted in a hot pan and cooled

First make the dressing by pulsing all ingredients in a food processor. The mixture can stay coarse; it does not have to be pureed smooth!

Cut the goat cheese into four equal portions. Roll the cheese in two slices of lamb gammon, once lengthways and once crossways. Distribute the arugula over four plates. Arrange the date strips on the arugula salad. Heat the olive oil in a nonstick skillet and pan fry the cheese for a few minutes on both sides, until light golden brown on the edges and relatively soft.

Place a slice on each salad, top with dressing, and sprinkle with the pine nuts.

Serve with warm Turkish bread from the oven.

LUNCH

# ZUCCHINI FLAPJACKS WITH BASIL CREAM

*For approx. 8 small flapjacks*

*For the flapjacks*
1 zucchini, washed
1 tsp. salt
2 egg whites
salt
2 tbsp cornstarch
freshly ground black pepper
¼ cup peanut oil
3 tbsp pine nuts, roasted
⅓ cup coarsely grated Parmesan cheese

*For the basil cream*
⅔ cup sour cream
¼ cup chopped fresh basil leaves
salt and freshly ground pepper
1 tbsp cold water

Grate the zucchini using a coarse grater and place in a colander. Fold in the salt and leave to stand over a bowl for 30 minutes to allow the moisture to drain. Rinse and thoroughly wring out the zucchini. Wrap the mixture in a dish towel and wring out again until it is truly "dry." Beat the egg whites until stiff with a dash of salt. Stir the cornstarch through the zucchini and generously grind pepper on the mixture. Carefully stir in the beaten egg whites. Heat a layer of oil in a nonstick skillet. Using two tablespoons, drop heaps of this mixture into the hot oil. Using the back of a spoon press against the flapjacks to make them a little flatter. Turn them over after approx. 3 minutes or when they are golden brown. Drain on paper towels and continue to pan fry until you run out of mixture.

In the meantime, make the basil cream: Blend all ingredients in a food processor; if necessary, add a tablespoon of water to make it a little thinner. Serve the flapjacks on a large plate, trickle sauce on them, and sprinkle with pine nuts and grated Parmesan cheese.

Aan de Amstel
Lunch rush

# TABOULEH WITH QUINOA, CORN, SCALLION, AND GOAT CHEESE

1¼ cups quinoa

4 fresh ears of corn or 1 large can of corn kernels

2 bunches scallions (about 6)

1 bunch flat-leaf parsley

2 small heads baby romaine lettuce

1¼ cups aged goat cheese

⅓ cup cashews

*For the dressing*

2 tbsp prepared mustard

1 clove garlic

1 tsp smoked paprika

¼ cup white wine vinegar

⅔ cup grape seed oil or sunflower oil

Cook the quinoa for 20 minutes in a large pan with salted water. Drain in a sieve and rinse thoroughly under cold running water. Leave to drain.

In the meantime, cook the ears of corn for approx. 15 minutes. Rinse under cold water and cut the kernels from the cobs. Cut the scallions into rounds; finely chop the parsley. Cut the romaine lettuce into strips and the cheese into small dice. Mix swiftly with the cashews.

Make the dressing by blitzing the mustard, garlic, paprika, and vinegar using a hand blender. Blend in the oil until a lovely dressing is obtained. If it is too thick, add some water. Pour the dressing over the salad.

# SAVORY PIE WITH SMOKED CHICKEN AND GOAT CHEESE

*I'm surprised how often I have to give out the recipe for savory pie or "quiche" to guests or friends, since I thought that by now everyone knows how to do it. But that is often not the case and that's okay. I will write it down again for you. Many people use puff pastry instead of shortcrust pastry. I'm not a great fan of it, especially since the bottom frequently remains soft. In our restaurant we often briefly turn the pie upside down and bake it for approx. 10 minutes on a baking sheet, creating a crispy bottom. This recipe is for approx. eight small pies or one large pie.*

60

*For the dough*
2 cups all-purpose flour
1¼ sticks butter, for greasing purposes
salt to taste
a few drops of cold water

*Basic mix for the filling*
3 eggs
¾ cup thick cream
salt and freshly ground pepper to taste

*This filling*
1 double-smoked chicken breast
1¼ cups goat cheese
a few sprigs of dill

Swiftly work the ingredients for the dough into a pliable ball. Add the water if the dough is too dry. Allow to rest in the refrigerator for 30 minutes. In the meantime preheat the oven to 350°F/Gas 4.
Cut the chicken into small cubes and the cheese into eight slices. Beat the eggs with the cream and season with salt and pepper. Divide the dough into eight equal parts. Grease eight quiche pans with butter and roll out the dough on a work surface dusted with flour. Cover the pans with the dough and trim the edges. Arrange the chicken and goat cheese on the pies, top with the cream mixture, and sprinkle with dill. Bake until golden brown for approx. 20 minutes.
Serve warm or cold.

## OTHER FILLINGS:

- Slice of crottin (small round goat cheese) with 1 tsp roasted fennel seeds.
- A few slices of very young zucchini, dill, and Parmesan cheese.
- Grilled winter squash, goat cheese, and spinach.
- Parma ham and blanched green asparagus.
- Gruyère and fried bacon bits.
- Leeks briefly stewed in butter, curry, and cashew nuts.
- Feta, green olives, and roasted bell pepper.
- Smoked mackerel, cream cheese, and dill.
- Parboiled broccoli, blue cheese (Roquefort!), and almonds.
- Onions stewed in butter for 30 minutes, anchovies, and fresh thyme.

# MUSSELS HORAS STYLE

*When my good friend Horas heard that I was writing mussel recipes for a magazine, he immediately gave me this recipe.*
*It was delicious and therefore I pass it on to you.*

Salt

1 bunch green asparagus

7 oz green beans

½ cup shelled fava beans and/or garden peas (frozen is okay)

4 shallots, peeled and finely chopped

2 cloves garlic, finely chopped

butter for frying and olive oil

2 cups fish broth

2 cups cream

approx. 40 mussels, or just a few handfuls

12 scallops (these can be found inexpensively today in large bags in the supermarket's frozen food section)

freshly ground pepper

Bring a pan with water to a boil. Add a pinch of salt. Trim away the bottom hard part of the asparagus and blanch for 2 minutes. Rinse under cold running water and cut diagonally in three parts. Then blanch the green beans for 2 minutes and rinse immediately under cold running water. Blanch the garden peas and lastly the fava beans. Fava beans will turn the water brown, which is why you have to cook them last. Remove the seeds from the pods, by making a small incision in the grey skin and pressing out the inner green beans. Thoroughly rinse all vegetables under cold running water to keep them green and crunchy.
Briefly pan fry the shallots with the garlic in a pat of butter. Add the fish broth and cream and reduce the liquid by half. Wash the mussels and cook them in the reduced sauce with the lid on the pot until they open up. Add the vegetables to the sauce. In the meantime briefly pan fry the scallops on both sides in a drop of olive oil and add to the mixture. Leave to heat for another minute, season as needed with salt and freshly ground pepper, and immediately arrange the warm salad on four plates. Serve with bread.

# RISOTTO FROM THE OVEN WITH SAUSAGE AND BELL PEPPER

*If you make this for an evening meal, double the quantities.*

1 tbsp olive oil

4 sausages (about 8 oz)

1 red bell pepper, cubed

1 green bell pepper, cubed

1 small onion, peeled and finely chopped

2 cloves garlic, slivered

2–3 sprigs rosemary, chopped

hot-pepper sauce to taste

⅔ cup Arborio rice

⅔ cup white wine

⅔ cup passato (smooth tomato pulp)

1 cup chicken broth

Heat the oil in a heavy skillet that can also go into the oven. Preheat the oven to 350°F/Gas 4. Cut open the skin on the sausages and crumble the meat over the hot oil in the pan. Turn over. Add the bell peppers, onion, and garlic. Sprinkle with two-thirds of the rosemary and dribble with the sauce. Pan fry the mixture while stirring for approx. 5 minutes. Fold in the rice and fry for another minute. Add the wine and stir in the passato and broth. Bring the mixture to a boil while stirring. Cover the pan with a lid and place in the oven. Bake the risotto for 18–20 minutes until done, or until all liquid is absorbed. Before serving sprinkle with the reserved rosemary. Serve with a small arugula salad.

# SALAD WITH SPELT, BARLEY, FOREST MUSHROOMS, AND BUTTERNUT SQUASH

*For the squash*

16–20 oz butternut squash

⅔ cup olive oil

1 clove garlic, crushed

2 tbsp fresh thyme

½ tsp each cumin, ground coriander, and cayenne pepper

1 tsp salt

*For the forest mushrooms*

5 cups mixed mushrooms

2 tbsp fresh thyme

2 cloves garlic, roughly chopped

1 tsp salt and freshly ground pepper

⅓ cup olive oil

*And also*

¾ cup spelt (organic store)

¾ cup barley (organic store)

⅓ cup red wine vinegar

a little fresh thyme

Peel the squash, quarter, and remove the seeds. Cut the pulp into ¾-inch chunks.

In a bowl, mix all the other ingredients and pour over the squash cubes. Stir thoroughly. Place a sheet of parchment paper on a baking sheet and arrange the squash on it. Bake the cubes in an oven preheated to 350°F/Gas 4 for 30 minutes until done or until the edges turn dark.

In the meantime, cook the spelt and barley in salted water until done approx. 40 minutes. Rinse in cool water.

Clean the mushrooms, tear or cut them roughly into pieces, and place them in an ovenproof dish. Sprinkle with all the ingredients on the list. Stir and place in the oven under the squash. The mushrooms will be ready after 8–10 minutes. Remove from the oven and leave to cool.

When all the ingredients are ready they can be loosely mixed in a large bowl including any liquid from the mushroom oven dish. Season the salad with red wine vinegar. Sprinkle with the remaining thyme leaves.

**TIP** This salad can be served lukewarm or at room temperature.

You can easily make it a day in advance.

# SALAD WITH LENTILS, APPLE, AND CILANTRO

1 cup lentils (use small greyish green [Puy] lentils that stay firm after cooking and do not become mushy)
1 whole celery, ribs washed, leaves removed (leaves can be used in soup)
2 handfuls golden raisins
2 heads Belgian endive
1 lemon
2 red crunchy apples, suitable for baking
1 bunch of cilantro, leaves pulled

*For the dressing*
1 clove garlic
⅓ cup red wine vinegar
¾ cup grape seed oil or mild olive oil
salt and freshly ground pepper

Cook the lentils in plenty of unsalted water for approx. 20 minutes until done, drain them in a colander, and rinse under cold running water. Cut the celery on a slicer, mandolin, or in the food processor, into very thin diagonal slices. Place them in a tray of ice-cold water until used, which will make them hard and crunchy. Soak the raisins in warm water, drain in a colander, and save until used. Trim away the ends of the endive, quarter, and then cut in two or three, removing the bitter core. Add the endive to the celery in the iced water, then add the juice of the lemon. Place the garlic and vinegar in a deep bowl and puree using a hand blender. While pureeing add the oil until a thick dressing develops. If necessary add a little water if the dressing is too thick and season with salt and pepper.

Cut the apple, skin and all, into thin strips. Drain the celery and endive; add the apple and lentils. Mix quickly. Stir in half of the cilantro leaves, coat with the dressing, and sprinkle the salad with the remaining cilantro leaves.

# EXTREMELY DELICIOUS DUCK BREAST SALAD WITH RICE

BOIL 300 G
(10 OZ / 1½ CUPS).
BROWN OR WILD RICE
FOR 40 MINS. (BE
CAREFUL RICE DOESN'T
DRY OUT).
ALLOW TO COOL.

RUB 2 DUCK BREASTS
WITH PEPPER & SALT
AND FRY ON BOTH
SIDES UNTIL GOLDEN
BROWN AND MEDIUM
RARE. I DO THIS IN
½ BUTTER & ½ OLIVE
OIL ⟶ SLICE!

CUT 3 SMALL GEM (COS)
LETTUCE INTO STRIPS.
COMBINE WITH THE RICE.
ADD 75 G. (3 OZ / ⅔ CUP)
HAZELNUTS,
200 G. (7 OZ / 1¼ CUPS)
RAISINS & ONE COARSLEY
CHOPPED BUNCH OF PARSLEY.

→ ARRANGE THE
SALAD ON 4
PLATES & COVER
WITH THE DUCK
SLICES.

WHISK
THE DRESSING WITH

2 CLOVES OF CRUSHED GARLIC
4 TBSP. (2 FL OZ / ¼ CUP)
WHITE WINE VINEGAR
ZEST & JUICE OF 1 LIME
PINCH OF CURRY POWDER
1 TSP CARAWAY SEEDS
2-3 TBSP APRICOT JAM
150 ML (5 FL OZ / ⅔ CUP)
OLIVE OIL &
75 ML (2½ FL OZ / ⅓ CUP)
SOUR CREAM.

# MAKING TEA

MAKING TEA IS VERY EASY AND FUN, SINCE YOU CAN MAKE UP YOUR OWN INGREDIENTS AS YOU LIKE THEM AND YOU WON'T HAVE TO DEPEND ON WHAT THEY PUT IN THOSE BOXES IN THE SUPERMARKET. YOU CAN MAKE TEA FROM FRESH PLANTS AND LEAVES, OR FROM DRIED ONES. YOU CAN ALSO MAKE TEA FROM SPICES. YOU CAN MAKE REFRESHING ICED TEA FOR A HOT SUMMER DAY OR A MEDICINAL TEA FOR YOURSELF IF YOU FEEL A LITTLE UNDER THE WEATHER. TEA IS ALWAYS GOOD, ESPECIALLY WITH CAKE, BUT THAT COMES LATER. HERE IS A STEP-BY-STEP GUIDE TO SEVERAL TEAS. I WILL START OUTDOORS, IN THE PARK OR IN THE GARDEN: MAKING TEA FROM FRESH HERBS AND PLANTS.

74

PLUCK PLANTAIN, DANDELION (WITH LEAF), NETTLES, GOLDEN RODS, HIBISCUS, HOLLYHOCK, HONEYSUCKLE BLOSSOMS,

VIOLETS, ROSE PETALS, OR ELDERBERRY BLOSSOMS. IT IS JUST LIKE MAKING MINT TEA:

PLACE YOUR OWN MIXTURE IN A GLASS OR POT. COVER WITH HOT WATER AND ALLOW TO BREW BRIEFLY. HERE: PLANTAIN-ELDERBERRY BLOSSOM TEA.

MAKE A SPICE MIXTURE—FOR EXAMPLE, CINNAMON, FENNEL SEED, AND STAR ANISE—

AND PLACE TEA IN SMALL BAGS. THESE TEA BAGS ARE AVAILABLE FROM TEA AND COFFEE STORES.

OR DRY SPICES TO ENJOY LONGER: FOR EXAMPLE, THYME, ROSEMARY, CHAMOMILE, LIME. TEATIME!

# LET'S GET GOING . . .

TEA IS HIGHLY VERSATILE. I WILL GIVE YOU A NUMBER OF TEA RECIPES THAT MAKE ME HAPPY, BUT EXPERIMENT AWAY. ALL RECIPES ARE FOR A 4-CUP TEAPOT, UNLESS INDICATED OTHERWISE.

## SAGE & LEMON TEA

*Sage can be used everywhere. It acts as an antiseptic and is therefore good for a sore throat or pain in your mouth or around your teeth. Sage calms the nervous system and also controls blood pressure and promotes digestion.*
*All the more reason to make tea!*

small sprig of fresh sage
zest of ½ lemon
1 generous tbsp honey

Bring 4 cups of water to a boil. Add the ingredients and simmer on low heat for a few minutes. Remove from the heat and allow the tea to brew for at least 20 minutes. Strain before pouring.

## LAVENDER & MINT TEA

*Lavender: Yes, you can make tea from it. Combined with mint it is delicious. Here's the recipe for fresh and dried lavender.*

2–3 tbsp fresh lavender leaves or 1–2 tbsp dried ones
small sprig of fresh mint leaves

Bring water to a boil. Pour over the herbs in a pot and allow to brew for 10 minutes. Strain into a cup, flavor with honey or sugar, as needed.

You can also strain this tea into a pot, flavor it with honey or sugar, and leave it to fully cool. Serve in tall glasses over ice cubes and with fresh mint leaves for show.

## ROSE HIP & LEMON TEA

*For this tea you will have to work a little first: Plucking and drying rose hips. The peels of a few lemons also have to be dried. However, stored in a glass jar, this tea looks very attractive! Here's a recipe that will make a considerable volume.*

4 oz dried rose hips
2 tsp dried lemon peel

Crush the rose hips in a mortar, thus releasing the seeds. Mix with the lemon peel. For one pot you will need 1 generous tablespoon of this mixture. Use a tea strainer or place the mixture in a tea bag.
Allow to brew for 10 minutes.

## THYME, VERBENA & TARRAGON TEA

*If you have access to fresh verbena, this tea is highly recommended. It also works well with dried verbena. But do use fresh tarragon and thyme.*

approx. 1 oz fresh verbena or 1 tbsp dried verbena
a few leaves of fresh tarragon
small sprig of fresh thyme

Bring 4 cups water to a boil with the herbs and remove from the heat. Allow the tea to brew for 10 minutes before pouring it. Add honey to taste. You can also sweeten the tea with honey and leave it to fully cool and serve over ice cubes on a hot day.

ANOTHER NAME FOR TARRAGON IS DRAGON'S WORT!

EUW...

# FRUIT TEA WITH CRANBERRIES & SPICES

*This tea is truly heart-warming. The longer you leave it to brew, the better. It almost tastes like lemonade.*

1½ cups fresh cranberries
2 cinnamon sticks
2 cloves
3 juniper berries
1⅓ cups sugar
2 cups orange juice
2 cups pineapple juice
juice of 1 lemon

Bring 4 cups of water to a boil with the cranberries, cinnamon sticks, cloves, juniper berries, and sugar. Stir occasionally until the sugar is dissolved and remove from the heat when all berries have burst. This only takes a few minutes. Leave to brew for a few hours. Strain and bring to a boil again. Add the juices, heat them briefly, and serve the tea in warm bowls.

# FRESH ICED TEA

*Tea for a hot summer day.*

1 handful or small bunch of fresh mint leaves
zest and juice of 1 lemon
juice of 2 limes
approx. 6 slices cucumber
honey to taste
1 tray ice cubes

Bring a kettle to a boil and pour water over the fresh mint in a heatproof glass pitcher. Leave the mint tea to slightly cool. Grate the lemon zest and squeeze, together with the limes. Stir the zest and juice through the tea. Add the cucumber slices and stir in the honey, until dissolved. Store the tea in the refrigerator to fully cool until used. Immediately before serving add half of the ice cubes to the pitcher and fill four large glasses with the other half. Pour the iced tea into the glasses through a tea strainer. You can garnish the glasses with a sprig of fresh mint and some extra cucumber slices.

# ELDERBERRY BLOSSOM TEA

*Elderberry blossom can be used in multiple ways. I will give you further recipes with elder blossoms or berries later in this book. Elder blossoms are good against colds, and they lower fever. If you pluck a lot of blossoms, dry them upside down in a dark and warm place. Dried elder blossoms are also available in organic food stores.*

*Basic tea for 4 cups*
4 umbels elder blossoms
honey or sugar, as needed

Allow the elder blossoms to brew for 10 minutes in boiled water.
As a variation on the basic tea, add mint leaves, a clove or two, 1 tbsp dried verbena, or some fresh lemon balm leaves.

# SPICY GINGER TEA

*Good for the throat and improves blood circulation.*

piece of ginger the length of your thumb
½ cinnamon stick
1 sprig of thyme
juice of 2 mandarins
freshly ground black pepper

Cut the ginger into fine slices. Pour 4 cups of water into a saucepan and add the ginger, cinnamon, and thyme. Allow to brew for approx. 20 minutes on very low heat. Squeeze the mandarins and strain the juice. Remove the tea from the heat and add the juice; flavor the tea with a little black pepper. Drink hot and flavor with high-quality honey, as needed.

# RHUBARB ICED TEA

*To be totally honest I actually did not want to include a recipe with store-bought tea to this section, but I will make an exception for this tea. A friend of my mother's gave me this recipe years ago and I have given it my own twist. Oh, so good.*

10 stalks rhubarb
3½ cups sugar
1 vanilla bean
2 star anise
4 tea bags Earl Grey tea
extra sugar (to taste)
lots of ice cubes

Wash the rhubarb and cut the stalks into sections. Place on low heat with the sugar in 4 cups water. Simmer for 2 hours on low heat until a syrup develops. Leave to fully cool. In the meantime, bring 4 cups of water to a boil. Cut the vanilla bean open lengthwise, scrape out the seeds, and add them to the water with the bean. Also add the star anise. Lastly, add the tea bags. Brew on low heat for 10 minutes and remove the tea bags.

Allow the tea to cool. Put in the refrigerator to fully cool.

Before serving, first pour the rhubarb syrup into an attractive glass pitcher. Add the tea and stir. Add extra sugar to taste. Serve with lots of ice cubes.

# FRESH CITRUS & CAMOMILE TEA WITH CATNIP

*Just like the previous recipe this one is also delicious as iced tea.*
*I bet that you had never thought of catnip, but it is delicious and readily available.*
*Catnip also cleanses the blood, which is another benefit.*

a few small leaves catnip
1 tsp camomile flowers
½ lemongrass stalk, crushed
1 tsp lemon balm
a few small leaves fresh mint

Combine all spices in a glass teapot and cover with boiling water. Allow to brew for 5 minutes and strain. If you dry all the spices first, you will need less than half. Crumble the dried spices in your hands, make a nice mix, and store sealed until used.

# gingerbread muffins

PREHEAT THE OVEN TO 200°C
(400°F / GAS 6)

COMBINE IN A BOWL:
- 125 G (4 OZ) BUTTER
- 125 G (4 OZ / APPROX ½ CUP) SUGAR
- 2 EGGS → ○ ○
- 125 G (4 OZ / APPROX 1 CUP) SELF-RAISING FLOUR
- 1 TSP VANILLA EXTRACT
- 1 TSP CINNAMON
- 1 TSP MIXED SPICE
- A PINCH OF SALT & 50 ML (1½ FL OZ / ¼ CUP) MILK

GREASE MUFFIN TRAY OR LINE WITH PAPER CASES

BAKE THE MUFFINS FOR 15-20 MINS UNTIL LIGHT BROWN. LEAVE TO COOL

MIX THE ICING IN ANOTHER BOWL

- 2 PACKS CREAMCHEESE (=250 G / 8 OZ) AT ROOMTEMPERATURE
- 375 G (13 OZ / 3 CUPS) ICING (CONFECTIONERS') SUGAR
- 1 TSP VANILLA EXTRACT
- ZEST & JUICE OF ½ LEMON

CAREFULLY SPREAD THE ICING ON YOUR MUFFINS, SPRINKLE WITH CINNAMON AND SERVE WITH A CUP OF TEA

TEA ANYONE?

# PEAR-HAZELNUT TART

*For the dough*

1⅓ cups all-purpose flour, plus some extra for rolling out the dough

½ cup sugar

1 stick butter

1 egg

pinch of salt

*For the pears*

6 cups water, or half water and half white wine

3 firm sweet dessert pears, peeled, with the stem

½ cup sugar

1 cinnamon stick

½ lemon

*For the filling*

⅔ cup hazelnuts

¼ cup sugar

2 tsp vanilla sugar

⅓ cup all-purpose flour

½ stick butter at room temperature

2 eggs

Work the dough ingredients into a nice dough and place in the refrigerator for 30 minutes wrapped in plastic wrap. Bring the water for the pears to a boil with the sugar, cinnamon stick, and squeezed ½ lemon. Poach the pears for 30 minutes. In a food processor, grind the hazelnuts and sugar into a powder. Then add the other ingredients.

Preheat the oven to 350°F/Gas 4.

Roll out the dough on a floured countertop. Use to cover a buttered 9-inch pie pan or 6 individual pie pans. First fill the bottom with the hazelnut mixture. Carefully halve the pears. Remove the cores and cut the pear halves in fan shapes, leaving the stems on. Arrange the pears on the filling with the stems facing inward. Bake the tart until golden brown, approx. 35 minutes. Smaller tarts are ready in approx. 25 minutes.

**TIP** For a shiny effect: Heat 3 tbsp apricot jam with a dash of rum, Calvados, or water. Press the jam through a sieve and brush the tart with it.

**TIP** Instead of hazelnuts you can use almonds.

# IRISH TEA BRACK

*A cake I remember well. The flavor is truly Irish. It looks a little like English Christmas pudding or those real Irish fruitcakes, also often used as the basis for those gorgeous wedding cakes with all that white frosting. But of course, those cakes contain a lot of alcohol and as children we were not allowed to eat them. Hence this more virtuous version, based on tea.*
*This recipe is for 1 cake.*

1⅔ cups boiling water

2 tea bags black tea; e.g., Ceylon or Earl Grey

3 cups mixed raisins, candied citrus, or dried semi-tropical fruit or a mixture thereof

1⅛ cups raw superfine sugar

1 egg

1 tsp mixed spices (or 1 tsp cinnamon, a pinch of nutmeg, and allspice)

1⅔ cups self-rising flour

pinch of salt

Brew strong tea with the water and tea bags. Remove the tea bags and stir in the raisins. Leave to steep, preferably for 1 day (for example, before you go to work). Preheat the oven to 340°F/Gas 3. Stir the sugar, egg, and mixed spices through the tea raisins. Lastly, fold in the flour and the salt. Stir briefly, otherwise the swollen raisins will break and the cake will not turn out well. Butter a loaf pan and cover the bottom with parchment paper cut to size. Butter. Pour the mixture into the pan and bake the cake for 90 minutes until done or until a skewer poked into it comes up dry.
Leave the cake to rest and turn out onto a board. Allow to further cool before cutting it. The cake must be a little moist and must be easy to cut. Preferably eat in thin slices and still warm, with butter.

# BANANA RUM CAKE

*A recipe from Koosjen, who used to bake delicious cakes for us at Aan de Amstel.*

*For 1 cake*

½ cup raisins

⅓ cup rum

4 ripe bananas

¾ cup walnuts or pecans, briefly toasted

1⅛ cups self-rising flour

½ tsp salt

1 stick butter, melted

⅔ cup sugar

1 tbsp vanilla sugar

2 eggs

zest and juice of 1 lemon

Heat the raisins and the rum for 1 minute in the microwave or in a small saucepan. Leave to steep for at least 1 hour, but preferably longer. Preheat the oven to 340°F/Gas 3. Cut the bananas into thick slices. Mix all ingredients swiftly into a firm batter. Butter a cake pan and cover the bottom with parchment paper cut to size. Butter. Fill with the batter. Bake the cake for approx. 1 hour. The cake is done when a skewer poked into it comes up dry.
Otherwise bake the cake a little longer. Leave the cake to rest for 5 minutes after it comes out of the oven and transfer to a rack in order to fully cool.

# CHOCOLATE-GINGER FUDGE CAKE WITH PECANS AND CINNAMON CREAM

*For the cake*

1 stick butter

8 oz semisweet chocolate, in chunks

½ cup raw superfine sugar

⅔ cup self-rising flour

½ cup grated fresh ginger

4 large eggs, beaten

*For the caramel nuts*

1½ cups pecans

dash of sunflower oil for greasing purposes

⅔ cup sugar

2 tbsp water

*For the cinnamon cream*

¾ cup thick cream

2 tbsp sugar

2 tsp cinnamon

*And also*

cocoa powder to garnish

Preheat the oven to 340°F/Gas 4. Briefly melt the butter and chocolate in the microwave or in a double boiler. Quickly mix all the cake ingredients, just until the batter is smooth. Butter an 8-inch springform pan. Cut a sheet of parchment paper to size and place it in the bottom. Butter. Pour the batter into the pan. Place the cake in the hot oven and bake for 30 minutes. The cake should not become completely dry, as in pound cake. Leave to fully cool on a rack. It will still sink a little; that is the idea. It is supposed to be a bit of a "boggy" pie. During the cooling process, make the caramel nuts.

Toast the pecans in a nonstick skillet; when they start smelling they are done. Grease a baking sheet with a dash of sunflower oil. Arrange the nuts on the tray, some distance apart. Heat the sugar and water in a heavy-bottomed saucepan, but stay close! Do not walk away, as this melting process is fast and caramel gets very hot. When the sugar starts to color around the edges, swirl the pan to ensure an even color.

Carefully trickle the caramel onto the loose nuts, making sure that each nut is covered with a layer of caramel. Leave to cool and harden. Break into pieces using a hammer or pestle.

Beat the cream with the sugar and cinnamon until thick. Dust the cake with cocoa powder. Cut the cake into wedges. Serve each wedge with a dash of cinnamon cream and sprinkle with the caramel nuts.

# DATE & LEMON RICOTTA CAKE

½ cup plain sugar

4⅓ cups ricotta

12 oz jar lemon jelly (you can also use lemon curd)

2 tsp vanilla sugar

zest of 1 lemon

⅓ cup cornstarch

6 eggs

3 cups Medjool dates (or just regular dates)

dash of Marsala wine

1⅓ cups jelling sugar or use granulated sugar and pectin (add pectin according to instructions on the package)

2 cinnamon sticks

6 cardamom pods

4 gelatin leaves (or 3 tsp powdered gelatin)


Preheat the oven to 340°F/Gas 4. Butter a 9-inch springform pan. Cut a sheet of parchment paper to size and place in the bottom. Butter. Combine the plain sugar, ricotta, lemon jelly, vanilla sugar, lemon zest, cornstarch, and eggs into a smooth batter. Pour into the pan. Bake the cake until done, approx. 1 hour. Leave to stand in the pan for 15 minutes and carefully transfer the cake to a plate to cool.

Halve the dates and remove the pits. Leave to steep in the Marsala.

In a saucepan bring the jelling sugar, ¾ cup water, the cinnamon sticks, and cardamom pods to a boil. Reduce. Add the dates and the Marsala and allow to slightly thicken. In the meantime, soak the gelatin leaves in cold water, squeeze, and stir into the warm jelly until dissolved. (Or dissolve the powdered gelatin in a small amount of warm water and then add to the jelly.) Briefly leave the jelly to cool. Using a spoon, first remove the spices and then the date halves. Arrange the dates neatly next to each other on the cake. Cover with the rest of the jelly and allow to set before slicing the cake.

# ALMOND & APPLE MUFFINS

*Recipe for 12 muffins*

1½ cups almond meal
1 cup all-purpose flour
1½ sticks butter, melted
⅔ cup superfine sugar
6 egg whites
pinch of salt
12 very small cooking apples, or 12 chunks of any apple, pear, or other fruit. Leave the peel; it looks good!

Combine all ingredients, except the apples. Butter 12 muffin cups. Distribute the batter in the cups. Press the apples into the cups and bake the muffins for 40 minutes in an oven preheated to 320°F/Gas 3 until golden brown and done.


# CHEWY CHOCOLATE RAISIN BROWNIES

*You probably are familiar with brownies, but brownies with chocolate raisins are devilishly addictive.*

1¼ sticks butter, cubed
8 oz semisweet chocolate, in chunks
2 eggs
⅔ cup plain sugar
2 tsp vanilla sugar
1⅓ cups self-rising flour, sifted
pinch of salt
1 cup chocolate-coated raisins

Preheat the oven to 340°F/Gas 3 and butter a 9-inch-square baking pan.
Melt the butter and chocolate in the microwave for 2 minutes or use a double boiler. Leave to slightly cool. Beat the eggs, the plain sugar, and the vanilla sugar into a light airy foam. Carefully fold in the melted chocolate-butter mixture. Fold in the sifted flour with a little salt. Lastly, fold in the raisins. Pour the mixture into the pan and bake the brownies for 25 minutes until done, or until a skewer poked into them comes up dry. Leave to cool and transfer to a board. Leave to fully cool and cut into equal chunks.

# ORANGE POLENTA CAKE

*For the cake*
2 oranges
juice of 1 lemon
½ cup polenta

1 tsp baking powder
1 tbsp vanilla sugar
1 cup almonds, finely ground
6 eggs
approx. 1¼ cups superfine sugar

*To garnish*
3–4 oranges
½ cup apricot jam or marmalade
2 gelatin leaves (or 1½ tsp powdered gelatin)

Preheat the oven to 350°F/Gas 4.
Cook the whole oranges for 1 hour in plenty of water. Leave to fully cool, then roughly chop, removing the seeds.
Place in a food processor and blitz with the lemon juice. Stir in the polenta, baking powder, and vanilla sugar and then the ground almonds. In another bowl, beat the eggs with the superfine sugar into a fine white foam.
Carefully fold the polenta mixture into the airy egg foam and pour into a thoroughly greased 10-inch cake pan.
Bake the cake in the hot oven for 35 minutes. Leave the cake to cool for 5 minutes and transfer to a rack to fully cool.
Peel the oranges for the garnish: Using a sharp knife, trim the top and bottom of an orange including the pith. Place the orange in front of you on the cutting board and cut the peel from top to bottom, removing all of the pith, leaving only the pulp. Cut the orange into slices. Continue until all oranges are cut.
Cover the top of your cake with overlapping orange slices.
In the meantime, soak the gelatin leaves in cold water. (Or dissolve the powdered gelatin in a small amount of warm water.) Heat the jam in a saucepan and press through a sieve. Squeeze the water out of the gelatin leaves and stir them into the hot jam until dissolved. (Or add the dissolved powdered gelatin.) Brush the oranges on the cake with the jam and allow to set.

Maxance

Pat

Mathis

*Apéro* is short for apéritif and really means pre-dinner drinks, which I learned all about in France. There things are not the same as in the Netherlands, where everyone drinks white wine or a glass of beer. In France, everyone gets their own personalized drink as an apéritif and wine is only drunk during meals. I felt I went from "country plain" to "posh Parisian." Now I have a lot of *apéros* behind me and many different and personalized mixed drinks. I learned to make a lot of apéritifs myself from my friends in Provence, since a drink sure hits the spot after a game of boules.

# DRINK

IN THIS SECTION I NOT ONLY GIVE YOU RECIPES FOR APÉRITIFS, BUT ALSO DRINKS YOU CAN SERVE WITH COFFEE AFTER A MEAL. TO MAKE THESE RECIPES YOU WILL NEED ALCOHOL, PURE ALCOHOL. IT IS NOT EASY TO FIND WHERE I LIVE IN THE NETHERLANDS, WHICH IS WHY I OFTEN REPLACE IT WITH VODKA, GIN, OR BRANDY. PAY ATTENTION TO THE ALCOHOL PERCENTAGE: THE HIGHER THE PERCENTAGE THE MORE SUGAR SYRUP OR WATER YOU HAVE TO ADD TO DILUTE IT. IT IS UP TO YOU. SHOULD YOU EVER BE IN A FRENCH SUPERMARKET, TAKE A LOOK AT THE ALCOHOL AISLE: YOU WILL FIND "ALCOOL DES FRUITS," WHICH IS 40% ALCOHOL. >FANTASTIC STUFF TO MAKE LIQUEUR AND IT COSTS NEXT TO NOTHING.

I MAKE LIQUEUR: DISTRIBUTE THE ALCOHOL AMONG SEVERAL BOTTLES. HERE I HAVE 4 CUPS 40% ALCOHOL, SO I HALVE IT, LEAVING ME WITH TWO BOTTLES THAT WILL BE 20% ALCOHOL.

ADD FLAVORING TO EACH BOTTLE. IN THIS CASE, ROSEMARY AND SPLIT VANILLA BEAN.

SEAL THE BOTTLES AND ALLOW TO STEEP IN A DARK PLACE FOR 2 WEEKS.

MAKE SYRUP: DISSOLVE 2 CUPS SUGAR IN I CUP WATER (YOU CAN USE LESS SUGAR).

POUR THE MARINATED ALCOHOL THROUGH A SIEVE OVER A LARGE PITCHER

ADD THE SYRUP AND TOP UP EACH BATCH TO 4 CUPS. IMMEDIATELY POUR INTO ATTRACTIVE BOTTLES AND SEAL.

# LET'S GET GOING . . .

SOME LIQUEURS HAVE TO STEEP FOR A LONG TIME, AND SOME CAN BE SERVED AFTER A DAY OR SO. TO THICKEN A LIQUEUR, ADD A TEASPOON OF GLYCERINE, WHICH IS AVAILABLE FROM THE PHARMACY, BUT IS ABSOLUTELY NOT A MUST. IT WORKS WELL WITHOUT IT TOO.

IN ANY GLASS
AS LONG AS
IT'S SMALL

## COFFEE LIQUEUR

*Coffee liqueur can be easily made at home, and what is great is that you can drink it the same day. It's a drink for those of us who tend to be impatient.*

*For 6 cups*
3½ cups sugar: half raw superfine and half granulated sugar
3 cups water
¾ cup very strong espresso coffee
seeds and pods of 4 vanilla beans
1⅔ cups vodka

In a saucepan, bring the sugar, water, coffee, and vanilla to a boil. Reduce for nearly 1 hour on a very low heat to a thick syrup. Allow the syrup to slightly cool. Remove the vanilla beans. Careful, they may still be hot! Swiftly add the vodka and stir into a smooth liqueur. Immediately pour through a funnel into bottles and seal. You can strain the liqueur through cheesecloth or a coffee filter if you prefer a clear liqueur.

## HAZELNUT LIQUEUR

2 cups hazelnuts
1 cup vodka
⅔ cup brandy or Cognac
seeds and pods of 2 vanilla beans
1¼ cups water
½ cup granulated sugar
½ cup raw superfine sugar

Coarsely chop the nuts (in the food processor), place in a large preserving jar, and cover with the vodka and brandy. Add the vanilla. Leave to stand for 6 weeks (yes, really!). Then strain through a sieve and then again through a coffee filter. Leave to stand for another 2 days, in order for the last residue to sink, and then strain again through a coffee filter. Heat the water with the sugars and briefly boil until the sugar is dissolved. Pour the sugar syrup into the nut drink in a bottle. Leave to cool until used.

## VERMOUTH

*This is my version of red vermouth. Do try it with white or rosé wine and add more cinnamon, for example, to taste. A tasty recipe that makes 4 cups*

juice and zest of ½ grapefruit
zest of 1 orange
1 tsp oregano, rosemary, basil, sage, and thyme (whatever you have in the house)
4 star anise

1 cinnamon stick
8 juniper berries
4 cloves
pinch of saffron
1 cup brandy, gin, or vodka
sugar: ½ cup sugar for sweet, ⅓ cup for medium-dry, or 1 tbsp for dry vermouth
1 bottle red wine

Add zests, juice, herbs, and spices to the brandy. Leave to stand for 2 weeks at room temperature to steep. Shake the bottle occasionally. After this period, pour the liquid through a coffee filter or fine strainer and add the sugar. Then add the wine. Stir to dissolve the sugar. Pour the vermouth into a 4-cup bottle and shake a little to fully dissolve the sugar. You can drink the vermouth immediately, but the longer you leave it, the more mature the flavor. Serve over lots of ice cubes and garnish with a curly orange peel.

HEY!
I ALWAYS THOUGHT THAT "VERMOUTH" WAS SPELLED WITH A TEE HA!

# VIN DE CHAMOMILE

*Chamomile wine*

1 bottle white wine
4 oz dried chamomile (from tea store)
1 cup sugar
½ cup rum
1 vanilla bean

Combine all ingredients and leave to stand in a clean preserving jar in a dark place for 14 days. Shake occasionally. Strain through a coffee filter and serve over ice cubes and garnish with a slice of lemon.

# CRANBERRY LIQUEUR

3 cups fresh cranberries
zest of ½ lemon
zest of ½ orange
1½ cups vodka
1 cinnamon stick
1 clove
¾ cup water
1⅔ cups sugar

Boil the preserving jars for 10 minutes in plenty of water and dry on a clean dish towel. You will need jars that total more than 4 cups in volume. Finely chop the cranberries in the food processor. Place in the preserving jars and add the lemon and orange zests. Add the vodka and spices. Bring the water and sugar to a boil. Add the syrup to the jars and immediately close the lids. Leave to steep in a dark place for 1 month. Shake the jars every day. Place a cheesecloth or dish towel in a strainer over a large jar. Strain the

liquid. Thoroughly wring out the cloth, removing all moisture. If necessary, again pour the liquid through a coffee filter for an attractive clear liqueur. Pour into a clean bottle. It can be drunk immediately, but you can save it for a year.

# BAY LIQUEUR

*Instead of bay leaves you can also use thyme, rosemary, or fresh mint. All very tasty!*

2 cups vodka
30 fresh bay leaves
1 cinnamon stick
zest of 1 lemon
2 cups water
1⅔ cups sugar

Combine the vodka, bay leaves, cinnamon, and lemon zest, and leave the mixture to steep in a clean container for 2 weeks. Bring the water and sugar to a boil and stir until the sugar is dissolved. Strain the bay drink and add the sugar syrup. Pour the liqueur into a bottle and leave to cool fully.

# GINGER BEER

*I call this beer (or ginger ale), since you carbonate this drink by adding yeast. It is, however, alcohol-free. And absolutely delicious!*

2-inch piece of fresh ginger
juice of 1 lemon
3 cups lukewarm water
¾ cup demarera sugar (or to taste)
¼ tsp yeast
1 clean 50-fl oz (6-cup) PET bottle

Grate the ginger to a fine pulp. Add to a bowl and stir in the lemon juice. Add a part of the lukewarm water and stir in the sugar and yeast until slightly dissolved (doesn't have to fully dissolve). Pour the mixture through a funnel into the PET bottle and add water to approx. 2 inches from the top. Leave to stand at room temperature for at least 12 hours or until the bottle feels rock-hard, which means that yeasting has taken place. Otherwise leave it a maximum of 48 hours. Immediately place the bottle in the refrigerator to cool. Be careful when unscrewing the cap! When pouring the drink you can strain it through a tea strainer. Most of the pulp will end up in the first two glasses, but it isn't disgusting, you can just drink it.

# ELDERBERRY SYRUP

*Pick elderberry blossoms in late spring. Take scissors and a large basket with you and dive in. Make enough syrup to last you to the following spring. Mixed with sparkling water this is the best-tasting drink I believe I know.*

2 oz elderberry blossoms, stems removed
½ lemon, sliced
4 cups lukewarm water
2¼ cups sugar

Place the blossom umbels in a tall clean container; add the sliced lemon. Then add the lukewarm water. Slightly press the mixture down in order for the blossoms to be fully immersed in water. Leave to stand for 24 hours in a warm and sunny place. Then strain the liquid into a large pan. Slowly bring to a boil and add the sugar. Keep on stirring until all the sugar is dissolved. Skim off and pour through a funnel into sterile jars. You can keep the syrup in the refrigerator for a few weeks. If you boil the jars for about 30 minutes in a pan of water they will have a shelf life of one year!

# LEMONADE

1 cup sugar
1 cup water
1 cup lemon juice (about 4–6 lemons)
approx. 3 cups cold sparkling water

Bring the sugar and water to a boil; stir until the sugar is dissolved. Add the lemon juice. Leave to cool. Pour the lemon juice into a large pitcher and top up with cold sparkling water. Garnish with slices of lemon and ice cubes.

# BLACKBERRY & THYME SYRUP

*You can also make raspberry, strawberry, or currant syrup.*
*I add thyme, but you can also leave it out. Or replace with basil or rosemary.*

4 cups blackberries
juice of 1 lemon
1 small bunch of thyme
2¼ cups sugar

Wash the berries and crush them in a large bowl using a masher. You can also blitz them briefly in a food processor. Place the fruit pulp in a large pan, add the lemon juice and thyme, and bring to a boil. Leave to simmer for approx. 10 minutes until the fruit is soft. Pour through a strainer into another pan. With the round side of a ladle press out all the juice. Heat the collected juice again and add the sugar. Stir until the sugar is dissolved and skim, if necessary. Pour the syrup into clean bottles.
Make a drink by pouring a bit of syrup into a glass and topping it up with fresh water. Or use in a cocktail.

# NUT WINE (BOERENPORT)

*This drink is very much like port, hence its second name. The recipe was given to me by a French farmer with whom I had become friendly and who served me this drink. Serve in tall glasses, with or without ice cubes.*
*You will need raw walnuts. Therefore the first thing you will have to do is find someone with a walnut tree in their garden. Pick the nuts when the hull or shell is still green.*

16 raw walnuts, without dents
8 cups reasonable quality red wine
2 cups Cognac
2¼ cups sugar

Quarter the nuts. Combine with the other ingredients in a sealable bucket or clean preserving jars. Leave to stand at least 3 months. Then pour through a strainer and then through a coffee filter. Pour into clean bottles ready for use.

# POMEGRANATE PROSECCO

*A great drink to welcome your guests at a party.*

approx. 1⅔ cups pomegranate juice in a carton (or juice of 4 pomegranates; see below)
1 cup sugar (to taste)
1 inch fresh ginger, sliced
1 bottle prosecco (Italian dry sparkling wine)
1 pomegranate

Make the pomegranate juice: Wear an apron; it can get a little messy! Cut the pomegranates into sections and fill a bowl halfway with water. Separate arils and pulp under water. The bitter white pulp will float to the surface and the arils (seeds) will sink to the bottom. Remove the pulp and strain the seeds from the water. You can now grind the seeds in a blender and then press the pulp with the round side of a spoon through a sieve over a bowl. If you don't own a blender, you can also push the seeds through the sieve by hand, it will only require a little more effort.
Top up the juice with water to 2 cups and place on the heat with the sugar and ginger slices. Reduce the syrup by half. Leave to fully cool and remove the ginger.

Before serving, pour a coffee spoon (to taste) of pomegranate syrup into an attractive glass. Add prosecco to fill the glass. Garnish the glass with a few loose pomegranate seeds.

# CASSIS & VERMOUTH COCKTAIL

*Use your own homemade white wine vermouth for a true homemade cocktail.*

*For 1 glass*
1 tsp crème de cassis
½ cup white vermouth
½ cup sparkling water
1 slice of lemon

First pour the crème de cassis into a glass; top up with vermouth and sparkling water. Garnish with a slice of lemon.

# CHAMPAGNE & CITRUS PUNCH

*For approx. 20 glasses*
½ cup sugar
½ cup water
2 cups juice: mix of lime, grapefruit, and orange
¾ cup Cognac
2 bottles Champagne, cava, or prosecco (or any dry sparkling wine)
leaves of 1 bunch fresh mint

Make sugar syrup with the sugar and water by heating them in a saucepan and slightly reducing. Leave to fully cool. Combine with the juices and Cognac. Place in the refrigerator until ice-cold. Before serving, pour into a large bowl (or a dash into a glass), add a lot of mint leaves, and pour plenty of Champagne over it.

# SAWASDEE KHA

*An alcohol-free cocktail, which I named after having had it in Thailand.*

*For 4 cups, or approx. 6 or 7 glasses*
8 lemongrass stalks
1-inch piece of ginger, peeled
1 carton pineapple juice, or 4 cups fresh pineapple juice (1 pineapple)
8 tbsp watermelon syrup or use grenadine syrup
maraschino cherries for a fancy garnish

Remove the outer leaves from the lemongrass. Cut the core of the lemongrass and the ginger into sections and puree with the pineapple juice in a blender. Then pour through a sieve into a tall jug. Serve the cocktail in tall glasses and pour 1 tbsp of watermelon syrup onto it. Such a posh alcohol-free drink surely has to be garnished with a cherry!

# SAVORY COCKTAIL NUTS

*Make your own cocktail nut mix—so much tastier, since the nuts are freshly toasted. I will give you mine here. Buy unsalted nuts, so you can add your own salt and spices.*

⅓ cup cashews
1 cup macadamia nuts
1 cup pumpkin seeds
1 cup Brazil nuts
1 cup peanuts
1⅓ cups raw superfine sugar
dash of chile powder (to taste)
2 tbsp butter
leaves and some sprigs thyme and/or rosemary
pinch of sea salt

Preheat the oven to 340°F/Gas 4. Arrange the nuts on a sheet of parchment paper on a baking sheet and bake until golden brown and crunchy approx. 15 minutes), turning over halfway through. Remove from the oven but leave the oven on. Heat the sugar and 3 tbsp water in a saucepan; gently shake the pan until all sugar is dissolved. Remove from the heat and stir in the chile powder, butter, herbs, and salt. Careful! It will spatter and the sugar gets very hot! Quickly fold in the nuts. Transfer them again to the baking sheet covered with the parchment paper. Arrange the nuts so that they do not touch. Bake for a few minutes in the oven until golden brown. Remove from the oven and allow to fully cool. Can be kept for at least 1 week in an airtight tin or canister.

# VITELOTTE POTATO CHIPS

*Making your own chips is extraordinarily simple. Here is the recipe for Vitelotte potato chips, as they look great too. But also try other types of waxy potatoes, or use beets, celeriac, or parsnip.*

6 Vitelotte noir potatoes (bluey-violet waxy potatoes originally from Peru), washed but not peeled
oil for deep-frying
Maldon sea salt or salt flakes

Very thinly slice the potatoes on a mandolin or in the food processor. Pat dry using paper towels. This is very important, because if there is too much moisture in the chips there will be unbelievable spattering during frying. Heat the oil to 350°F. Deep-fry only a handful of potato slices at one time and leave to drain on paper towels.
Sprinkle with sea salt before serving.

# CROSTINI

*This is a quick recipe for crostini, or just toasts. Carefully select the bread you will be using. Good sourdough bread makes a very different toast from brioche bread. You can vary the spices and garlic, or just use nothing at all. From an average baguette you will get approx. 40 thin slices of bread.*

¾ cup olive oil

salt and freshly ground pepper

garlic, oregano, thyme, rosemary, paprika, as desired or to taste

1 baguette or other bread

Combine the olive oil, salt and pepper, garlic, and any other spices. Arrange the bread slices on a baking sheet. Brush with the olive oil mixture. Bake for 5 to 10 minutes in an oven preheated to 350°F/Gas 4; turn over halfway through. Leave to fully cool before filling. Can be stored for at least 1 month in an airtight bag.

# LAVASH CRACKERS

*Make these crackers in large quantities, break into pieces on the table, and spoon dips on them. Yummy!*

pinch of yeast (a pinch between index finger and thumb)

1⅓ cups all-purpose flour

pinch of salt

1 tbsp vegetable oil

approx. ⅔ cup lukewarm water

*For the garnish:*

poppy seeds, sesame seeds, caraway seeds, paprika, cumin seeds, coarse sea salt

Dissolve the yeast in an eggshell full of lukewarm water and combine with the flour, salt, and oil. Pour the water into the mixture until a pliable dough ball is formed. Pay attention; sometimes you just need a little less water. Work the dough for at least 10 minutes on a countertop dusted with flour, or in a food processor, until smooth and silky. Leave to rise for 1 hour. Roll the dough into a thin sheet (you might have to cut it in half), place on parchment paper, and then on a greased cookie sheet. Lightly brush with water and sprinkle with seeds or salt to garnish. Do this in nice strips, for example. Bake the dough in an oven preheated to 340°F/Gas 4 for 12–15 minutes or until the crackers turn an even golden brown. Break into equal parts and serve with dips and sauces (see next page).

110

# SPICY ZUCCHINI, RICOTTA & MINT SALAD

4 zucchinis
1 small green bell pepper
dash of olive oil
1–2 cloves garlic, crushed

salt and freshly ground pepper
1 bunch fresh mint
1½ cups ricotta
juice of ½ lemon

Wash and slice the zucchinis, cut the slices into strips, and then cut into very small cubes. Halve the bell pepper and remove its seeds. Cut into thin strips. In a large pan or wok, heat the olive oil and briefly pan fry the garlic, otherwise the garlic will turn bitter. Add the zucchini and bell pepper and quickly stir. Season with salt and pepper and, when the zucchini is cooked *al dente*, transfer the mixture to a large plate to cool. Wash and finely chop the mint. Add the zucchini and ricotta to a bowl with the mint. Stir well and season with lemon juice. Serve the salad on crostini.

# APRICOT TAPENADE

1⅓ cups dried apricots, soaked
2 sprigs rosemary
½ cup olive oil

juice of ½ lemon
1 clove garlic
salt and freshly ground pepper

Blitz all the ingredients in a food processor. If necessary, add some more oil. You can keep the tapenade in the refrigerator for some time. Make sure the tapenade is always covered with a thin layer of oil. This tapenade is great on toast, as is, or with cheese or cured ham.

# FIG BUTTER

1 cup dried figs
1 tsp cinnamon
½ tsp nutmeg
Salt

Blitz the dried figs, without the hard stem, in a food processor; add the spices and a pinch of salt. Roll the mixture into a log in plastic wrap. Leave to cool in the refrigerator and cut into attractive slices.

# FAVA BEAN MINT DIP

2½ cups frozen shelled fava beans
4 tbsp grated Parmesan or pecorino
2 cloves garlic
½ cup olive oil
3 tbsp chopped mint

Cook the fava beans for 5 minutes in salted water and drain. Pod again, leaving you with nice bright green beans. Grind in a food processor with the other ingredients into a coarse pesto.

# SARDINE SALAD

4 oz can sardines
2 tomatoes, seeds and skin removed, cubed
⅓ cup mayonnaise (page 380)
¼ cup sour cream
a few sprigs of parsley, chopped
a few drops of lemon juice
salt and freshly ground pepper

Drain the sardines and remove the bones. Combine the fish and the other ingredients; season generously with pepper and a pinch of salt.

# GRILLED SWEET PEPPERS FILLED WITH GOAT CHEESE, PRESERVED IN OLIVE OIL

*Cut into thick slices these are delicious snacks with a drink. Dip the bread in the remaining oil.*

6 green, orange, and/or red pointed peppers (sweet peppers, available from Turkish stores and supermarkets)
1½ cups soft goat cheese
2 tbsp finely chopped parsley
2 tbsp finely chopped fresh oregano and a few sprigs for the jar
freshly ground black pepper
generous amount of high-quality olive oil, approx. 4 cups
3 dried peppers, or more if you love them
a few cloves garlic, peeled and blanched for 10 minutes
clean sealable jar, approx. 4 cups

Place a griddle pan on the heat. Put the peppers in it and regularly turn them over until cooked. This is a relatively fast process and takes approx. 10 minutes. Leave to cool. Trim away the stems and remove the seeds and membrane from the peppers using a sharp knife. Combine the goat cheese, parsley, and oregano; season generously with black pepper. Fill the peppers with the cheese using a small spoon. Wash your hands in between so that the peppers stay clean on the outside. Fill a deep preserving jar with the peppers and cover them with olive oil. Add the dried peppers, garlic, and a few sprigs of oregano, which will sink to the bottom.
These can be kept for more than a week or two. The flavor will become increasingly spicy.

# BLACK OLIVE MINI BLINIS WITH PINK MASCARPONE, SALMON, AND PRESERVED BEET

*You will want to make these snacks simply because they look so good. Don't you agree?*

*For the blini batter*
¾ cup pitted black olives
⅓ cup buckwheat flour (organic store)
⅓ cup all-purpose flour
1 egg
1 package dried yeast (2¼ tsp)
1 cup lukewarm low-fat milk
a pinch of salt

*For the filling*
1 small beet, parboiled
½ cup raspberry vinegar
1 tbsp honey
salt and freshly ground pepper
approx. ⅓ cup mascarpone
4 oz smoked salmon

*And also:*
butter or oil for pan frying

Grind the olives in a food processor. Add the flours, egg, and yeast. Add the milk in a trickle while stirring. Add a pinch of salt. Cover the batter with plastic wrap and leave to rise for 1 hour in a warm place.
Cut or slice the beet into very fine slices. Collect the red juice by cutting it over a bowl. Combine the vinegar and honey, season with salt and pepper, and pour over the beet slices. Set aside.
Stir the collected red juice into the mascarpone and season with salt and pepper. Heat a flapjack pan, butter the cavities, and pour a spoonful of batter into each cavity. If you don't own a flapjack pan, you can also pour small spoonfuls into a shallow skillet. You may find it easiest with a squeeze bottle if you have one available. Cook until slightly risen and done in a few minutes.
Cover the blinis with a layer of pink cream, a slice of salmon, and a slice of beet.

# DRUNKEN AVOCADO SOUP SHOT

*A small shot of soup (hot or cold) is often a fun change of pace, whenever you serve several different snacks. It is also a good way to get rid of leftover soup. Make sure to season regular soup (the one from last night), as such a small glass has to make an impression!*

*For 6–8 small shot glasses*
2 ripe avocados, quartered, peeled, and pitted
⅓ cup milk
1 cup chicken broth
juice of ½ lemon
1 diced shallot
1 tsp hot-pepper sauce (to taste)
1–2 tbsp good-quality sherry
2 tbsp sour cream, slightly beaten
some chive sprigs, finely chopped
pinch of paprika

Place the avocados in a blender or food processor and puree with the milk and broth, lemon juice, shallot, hot-pepper sauce, and sherry. Taste to check if it needs more salt and pepper and place the soup in the refrigerator to fully cool for at least 4 hours. Serve in small shot glasses topped with a teaspoon of sour cream, plenty of chives, and paprika.

# SMALL CHESTNUT SOUP

*This recipe is for approx. 6 shot glasses. If you want to make it as a main course serving 4, double the quantities and dilute with broth to the desired consistency.*

2½ oz chestnuts, vacuum-packed (peeled and cooked)
⅓ cup white vermouth
⅔ cup thick cream
⅔ cup chicken broth
salt and freshly ground pepper
2–3 small chestnut mushrooms
2 tbsp olive oil, for frying
a few drops of hazelnut oil

Cook the chestnuts for approx. 15 minutes in the vermouth, cream, and broth. Puree the soup until smooth and add salt and pepper to taste. Leave to fully cool in the refrigerator. If too thick add a little water. Before serving, thinly slice the mushrooms and briefly pan fry in a little olive oil in a nonstick skillet. Leave to drain on paper towels. Pour the cold chestnut soup into small shot glasses. Place a mushroom on each glass as well as a drop of nut oil.

# POLENTA BISCUITS WITH SAGE, GOAT CHEESE & PARMA HAM

*For at least 20 biscuits*
3 cups water
salt
¾ cup polenta
½ stick butter
3 cups crumbled goat cheese
2½ oz Parma ham, finely chopped
a few sage sprigs, finely chopped

Bring the water to a boil with a generous pinch of salt and trickle in the polenta while stirring. Lower the heat and leave the polenta to simmer for 30 minutes. Lastly, stir in the butter, goat cheese, ham, and sage, and melt the butter and cheese. Pour the polenta onto a baking sheet to cool. If you own a mini muffin tin, you can also fill these cups. Leave to fully cool for a couple of hours. Cut out rounds using a cutter. Preheat the broiler to 350°F/Gas 4 and broil the polenta biscuits for 10 minutes until golden. Serve immediately.

# POLENTA MUFFINS FILLED WITH SALMON IN CHAMPAGNE AND SQUASH PICKLES

*For the salmon*
8 oz raw salmon
1 glass Champagne or prosecco (dry sparkling wine)
salt and freshly ground pepper

*For 24 mini muffins*
⅔ cup self-rising flour
2 tbsp cornstarch
½ tsp baking powder

½ cup polenta
1½ tbsp sugar
¾ cup milk
1 egg
approx. 4 tsp melted butter

*And also*
approx. 6 tbsp butternut squash pickles
(recipe on page 162)

Place the salmon in a bowl and cover with the Champagne, sprinkle with salt and pepper. Cover with aluminum foil and place in the refrigerator until used.
Beat the muffin ingredients into a batter; lumps are allowed. Grease mini muffin cups with baking spray or oil and bake the polenta muffins in an oven preheated to 350°F/Gas 4 for 12 minutes until golden brown. Leave to cool.
Cut the salmon into thin slices. Make a deep incision in the polenta muffins and top with a slice of salmon and some squash pickles; serve immediately.

# CRAB CAKES WITH FRESH LEMON AND TOMATO MAYONNAISE

*For the crab cakes*
1 tbsp butter
1 onion, chopped
2 ribs celery, cleaned and finely chopped
1 small can of crab meat (approx. 4 oz)
2 cups fresh or dry bread crumbs, but fresh ones taste much better
½ cup crème fraîche
a few chives, finely chopped
1 egg
salt and freshly ground pepper
light oil for frying

*For the mayo*
1 egg yolk
juice and zest of 1 lemon
1 tbsp prepared spicy mustard
sufficient sunflower or maize oil approx. 2 cups)
2 tomatoes, seeds removed, peeled and cubed
pinch of cayenne pepper
salt

Melt the butter in a skillet, add the onion and celery, and cook, stirring, for approx. 4 minutes.
Leave to slightly cool on a plate. Open the crab can, drain, and shred. Blend with the onion-celery mix from the pan, half of the bread crumbs (from old bread in the food processor), the crème fraîche, the chives, and the egg. Season the mixture with salt and pepper. Roll into approx. 12 small balls. Slightly flatten and dip in remaining bread crumbs.
Heat a thin layer of oil in a nonstick skillet. Pan fry the cakes on both sides until golden brown. Drain on paper towels.
Make the mayonnaise: In the food processor beat the egg yolk, lemon juice, zest, and mustard into a foamy mixture. Add the oil in a thin trickle until it becomes a thick mayonnaise. Briefly pulse the tomato cubes and season with cayenne pepper and salt. Serve with the cakes.

# LAMB BALLS WITH SESAME & CILANTRO SALSA

*For 30 balls*
2 lb ground lamb
1 egg
3 tbsp ground cumin
2 tbsp cinnamon
2 tbsp paprika
2 tbsp prepared mustard
3 tbsp soy sauce
a little oil to grease the baking sheet
⅓ cup sesame seeds

*For the cilantro salsa*
1 large bunch cilantro, at least 2½ oz
1 red onion
1 clove garlic
2 tbsp white wine vinegar
1 generous tbsp honey
5 tbsp olive oil
salt and freshly ground pepper

Preheat the oven to 340°F/Gas 4. Combine the ground lamb with the egg, spices, mustard, and soy sauce and roll into approx. 30 balls, each the size of a walnut. Slightly grease a baking sheet with olive oil. Pour the sesame seeds into a plate and roll a few balls at the same time through the seeds until all balls end up coated with a layer of seeds. Arrange on the baking sheet and bake in the oven until done approx. 20 minutes. Pulse all ingredients for the salsa on the pulse setting on the food processor to coarsely chop the mixture. Season the salsa with salt and pepper. Serve with the hot balls.

# SHISH KEBABS WITH YOGURT SAUCE

*For the marinade*
1 tbsp cumin seeds
juice and zest of 2 limes
fresh ginger the length of your thumb, peeled and thinly sliced
1 tbsp ginger syrup
1 tbsp tamarind paste
3 tbsp olive oil
1 tsp ground cumin
1 clove garlic, crushed
salt and freshly ground pepper

*For the yogurt dip*
¾ cup yogurt
2 scallions, finely chopped
1 red bell pepper, cut lengthwise, seeds removed
salt and freshly ground pepper

*And also*
14 oz beef steak, cut into long strips
8 wooden skewers, soaked in water for 30 minutes, or metal skewers

Briefly roast the cumin seeds in a skillet until they release an aroma. Blend with the other ingredients for the marinade and add the steak. Leave to marinate for 3 hours. In the meantime, make the yogurt dip by combining the ingredients in a bowl. Set aside. Skewer the steak strips, in and out, like a simple basting stitch, if you like. Heat a griddle pan until it smokes. Sauté the steak on both sides on high heat: It can still be a little red on the inside. Serve with the yogurt dip.

Soup, yesssss! Soup is good.
There is a soup for every season . . .
Soup can make me intensely happy. The richer the better. But . . . is this actually the case?
I can't say no to a bowl of hot veal broth with fresh chervil and a poached egg, either.

*George*

# MAKING BROTH

ALL SOUPS ARE MADE ON THE BASIS OF A GOOD BROTH.

IN OUR RESTAURANT A POT OF BROTH CAN ALWAYS BE FOUND ON THE STOVE. IN YOUR HOUSE THIS IS NOT ALWAYS THE CASE, BUT IT IS WORTHWHILE TO MAKE A BATCH EVERY ONCE IN A WHILE. LEFTOVERS CAN ALWAYS BE FROZEN.

BROTH ENSURES THAT EVEN THE SIMPLEST OF SOUPS HAS MORE DEPTH, AND THEREFORE MORE FLAVOR. HERE I'M MAKING A VEAL BROTH IN OUR RESTAURANT KITCHEN TOGETHER WITH SOPHIE. FOR A RICH COLOR, WE FIRST ROAST THE BONES BEFORE MAKING THE BROTH.

ARRANGE ON A BAKING SHEET: VEAL BONES AND SHANKS, THYME, BAY, GARLIC, ONIONS WITH PEEL & TRICKLE SOME OIL OVER THE BAKING SHEET.

MIX THOROUGHLY.

PLACE IN AN OVEN PREHEATED TO 180°C (355°F / GAS 4). BAKE THE BONES UNTIL GOLDEN BROWN (APPROX. 45 MINUTES).

REMOVE FROM THE OVEN.

TRANSFER THE CONTENTS OF THE OVEN TRAY TO A LARGE POT.

WASH THE VEGETABLES: CELERY, LEEKS, CARROTS, AND PARSLEY. PREPARE THE SPICES: MACE, PEPPERCORNS, CORIANDER SEEDS.

**7** ADD ALL THE INGREDIENTS TO THE BONES IN THE PAN AND TOP UP THE PAN WITH WATER.

**8** COVER THE PAN, LEAVING THE LID AJAR AND ALLOW THE SOUP TO SIMMER ON LOW HEAT FOR AT LEAST 90 MINS.

**9** OCCASIONALLY SKIM THE TOP OF THE BROTH.

**10** PLACE A COLANDER OR STRAINER OVER ANOTHER POT AND COVER WITH A CLEAN DISH TOWEL.

**11** STRAIN THE PAN CONTENTS.

**12** VOILÀ! A CLEAR BROTH OR STOCK, WHICH YOU CAN NOW SEASON WITH A LITTLE SALT AND A DASH OF SOY SAUCE OR WORCESTERSHIRE SAUCE.

# LET'S GET GOING . . .

I WILL INCLUDE A NUMBER OF BROTHS, ENABLING YOU TO MAKE ANY KIND OF SOUP. ONCE YOU HAVE ACQUIRED A TASTE FOR IT, YOU CAN ALSO TAKE IT FURTHER: REPLACE THE VEAL BROTH WITH GAME CARCASSES FOR GAME BROTH. REPLACE THE CHICKEN WITH THE CARCASSES OF PHEASANT, PIGEON, OR PARTRIDGE FOR A GAME BIRD BROTH. REPLACE THE VEGETABLES IN VEGETABLE BROTH WITH DRIED AND FRESH MUSHROOMS FOR MUSHROOM BROTH. ADD SPICES TO TASTE.

## VEAL BROTH

*I will give you the recipe for approx. 6–8 servings of the broth I described on the previous page. You can also use beef bones, turning it into a beef broth.*

1 lb veal bones (ask the butcher)
2 veal shanks
2 onions, with the peel, halved
1 small bunch of thyme
a few bay leaves
a few cloves garlic, unpeeled
4–5 tbsp olive oil
1 rib celery, cut into three sections
2 leeks, roughly chopped and washed
1 carrot, scraped and roughly sliced
1 small bunch of parsley
3–4 blades mace
1 tbsp black peppercorns
2 tbsp coriander seeds
2 bunches chervil, chopped

Place the bones, shanks, onions, thyme, bay, and garlic in a roasting pan. Pour over a little oil and stir. Roast in an oven preheated to 350°F/Gas 4 until the bones start to color in about 30 minutes. Transfer to a large soup pot. Add at least 16 cups of water as well as the remaining ingredients. Bring the liquid to a boil. Lower the heat once it boils and let the broth to simmer on low heat.
During this time, carefully skim the foam from the broth using a skimmer. If you don't do this, the broth will become cloudy. Simmer on very low heat for approx. 3 hours until reduced by half. Strain the broth or pour through a colander in which you have placed a clean(!) dish towel. Leave to cool. Place the broth in the refrigerator. As soon as it is very cold, skim off the solidified fat. Season the broth with salt and pepper.

## CHICKEN BROTH

*This recipe is for a good-sized pot. I will just assume that you will make a little extra for the freezer. Should you wish to make less, use chicken legs and halve the ingredients.*

1 whole boiler (stewing chicken)
2 onions, with peel, halved: insert
4 cloves in the onions
½ rib celery, cut into three sections
2 leeks, roughly chopped and washed
1 carrot, scraped and roughly sliced
3 cloves garlic, unpeeled
3 bay leaves
1 small bunch of parsley and thyme
1 tbsp black peppercorns
2 tbsp coriander seeds
3–4 blades mace

Combine the ingredients in the largest pot you can find. Add at least 20–24 cups cold water and bring the liquid to a boil. Then lower the heat and allow the broth to simmer.
During this time, carefully skim the foam from the surface. If you don't do this, the broth will become cloudy. Reduce the broth by half on very low heat for approx. 3 hours. Strain or pour through a colander in which you have placed a clean(!) dish towel. Leave to cool. Place the broth in the refrigerator. Skim off the solidified fat, as soon as it is very cold. Season the broth with salt and pepper.

## FISH BROTH

approx. 3 lb fish bones
2 onions, with peel, halved
½ rib celery, cut into three sections
1 fennel bulb, quartered
1 leek, roughly chopped and washed
1 carrot, scraped and roughly sliced
3 cloves garlic, unpeeled
1 bay leaf
1 small bunch of parsley, dill, and thyme
1 tbsp black peppercorns
2 tbsp coriander seeds
3–4 blades mace
½ bottle white wine
a dash of Pernod, if desired

Combine the ingredients in the largest pot you can find. Add at least 20–24 cups cold water and bring the liquid to a boil. Then lower the heat and allow the broth to simmer. During this time, carefully skim the foam from the surface. If you don't do this, the broth will become cloudy. Reduce by half on very low heat for approx. 3 hours. Strain the broth or pour through a colander in which you have placed a clean(!) dish towel. Season the broth with salt and pepper. I personally like to add a dash of Pernod.

# VEGETABLE BROTH

*If they are available I also sometimes add turnips to the broth. The more vegetables, the better, actually.*

2 onions, with peel, halved: insert
4 cloves in the onions
1 celeriac, peeled and cubed
1 rib celery, cut into three sections
2 leeks, roughly chopped and washed
3 carrots, scraped and roughly sliced
6 cloves garlic, unpeeled
3 bay leaves
1 small bunch of parsley, rosemary, and thyme
1 tbsp black peppercorns
2 tbsp coriander seeds
3–4 blades of mace

Combine the ingredients in the largest pot you can find. Add at least 20–24 cups cold water and bring the liquid to a boil. Then lower the heat and allow the broth to simmer.
During this time, carefully skim the foam from the surface. If you don't do this, the broth will become cloudy. Reduce by half on very low heat for approx. 2 hours. Strain the broth or pour through a colander in which you

have placed a clean(!) dish towel. Leave to cool. Season the broth well with salt and pepper.

# BISQUE À MA FAÇON

*Bisque is, I believe, one of the tastiest soups ever. It involves a lot of work, but with a bit of humor you will get through it. Do not use fresh lobster for soup. You can find excellent frozen lobsters that you can use to make soup. If you can't find lobster, use shrimp shells, which also work well.*

approx. 2 lb frozen lobster(s)
4 shallots, chopped
1 leek, chopped and washed
6 cloves garlic, crushed
1 carrot, scraped and cubed
1 celeriac, peeled and cubed
3 bay leaves
a few sprigs of thyme
a few sprigs of rosemary
2 tbsp fennel seeds
2 tbsp tomato puree
¾ cup Cognac
½ bottle white vermouth (Noilly Prat)
12 cups rich fish broth
2 sticks chilled butter
cayenne pepper to taste
1 tsp paprika
salt and freshly ground pepper

If raw, briefly cook the lobster(s) in a large pan with water and salt:
Bring the water to a boil, add the lobsters, and when the water boils again, remove the lobsters. Leave to cool and remove the tail and claws from the shell. Remove the gills from the lobster; remove the meat from the tail and claws. Set the meat aside in the refrigerator and crush the remaining shell as finely as possible. I do it first with a pestle and then in the food processor. You do need a good food processor with a strong motor. Keep the appliance steady during the grinding process! Your workplace will certainly not stay clean, but you have to remember that it will be quickly tidied up.
Sauté the crushed shells in a dab of butter in a large pan. Add the vegetables, herbs, fennel seeds, and tomato puree. Stir while frying and add Cognac and vermouth. Slightly reduce the liquid. Pour in the fish broth and let the soup simmer on low heat for 2 hours. Do not boil, since it will make the soup bitter. Strain the soup through a fine sieve. Return to the pan and again bring it close to a boil. Cut the chilled butter into cubes and stir the cubes into the bisque one by one. Season with cayenne pepper, paprika, salt, and possibly some freshly ground pepper. Cut the lobster meat into small chunks and stir into the soup. Briefly heat and serve immediately.

# CREAMY CELERIAC & SAFFRON SOUP

1 onion, diced
2 tbsp olive oil
1 celeriac, peeled and cubed
a few strands of saffron
dash of white wine approx. ⅓ cup)
6 cups chicken or vegetable broth
¾ cup crème fraîche
salt and freshly ground pepper
hazelnut or walnut oil

Sauté the onion in the olive oil in a heavy-bottomed skillet. Add the celeriac and saffron, stirring occasionally. Add the white wine and broth. Allow the mixture to simmer for 25 minutes, until the celeriac is cooked. Puree the soup until smooth using a hand blender.
Fold in the crème fraîche and season the soup with salt and pepper. Reduce until it slightly thickens. Pour into attractive bowls and top with a little hazelnut or walnut oil.

## TIP FOR A CHANGE

Leave the soup to fully cool and place in the refrigerator until ice-cold. Serve cold (with drinks, for example) in small shot glasses topped with a drop of quality oil.

# RED BELL PEPPER SOUP WITH ORANGE AND TARRAGON-BASIL OIL

*This soup can be served hot in the winter or cold in the summer.*

*For the soup*
4 red bell peppers
3 tbsp olive oil
1 large onion, diced
3 cloves garlic, crushed
1 can of peeled tomatoes (14 oz)
1⅔ cups chicken or vegetable broth
zest and juice of 1 orange
salt and freshly ground pepper

*For the tarragon-basil oil*
1 bunch basil
1 bunch tarragon
sea salt to taste
⅔ cup extra-virgin olive oil

If you have a gas range, light the burners. Lay the bell peppers on the burners and scorch the peppers until black. Turn regularly. (If you do not have a gas range, it can also be done under the broiler.) Place the blackened peppers in a plastic bag and seal. In the meantime, put a large pot on the heat. Heat the olive oil and pan fry the onion. Then add the garlic and tomatoes. Pour in the broth and simmer for at least 30 minutes. Remove the peppers from the bag and peel off the skin. This is easier under running water. Remove the seeds and cut the pulp into large sections. Add to the soup in the pan and briefly puree the mixture using a hand blender. Fold in the orange zest and juice.
Taste! Season with salt and pepper.
Leave the soup to fully cool for a warm summer eve or serve hot topped with a few drops of herb oil.
For the oil, crush the herbs and salt in a mortar. Carefully add the oil and stir with the pestle into an attractive dark green oil.

# CHUNKY CHOWDER

*This typical main course soup from New England is one of my favorites: a rich, creamy soup with large chunks of fish, potato, corn, strips of cured or cooked ham, and a lot of fresh thyme and parsley.*

8 oz cured or cooked ham, in thick slices, cut into strips
2 tbsp butter
2 onions, diced
1 tbsp fresh thyme leaves
2 bay leaves
4 potatoes, peeled and diced
4 cups fish broth
2 ears of corn
salt and freshly ground pepper
2 lb cod fillet or other white fish
1 cup cream
1 bunch of flat-leaf parsley, washed and chopped

Heat a large heavy-bottomed pot and fry the ham in a spoonful of butter until golden brown. Remove from the pot and set aside. Then sauté the onions, thyme, and bay leaves in the remaining fat until glassy but not brown. Add the potatoes and fry briefly. Pour in the broth. The potatoes should be under water; if this is not the case, add some extra broth. Cut the corn kernels away from the cobs and add them to the broth. Simmer for approx. 10 minutes. Stir the pot in order for some potato cubes to break and others not. The soup must be thick, but have texture. Season the chowder well with salt and pepper. Make sure it is very well seasoned, as when the fish is added it's best not to stir the broth much. Add the fish and ham.

Cook for approx. 5 minutes. Remove from the heat and leave the soup to stand for 10 minutes. Stir in the cream and taste to check whether it needs more salt or pepper. Leave the chowder to stand for at least 1 hour.

You can also store the soup in the refrigerator until the following day. Gently heat before serving, but do not boil. First scoop chunks of fish and potato into the bowl and then top with the creamy soup. Generously sprinkle with parsley. Serve with crusty bread.

# HOT CUCUMBER SOUP WITH DEEP-FRIED PARSLEY

*You can make this soup in advance, since it first has to be cooled, allowing for the flavors to fully develop. It is, for that matter, particularly tasty when topped with small pieces of smoked eel before serving.*

6 cups vegetable broth

2 potatoes, peeled and cubed

1 onion, peeled and chopped

3 ribs of celery, cleaned and chopped

1 bay leaf and a few thyme sprigs, tied together

2 cucumbers, in coarse chunks

½ cup thick cream

½ cup milk

*And also*

1 bunch parsley

oil for frying

Heat the vegetable broth and add the potatoes, onion, celery, and bay and thyme. Let simmer for 20 minutes or until the vegetables are cooked. Remove the bay and thyme. Add the cucumbers and cook for a few minutes. Puree the soup using a hand blender. Add the cream and taste, adjust seasoning, if necessary. Leave the soup to cool until used.

Briefly deep-fry the parsley in hot oil and drain on paper towels. Careful! It will splatter quite a lot.

Heat the soup close to the boiling point, but do not boil; add the milk and beat the soup with a hand blender. Pour into bowls and serve immediately, topped with the parsley.

# SUMMER MINESTRONE FROM YOUR OWN GARDEN

*I used to have a vegetable garden and in the summer we had so many vegetables that I was at my wit's end as to what to do with them. Into the soup they went. You can use anything you have on hand. And since it is great if all the vegetables remain crunchy, this soup is actually ready in a jiffy. Excellent soup!*

3–4 tbsp olive oil
1 onion, chopped
3 cloves garlic, finely chopped
16–26 oz vegetables from your vegetable garden, from the greengrocer, or even frozen (just don't tell!): garden peas, fava beans, broccoli florets, and cubed zucchini and bell peppers
2 x 14 oz cans diced tomatoes
4 cups chicken or vegetable broth, heated
8 oz small pasta: mini penne, ditalini (small tubes), conchigliette (small shells), rotelline (small wheels)
1 can cannellini beans or white beans approx. 14 oz), or fresh from the garden, of course!
salt and freshly ground pepper
a piece of Parmesan cheese to grate over the soup, if desired

Heat the oil in a large pan and sauté the onion until light brown. Add the garlic. Then add all the vegetables that require some cooking, such as broccoli, bell pepper, and zucchini. Fry briefly and add the tomato.
Allow to cook for approx. 5 minutes and cover with the (hot) broth and pasta. Simmer the soup for 10–12 minutes, leaving the lid slightly ajar. Add the smaller vegetables. Coarsely mash the cannellini beans, leaving some of them pureed and some whole. Add to the soup. Briefly heat the soup and allow to slightly thicken. Add salt and pepper to taste.
Serve the minestrone in large bowls and top with grated Parmesan cheese, if desired. Serve with country bread and tasty olive oil for dipping.

# CREAMY CAULIFLOWER SOUP WITH STILTON

*I find cauliflower to be such an undervalued vegetable, you really should start eating it more often; it is especially worthwhile in soup. It also easily purees.*

*This velvety soup is served topped with garlic crostini, on which a little Stilton combined with crème fraîche is melted.*

1 onion, diced

2 ribs blanched celery, peeled and chopped

8 oz cauliflower, cut into florets

3 tbsp butter

2 cups veal or chicken broth

1 cup milk (reserve 2 tbsp)

1 tbsp cornstarch

2½ oz Stilton, crumbled

⅔ cup cream

salt and freshly ground pepper

*For the crostini*

1 ciabatta (Italian white loaf)

½ cup olive oil

1 clove garlic, crushed

salt and freshly ground pepper

approx. 2 oz Stilton

3 tbsp crème fraîche


Sauté the onion, celery, and cauliflower on low heat in the butter until the celery and onion are soft, approx. 10 minutes. Add the broth and milk and simmer for approx. 20 minutes on low heat until the cauliflower is fully cooked. Puree the soup until smooth using a hand blender. Combine the cornstarch with the reserved milk, add to the soup, and briefly bring to a boil. Cook for a few minutes, slightly thickening the soup. Turn down the heat, fold in the Stilton, and then the cream. Simmer on low heat until the cheese has melted. Season the soup with salt and pepper.

Meanwhile, make the crostini: Using a sharp knife, cut the bread into thin slices. Careful, the bread breaks easily. Preheat the oven to 350°F/Gas 4. Combine the oil and garlic and add generous amounts of salt and pepper. Heat in the microwave for 1 minute, or in a saucepan, allowing the garlic to infuse the oil, and pour over the bread slices. Carefully mix until all slices have absorbed some of the oil. Arrange the bread slices on an oven rack. Bake a few minutes until light brown and remove from the oven to slightly cool.

Heat the oven on the broiler setting. Crumble the Stilton and combine with the crème fraîche. Stir thoroughly and place a tablespoon of the mixture on each bread slice. Put briefly under the broiler. Place one or two crostini with melted cheese in each bowl of soup and serve immediately.

# SWEET POTATO SOUP WITH BUTTERED CASHEWS

1 onion, diced

2 leeks, washed and cut into rounds

3 sweet potatoes, peeled and cubed

2 cloves garlic, chopped

dab of butter

1 glass white wine

4 cups veal or chicken broth

1 bay leaf

pinch of cayenne pepper (to taste)

1 can chickpeas (14 oz)

a few sprigs fresh oregano

*Before serving*

4 tbsp cashews

5 tsp butter

sea salt

for each bowl, 1 tbsp crème fraîche


Braise the onion, leeks, sweet potatoes, and garlic in the butter and add the white wine. Blend in the broth as well as the bay and cayenne pepper. Simmer on low heat for 25 minutes. Remove half of the vegetables from the pan and puree the other half with a hand blender. Replace the removed vegetables and add the chickpeas and a few leaves of fresh oregano.

Serve the soup in individual large bowls each with 1 tbsp cashew nuts (briefly fried in the butter and sprinkled with a little sea salt) and a generous dollop of crème fraîche.

# Italian bread soup

This is my all-time favourite soup. The recipe was given to me by my friend Claartje and I still make it often. This is the basic recipe, just add whatever you have available or leave it as it is. → USE HIGH-QUALITY OLIVE OIL ←

Sauté 1 onion  in plenty of olive oil until soft.

Add 1 garlic clove, freshly crushed, 2 x 400 g (14 oz) cans of peeled tomatoes, a dash of vegetable stock or broth, chili to taste & 2 handfuls of old bread, cut into coarse chunks.

Gently simmer for **30** mins.

Add 1 zucchini (courgette), cubed and cook for a further 10 minutes.

Add salt & pepper to taste.

Serve in large bowls splashed with olive oil.

mamma mia!

# CREAMY SUNCHOKE SOUP WITH FRIED PARSNIP AND MUSHROOMS

*I make delicious sunchoke soup, velvety smooth, if I say so myself. Briefly sauté the sliced parsnip with salt and pepper, as well as sliced mushrooms. Serve on the soup.*

2 lb sunchokes
juice of ½ lemon
3 tbsp olive oil
2 shallots, diced
¾ cup white wine
3⅓ cups chicken or vegetable broth
⅔ cup cream
1 parsnip
5 tsp butter
1⅔ cups mixed forest mushrooms, torn into strips
salt and freshly ground pepper

Peel the sunchokes, cut in equal slices, and add the lemon juice to prevent discoloration. Heat a little oil in a large pan. Sauté the shallots, add the sunchoke, fry briefly, and add the white wine. Slightly reduce and add the broth. Allow to simmer on low heat until the sunchoke is cooked. Puree the soup until smooth using a hand blender. Add the cream and stir well. Peel the parsnip and cut into thin slices. Heat the butter and reserved olive oil in an nonstick skillet and pan fry the parsnip and mushroom slices on both sides until crunchy. Generously add salt and pepper. Pour the soup into bowls and top with the parsnip and mushrooms.

# FAST BOUILLABAISSE

*Look, I understand that real bisque is much tastier, but sometimes you just don't have the time or you don't feel like making it.*
*This recipe provides a solution. Made in no time at all and, honestly, almost as good!*

1 onion, diced

2 cloves garlic, crushed

1 fennel bulb, cleaned and diced

3 tbsp olive oil

1 small can tomato puree (6 oz)

a few strands saffron

½ cup Pernod (Cognac is also good, for that matter)

4 cups fish broth (homemade is obviously always best, but as this soup is called "fast," bought stock is fine)

2 lb fish (any white fish will do)

1 handful of mussels, cockles, and shrimp (ask the fishmonger for a mixture)

*And also*

1 baguette (preferably a little stale)

2 cloves garlic, crushed

4 tbsp mayonnaise

2 tsp harissa or 1 tbsp ketchup and a pinch of cayenne pepper (to taste)

Braise the onion, garlic, and fennel briefly in the olive oil until the onion turns glassy. Add the tomato puree and saffron.
Keep stirring until the tomato puree begins giving off a sweetish aroma. Add the Pernod and the fish stock and simmer for
20 minutes. Five minutes before the end, add the fish and shellfish and cook in the soup until done.

In the meantime, make the "rouille" and the croutons: Preheat the oven to 350°F/Gas 4. Cut the baguette into thin slices
and arrange on a baking sheet. Bake the croutons until golden brown, approx. 5–6 minutes. Turn them over halfway through
the process.

Grind approx. 6 croutons in the food processor. Fold in the garlic, mayonnaise, and harissa and blend into a smooth sauce.
First transfer the fish from the soup into 4 bowls and then cover with the soup. Serve with the rouille and the croutons.

*150*

# FOAMY GARDEN PEA SOUP WITH BASIL AND AVOCADO CREAM

2 cups organic garden peas (frozen is okay, but preferably fresh!)
4 cups chicken or vegetable broth
2 to 3 scallions, chopped
1 bunch of basil
1 avocado
1 small clove garlic, crushed
½ cup crème fraîche
salt and freshly ground pepper

Cook the garden peas with the broth. Simmer for 15 minutes. Add the scallions and half of the basil. Puree the soup for approx. 6 minutes using a hand blender. Continue until the soup is nice and smooth. Puree the avocado, garlic, and the reserved basil in a food processor. Reserve a few basil leaves to garnish. Fold in the crème fraîche and season the avocado cream with salt and pepper. Transfer the soup to four plates. With an ice-cream scoop place a dollop of avocado cream in the middle of each plate and garnish with torn basil leaves.

# IRISH OYSTER SOUP WITH MUSSELS AND SAMPHIRE

*Ah, as a true Irish woman I didn't want to keep an oyster soup recipe from you.*
*I also add mussels, but you can leave them out and add an entire crate of oysters, if you wish.*
*Eat the soup on St. Patrick's Day, or, actually, any other day.*

2 shallots, chopped

2 tbsp butter

2 cloves garlic, chopped

2 tbsp all-purpose flour

1 bottle beer (not dark beer)

2 tbsp smooth or grainy mustard

3 cups fish broth

⅔ cup cream

2 waxy potatoes, peeled and cubed

1 carrot, peeled and cubed

7 oz green mussels, cooked, without shell (from the fishmonger)

7 oz samphire (glasswort/seabean)

12 oysters or more (shucked)

2 tbsp finely chopped chives

salt and freshly ground pepper

In a heavy-bottomed pot, braise the shallots in the butter and add the garlic when the shallots have turned a golden brown. Sauté for a minute and add the flour. Continue to stir until the flour has absorbed all of the butter. Slowly add the beer and stir until the mixture thickens. Fold in the mustard, followed by the broth and cream. Add the potatoes and carrot, bring the soup to a boil, turn the heat to low, and simmer for 30 minutes. Then add the mussels and heat thoroughly. You can keep the soup in the refrigerator until served.

Heat the soup again before serving. Add the samphire, and heat briefly. Open/shuck the oysters (if necessary) and poach in the hot soup for 1 minute before serving. Immediately serve the soup, sprinkled with the chives and pepper.

# PRESERVING VEGETABLES

PEOPLE USED TO PRESERVE FRUIT AND VEGETABLES IN ORDER TO BE ABLE TO ENJOY THEM THROUGHOUT THE WINTER. CURRENTLY THIS FORM OF PRESERVING IS ONCE AGAIN IN VOGUE. PROBABLY BECAUSE WE LIKE TO KNOW WHAT WE EAT, WE FIND IT IMPORTANT TO KNOW WHERE OUR FOOD COMES FROM AND NO LONGER WANT ARTIFICIAL ADDITIVES. BUT IT IS ALSO JUST FUN TO DO AND OFTEN NOT ALL THAT MUCH WORK. THERE ARE MANY DIFFERENT WAYS OF PRESERVING: YOU CAN PICKLE VEGETABLES, PRESERVE FRUIT IN ALCOHOL, MAKE CHUTNEYS AND JAMS, OR BOTTLE. > WHEN YOU COOK THE JARS WITH THEIR CONTENTS FOR A WHILE, IMMERSED IN WATER, YOU CREATE A VACUUM. THEREFORE ALWAYS WORK WITH PRESERVING JARS (YOU KNOW, THE ONES WITH THAT RUBBER RING), OTHERWISE THE JAR WILL BURST. > A JAR OF PRESERVED VEGETABLES CAN BE KEPT FOR ONE YEAR IN A DARK COOL PLACE.

156

TO PRESERVE CAULIFLOWER: I CAULIFLOWER, SALT, I TBSP CURRY POWER, MUSTARD SEEDS, PEPPER, I RED ONION, AND ½ LEMON.

CLEAN THE CAULIFLOWER, WASH, AND CUT INTO FLORETS.

BRING A PAN OF WATER TO A BOIL AND BLANCH THE CAULIFLOWER FOR 4 MINUTES.

FILL A LARGE BOWL WITH ICE CUBES AND WATER.

LEAVE THE BLANCHED CAULIFLOWER TO COOL IN IT.

PEEL THE ONION AND CUT INTO ROUNDS.

7

FILL THE JARS WITH ONION AND CAULIFLO-
WER, AND SQUEEZE IN THE LEMON JUICE.

8

FILL A PITCHER WITH APPROX. 4 CUPS
BOILING WATER.

9

SEASON WITH THE CURRY POWDER AND
1 TSP SALT PER 4 CUPS WATER.

10

PUT THE MUSTARD SEEDS AND PEPPER-
CORNS IN THE JARS.

11

IF DESIRED, ADD A BAY LEAF AND COVER
WITH THE LIQUID.

12

CAREFULLY SEAL THE LID.

13

FILL A PAN WITH WATER. PLACE THE JARS
IN IT. THEY NEED TO BE IMMERSED.

14

COOK FOR SOME 45 MINUTES AND DO
THE VACUUM TEST:

15

IF THE RING IS STUCK, IT'S A SUCCESS!
COOL AND REFRIGERATE.

# LET'S GET GOING

158

## PICKLED CUCUMBER

*You will find fresh Kirby cucumbers in the summer in organic food stores. This recipe is for 2 lb vegetables.*

2 lb Kirby (small pickling) cucumbers
plenty of salt
a few sprigs of dill
2 cups vinegar
2 cups water
1⅔ cups sugar
4 cloves
1 tbsp caraway seeds
12 peppercorns
2 bay leaves

Place the cucumbers in a baking pan and generously rub them with salt. Leave to stand in a cool place for 24 hours. Wash them thoroughly. The salt is necessary to slightly strengthen the peel and ensure that the pulp is firm and well seasoned. Quarter the cucumbers lengthwise. Then cut to size, to fit nicely in the jars. Insert the dill sprigs.
Bring the vinegar, water, sugar, and all spices to a boil. Reduce for 10 minutes and cover the cucumbers in the jar with the liquid. Seal the lid. Cover the jars of pickled cucumber for 20 minutes in a pot of boiling water and boil.

## PRESERVED LEMONS

*For approx. 2 preserving jars (4–6 cups)*

12 organic lemons (unsprayed and without wax coating)
1¼ cups lemon juice
boiling water and plenty of sea salt

Thoroughly wash the lemons, then generously rub them with salt and divide them between the jars. Sprinkle 3 tbsp salt over each jar of lemons. Distribute the lemon juice over both jars and top up with boiling water. Seal the jars and leave to rest in a dark place for 2 to 4 weeks. Thoroughly rinse the lemons before use.
Use the preserved lemons in stewed dishes; in Arab cuisine it is an essential ingredient. The peel cut into strips is also very good in salads or with chicken. The lemon water remaining in the jar is tasty as flavoring for your dressings!

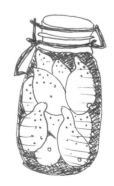

## CRANBERRY, WALNUT & PEAR CHUTNEY

*Almost any fruit and vegetable is fine in a chutney. This chutney can be kept for approx. three months. After filling, turn the jars upside down to allow them to create a vacuum.*
*(You have no doubt read the section on jam making.)*

*This recipe is for 4 x 1-cup jars*

⅓ cup cider vinegar
¼ cup grated ginger
3 onions, peeled and chopped
zest of ½ lemon and 1 orange
1 cinnamon stick
1 handful of walnuts
1 dried bell pepper
1⅔ cups cranberries
2 pears, peeled and cubed
½ cup raw superfine sugar
salt and freshly ground pepper

Reduce the vinegar, ginger, onions, lemon and orange zest, cinnamon stick, and bell pepper for approx. 10 minutes, on medium heat. Roast the walnuts in a pan until they release an aroma. Transfer to a board and roughly chop.
Add them to the vinegar mixture together with the fresh cranberries, the pear cubes, and the sugar.
Allow to simmer for 30 minutes.
Taste and add salt and pepper to taste.

Fill 4 clean jars. Cool to room temperature. Cap the jars and refrigerate for at least 24 hours before serving.

# PICCALILLI

*For approx. 8 cups*

2 zucchinis, diced
1 cauliflower, in small florets
2 cups green beans, sliced
1 lb fresh pearl onions, peeled
1 cucumber, peeled and diced
¾ cup salt
⅔ cup sugar
4 cups vinegar
2 tbsp all-purpose flour
3 tbsp mustard seeds
1 tbsp ground ginger

Mix all the vegetables. Generously cover the bottom of a large bowl with the mixture. Sprinkle with salt. Cover this layer with another layer of vegetables and also sprinkle with salt. Continue until all vegetables and salt are used. Cover the bowl and leave to stand for 24 hours.
Drain the released moisture from the vegetables and rinse thoroughly under running water. Place in a large pot and add the sugar and 3 cups of the vinegar. Bring to a boil and simmer for approx. 15 minutes. Stir the remaining vinegar through the flour, add the spices, and, while stirring, pour onto the vegetables in the pot.
Bring to a boil and heat through for 3 minutes. Remove from the heat and immediately pour into clean jars. Turn the jars upside down and leave to cool until used.
You can keep your homemade piccalilli for approx. 2–3 months. Once opened, keep in the refrigerator!

# RHUBARB COMPOTE

*Oh, this is so good.*

3 lb rhubarb, cleaned and cut into pieces of approx. ½ inch
3½ cups sugar, or more
2 cinnamon sticks
8 cardamom pods
2 vanilla beans, split with the seeds scraped
3 mandarins

Fill a large baking pan with the rhubarb, sugar, cinnamon, cardamom, and vanilla beans and seeds. Halve the mandarins, squeeze them over the rhubarb, and add the peels. Stir thoroughly and cover with aluminum foil. Place in an oven preheated to 350°F/Gas 4 for approx. 20 minutes and stir occasionally. Fill two 4-cup preserving jars with the hot compote, put the lids on, and sterilize by covering the jars with boiling water and boil for another 20–30 minutes. If you want to eat the rhubarb immediately, leave the jars in the oven for another 10 minutes. Before serving, remove the mandarin peel and the spices.

# APPLE–DATE CHUTNEY

*For 4 jam jars or 4 cups*

1 dab butter
2 lb tart/sour apples (Granny Smith)
½ cup raw superfine sugar
1 piece of ginger the length of your thumb, peeled and finely chopped
1 cup white wine vinegar or cider vinegar
1 cup water
1 cinnamon stick
1 tbsp cumin
2 tbsp ground cardamom
1 clove garlic, crushed
2 cups pitted dried dates, cut into chunks
1 cup golden raisins

Heat the butter in a heavy-bottomed pot and sauté the apple cubes together with the sugar and ginger on all sides. Add the vinegar and water and, together with the spices and garlic, slowly bring to a boil. Add the dates and raisins. Leave to cook for 15 minutes. Fill 4 clean jam jars with the chutney and seal with the lids. The chutney can be kept for at least 2 months. Serve as an appetizer with some pâté, or after a meal with cheese.

159

# PINK PEARS IN SYRUP

*For the syrup*

1 bottle red wine

2 cinnamon sticks

3 star anise

1 vanilla bean, split, with the seeds scraped

4 cloves

1 cup sugar

1 sliced orange

rind of 1 lemon

*and of course also*

4–6 ripe pears (Comice)

Bring all the ingredients for the syrup to a boil, stir gently until the sugar is dissolved, then lower the heat, allowing the mixture to infuse. Peel the pears and add to the syrup. Allow them to cook for 30 minutes and then remove them. (The longer you let them stay in the syrup, the darker they will become.) Strain the syrup and reduce to at least half its volume, or until you like its consistency as a sauce, but note that once cooled it will thicken considerably more. Leave to cool.

You can also preserve the pears in this syrup: Add at least 7–8 uncooked pears to a sterilized 8-cup preserving jar. Add the unreduced syrup. Cover with the lid and cook the jar immersed in a tall pot of boiling water for 30 minutes. Pears can be processed both savory and sweet. A savory example is provided below, and when sweet they taste good with vanilla cream, a little syrup from the jar, and almond biscuits (recipe on page 362).

# SALAD WITH SPINACH, PEAR, STILTON, AND CURED HAM

*For this salad you can use the pears you have already preserved (see above).*

*For the dressing*

6 tbsp white wine vinegar

1 generous tsp Dijon mustard

6 tbsp hazelnut oil or other nut oil

6 tbsp olive oil

approx. ½ cup hazelnuts, chopped

salt and freshly ground pepper

*For the salad*

1 tbsp olive oil

7 oz cured ham, sliced

2 ripe pears (Comice)

5 oz Stilton, crumbled

1 red onion, cut into thin rings

1 lb spinach leaves, washed

Fill a jar with all the ingredients for the dressing and cover with the lid. Shake well, taste for salt and pepper, and save the dressing until used. Heat a nonstick skillet and add a teaspoon of olive oil. Sauté the ham on both sides until crunchy and drain on paper towels. Do not fry too many slices at the same time, but two by two, keeping them whole. Quarter the pears and remove the cores. Cut into strips. Toss the cheese, onion rings, and ham with the spinach leaves. Transfer the salad to a plate, arrange the pears on it, and top with the dressing. Serve with winter squash buns (page 24) and eat immediately.

# BUTTERNUT PICKLES

¾ cup white wine vinegar

1¼ cups water

3 tbsp sugar

6 cloves

1 blade mace or a pinch of freshly grated nutmeg

1 cinnamon stick

6 cardamom pods

1–2 red bell peppers

1 lb butternut squash, peeled and cubed (½ inch)

Bring all the ingredients except the butternut squash to a boil in a saucepan. Reduce for 10 minutes on low heat. Add the butternut cubes and cook for 5 minutes.

Transfer the mixture to a preserving jar, let cool, then put the lid on and refrigerate for at least 3 days before consuming, but preferably longer. Serve the pickles with meat, vol-au-vent, fish, or on a snack, as on page 120.

# VEGETABLE TERRINE

*Vegetables can be kept for a long time when preserved in oil. By applying pressure, the moisture is pressed out and you are left with flavor. A perfect appetizer for approx. 10 people and served with leftovers for a tasty lunch.*

*For the terrine*
3–4 eggplants
2–3 zucchinis
generous splash of good olive oil
salt and freshly ground pepper
1 lb roasted red bell peppers (you will need 2–3)

*For the basil oil*
1½ cups olive oil
1 bunch basil
2 cloves garlic
juice of ½ lemon
salt and freshly ground pepper

*For the cottage cheese*
2 tbsp chives
2 tbsp parsley
2 tbsp dill
1 cup low-fat cottage cheese
salt and freshly ground pepper

Cut the eggplants and zucchinis as thinly as possible on a mandolin or with a large sharp knife. Preheat the oven to 350°F/ Gas 4. Grease 1 or 2 baking sheets with olive oil, rub with salt and pepper, and cover with the eggplant slices. Trickle olive oil on the eggplants and sprinkle with salt and pepper. Bake for 8–10 minutes until done. Repeat this process until all eggplant slices are baked.

Make the basil oil: Blitz all ingredients using a hand blender in a deep container. Taste and add salt and pepper, as needed. Generously line a cake loaf with plastic wrap, allowing the edges to hang over the rim. Then cover the bottom with a layer of eggplant slices. Arrange them overlapping in the pan. Continue to fill the pan with layers of raw zucchini and roasted bell peppers. Every three layers, cover with a dash of basil oil. End with a layer of eggplant. Fold the plastic wrap closed over the terrine. Place something heavy (cans, carton of milk) on the terrine and place in a deep bowl, to prevent leaking, for at least 1 day in the refrigerator.

Make the cottage cheese with herbs immediately before serving: Finely chop all the herbs, stir through the cottage cheese, and season with salt and pepper.

Remove the vegetable terrine from the refrigerator. Thoroughly drain all oil. Open the plastic wrap at the top. Cover with a plate and transfer the terrine by turning it over onto the plate. Be careful, since moisture will be released from the dressing and vegetables. Pat the plate dry with paper towels. Cut the vegetable terrine into thick slices (use a sharp knife!) and serve with a dollop of cottage cheese with herbs.

# LENTIL SALAD

*You can serve this salad immediately, as you can the previous ones, but you could also make more and save it in the refrigerator for later in the week when you do not feel like cooking.*

*For the lentil salad*
1 small carrot
½ bunch celery (some 6–8 ribs)
1 leek
2 shallots, diced
3 cloves garlic, chopped
2 cups chicken broth
3 tbsp olive oil
1 cup lentils (good-quality gray/green [Puy] lentils)
⅔ cup white wine
1 bunch flat-leaf parsley, chopped
salt and freshly ground pepper

*For the green herb oil*
1 cup high-quality olive oil
1 small bunch of chives and parsley
salt and freshly ground pepper

*And also*
12 oz smoked sausage
butter or oil for frying
prepared mustard

Peel the carrot and finely dice all the vegetables (this is called "brunoise"). Heat the broth in a large pot. Heat the oil in a wide pan and add all the vegetables, and the lentils, and stir-fry until hot, just as for risotto. Add the wine and continue to stir. Add the hot broth slowly and continue to stir until the lentils are cooked *al dente*. Remove from the heat. Taste, and add salt and pepper, as needed. Chop the parsley and add to the mixture.

In the meantime, make the herb oil: Heat the oil close to the smoking. Roughly chop the herbs and add them to a deep heatproof pitcher. Blitz with a hand blender and add the hot oil in a thin trickle. Season with salt and pepper and set aside until used.

Cut the sausage into thin slices. Heat the butter in a skillet and swiftly sauté the sausage slices on both sides until golden brown. Transfer the lentil salad into a ring mold on the plate, remove the ring. Add the sausage and garnish the lentil salad with a nice sprig of parsley. Trickle the herb oil on the plate and serve with mustard. This appetizer is also good as a main course served with boiled potatoes.

# BRUSCHETTA WITH MARINATED EGGPLANT AND MINT

*Immersed in oil, the preserved eggplant can easily be kept for 2 weeks. It will become more oily, but the flavor will be more intense!*

2 eggplants
1 cup extra-virgin olive oil and a little extra
2 tbsp honey
⅔ cup red wine vinegar
salt and freshly ground pepper
1 green bell pepper
1 bunch of fresh mint leaves, cut into strips
4 slices of coarse Italian bread
1 clove garlic

Cut the eggplants into slices approx. ⅛ inch thick. Heat a broiler to high. Brush the slices on both sides with a thin coat of olive oil. Broil the eggplant on both sides until done. Save until used.

Stir the honey through the vinegar. Beat in a trickle of olive oil until the dressing thickens. Season with salt and pepper.

Halve the bell pepper, remove the seeds, and finely chop. Stir two-thirds of the mint through the dressing. Stir the dressing into the eggplant and leave to stand for at least 30 minutes.

Before serving heat the broiler. Broil the bread slices on both sides until brown. Trickle with olive oil and rub the garlic clove on the bread. Cover with a few eggplant slices. Garnish with the fresh mint and freshly ground pepper, and serve with the remaining eggplant.

**TIP** Good served with seasoned labneh balls (see recipe on page 298).

# GREEN VEGETABLE SALAD

*For serving I will give you a recipe for a dressing and will recommend what to have with it. It is a good lunch or appetizer. In our restaurant we also often serve it as a side dish. You can also preserve the salad.*

*For the salad*
5½ lb green vegetables: green beans, fava beans, dried peas, snow peas, green asparagus, or a mixture thereof
4 ribs celery, washed and sliced diagonally in 1-inch slices
1 bunch parsley, tarragon, mint, or dill, or a mixture thereof, roughly chopped
2 sterile preserving jars of approx. 4 cups, or smaller ones (see page 12 for sterilizing jars)

*For the yogurt-dill dressing*
½ cup yogurt
juice of 1 lemon
1 tbsp apricot or peach syrup
1 scallion, finely chopped
1 clove garlic, crushed
1 tbsp finely chopped dill
salt and freshly ground pepper
¼ cup hazelnut oil

*As a dressing, or side dish as an appetizer, or lunch dish, calculate 2 oz of the following ingredients per person*
tasty crumbles such as goat cheese or feta
ham, smoked fish, wafer-thin smoked chicken, or thinly sliced beef loin (described on page 256)

Cut the long vegetables, such as asparagus or green beans, in half. Blanch all vegetables for 2 minutes, in turn, in a pan with plenty of boiling water. Finish with the fava beans, since they will color the water purple. Rinse everything immediately under cold running water. Mix the vegetables, stir in the herbs (reserve some for the garnish if you intend to serve the salad later that day), and scoop into two 4-cup preserving jars. Top up the jars with hot water and 1 tablespoon salt per 4 cups of water used. Make sure all the vegetables are immersed. Cool to room temperature. Keep this salad in the refrigerator.

To make the dressing, thoroughly blend all the ingredients, except the oil. Lastly, beat in the oil in a thin trickle. Distribute the bean salad over the plates and garnish with cheese, meat, or fish, or serve as is, as a side dish. Trickle the dressing on the salad and sprinkle with some of the reserved chopped herbs.
You can keep the leftover dressing carefully covered in the refrigerator for about a week.

# BEET SALAD WITH ASH-COVERED GOAT CHEESE

*Serve this beet salad as an appetizer with smoked fish, or as a side dish with meat. Here I serve it with a goat cheese. You can also serve it with a small green salad. The recipe for the beet salad makes about 8 cups. So you had better clear a shelf in the refrigerator. If you want to make less, just halve the quantities.*

1½ lb sweet/sharp apples, peeled and cut into slices or sections

1 red onion, peeled and in rings

2–3 slices fresh ginger, leave the skin

½ tsp cinnamon

pinch of nutmeg

1 tbsp mustard seeds

¾ cup raspberry vinegar, otherwise red wine vinegar

½ cup sugar

salt and freshly ground pepper

3¼ lb parboiled beets, in slices or sections

*For an appetizer, 4 servings*

1 lb beet salad

4 cups arugula, mesclun, or a mixture thereof

1½ cups ash-covered goat cheese

olive oil

In a large pan bring all the ingredients, except the beets and salt and pepper, to a boil and simmer for 5 minutes. Season with salt and freshly ground pepper. Add the beets. Stir until the beets are heated but be careful not to break the apples and the beets. Transfer the salad to two clean 4-cup jars or four 2-cup preserving jars. Cool to room temperature and put the lids on. Store in the refrigerator for at least 1 hour and up to several weeks.

Serve a nice helping of preserved salad with fresh green salad, adding approx. 3 slices of goat cheese per serving. Trickle olive oil on the salad immediately before serving.

# DOLMAS FILLED WITH WILD RICE

*You will make 20 dolmas with this recipe. Keep dolmas longer by covering with olive oil. Tap the bowl in which you will store the dolmas a few times on the countertop, releasing as much air as possible to prevent spoilage. Store in the refrigerator.*

9 oz jar vine leaves (I use the Drossa brand, available from the supermarket)
1 onion, peeled and finely chopped
2 tbsp olive oil
¾ cup white and wild rice (mixture)
¾ cup water
½ cup raisins, roughly chopped
⅔ cup pine nuts
2 tbsp finely chopped parsley
2 tbsp finely chopped mint
1 generous pinch of ground cinnamon
2 peeled tomatoes (canned), in chunks
salt and freshly ground pepper
juice of 1 lemon, plus 1 extra lemon for garnish

*For the dressing*
¾ cup yogurt
juice of ½ lemon
½ clove garlic
pinch of cayenne pepper (to taste)
salt and freshly ground pepper

Carefully rinse the vine leaves under running water. Sauté the onion in the oil until golden brown. Add the rice and sauté for 3 minutes while stirring. Add the water, salt, raisins, and pine nuts. Stir briefly and cover the pan. Let the rice cook on very low heat for 15 minutes until nearly done, and all the water is absorbed. Stir, transfer to a large tray, and leave to slightly cool. Stir in the parsley, mint, cinnamon, and tomatoes. Taste the mixture and add salt and pepper, as needed.

Fill the vine leaves with 1 generous tablespoon of the rice mixture. Roll up the leaf by first folding the sides over the filling and then rolling it. They are most attractive if the dolmas are of equal size. Arrange the rolls next to each other in a baking pan and completely cover with water. Add the lemon juice. Cover the pan with aluminum foil and place in an oven preheated to 350°F/Gas 4 for 1 hour. Occasionally check whether there is enough water to cover the bottom of the pan. It should not boil dry. Leave to cool.

In the meantime make the dressing by mixing the ingredients into a smooth sauce using a hand blender. Season with salt and pepper. Serve three or four dolmas per person, drizzle with the dressing, and serve with slices of lemon and crusty bread.

# SALAD WITH CELERIAC, GOAT CHEESE, POMEGRANATE & TARRAGON

*For the salad*
1 celeriac
juice of 1 lemon
1 bunch celery (reserve 2 ribs for the dressing)
1 bunch flat-leaf parsley
1 bunch tarragon
seeds of 2 pomegranates (read how to release them on page 102)
1¼ cups goat cheese, crumbled

*For the dressing*
2 ribs celery
1 clove garlic
½ tbsp freshly grated horseradish or 1 tbsp from a jar
¼ cup red wine vinegar
½ cup grape seed oil (or otherwise sunflower oil)
salt and freshly ground pepper

Peel the celeriac. Wash and slice, then cut the slices into strips and then into matchsticks. If you are the proud owner of a food processor or mandolin with chip cutter, it will take you even less time. Save the matchsticks immersed in a container with water with the squeezed lemon juice until used. You can also add the squeezed lemon halves. Bring a pan with plenty of water to a boil and briefly blanch the celeriac.

Immediately rinse under cold running water or in ice water. Wash the celery ribs. Cut into thin strips, more or less the same size as the celeriac. Mix the celery matchsticks with the celeriac matchsticks.

If serving the salad immediately, make the dressing using a blender or hand mixer in a deep container. Roughly cut the reserved celery, cook until done (15 minutes), and puree with the other ingredients into a smooth dressing, taste and add salt and pepper, as needed. Trickle half of the dressing on the salad and leave to stand for 1 hour, allowing the flavors to infuse. Make the salad: Chop the herbs and toss them, together with the pomegranate seeds, lightly with the salad. Transfer a good amount to each plate. Distribute the goat cheese over the salads and trickle with some extra dressing.

PRESERVING MEAT & FISH

# MAKING TERRINE

MY GOOD FRIEND FLORIS TAUGHT ME HOW TO MAKE EXCELLENT TERRINES. TOGETHER WITH DINY HE NOW RUNS HIS OWN SHOP IN AMSTERDAM. THEY MAKE THE TASTIEST (AND BEST-LOOKING) FRENCH CHARCUTERIE I HAVE EVER HAD. >>> PRIOR TO THAT, FLORIS WORKED FOR US IN THE KITCHEN. WE OFTEN TRIED OUT ALL MANNER OF DISHES AND DISCOVERED THAT A SIMPLE PÂTÉ OR TERRINE IS ACTUALLY EASY TO MAKE. ONCE YOU HAVE MASTERED THE BASICS, YOU CAN MAKE ENDLESS VARIATIONS. I INCLUDE MORE THAN NORMAL HERE, ALLOWING YOU TO LEARN HOW IT'S DONE! IT'S IMPORTANT THAT YOU GRIND THE MEAT: NOT AS FINELY AS NORMAL, BUT A LITTLE COARSER, USING A GRINDER. IF YOU DON'T OWN ONE, USE A GOOD FOOD PROCESSOR, PROVIDED YOU CUT THE MEAT INTO SMALL CHUNKS FIRST. YOU CAN ALSO JUST ASK YOUR BUTCHER TO GRIND THE MEAT. THIS IS ACTUALLY THE EASIEST AND IT MAKES A HUGE DIFFERENCE IN TERMS OF WASHING DISHES.

NEEDED FOR 1 TERRINE DE CAMPAGNE:

8 OZ PORK SHOULDER
15 OZ PORK JOWL
14 OZ PORK LIVER

AFTER CLEANING AND GRINDING YOU WILL BE LEFT WITH 2 LB.

FOR THIS RECIPE YOU WILL NEED:
1.5 TSP PINK SALT AND 1 TSP REGULAR SALT. >>> MEASURE VERY PRECISELY!!
1 SHALLOT
1 DAB OF BUTTER, SHORTENING, OR LARD
1 SPRIG THYME
1 TBSP JUNIPER BERRIES
4 DRY BAY LEAVES
1 TBSP BLACK PEPPER
1 SMALL GLASS COGNAC
2 EGGS
PIECE OF CAUL FAT OR 10 OZ BACON STRIPS

START BY DICING THE SHALLOT AND . . .

SAUTÉ IT VERY SLOWLY IN A LITTLE BUTTER, ADD SOME THYME SPRIGS.

GRIND THE BAY LEAVES, JUNIPER BERRIES, AND PEPPER INTO POWDER.

FLORIS SAYS A TERRINE MUST BE FATTY, COARSE, SLICEABLE! IMPORTANT STUFF!

CUT THE PORK SHOULDER AND JOWL INTO STRIPS THAT NEATLY FIT INTO THE GRINDER.

COARSELY GRIND THE MEAT. BUT YOU CAN ALSO ASK THE BUTCHER TO DO IT FOR YOU.

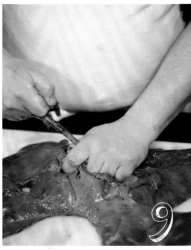

PULL OUT LIVER BILE DUCTS (TOUGH THREADS THAT MAKE THE TERRINE BITTER). COME ON, YOU ARE UP FOR IT!

COARSELY GRIND THE LIVER IN THE FOOD PROCESSOR (OR GRINDER).

COMBINE EVERYTHING; CAN YOU SEE THE AMOUNT OF FAT? THAT'S OK!

NOW YOU CAN ADD THE OTHER INGREDIENTS, EXCEPT THE SALTS.

WASH YOUR HANDS AND START WORKING THE MIXTURE. ADD THE SALTS.

WORK THE MIXTURE THOROUGHLY INTO A TACKY CONSISTENCY.

IN THE MEANTIME I GREASE THE TERRINES.

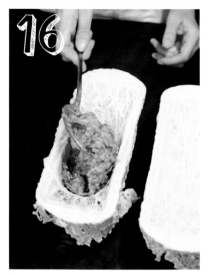

LINE THE MOLD WITH BACON STRIPS, OR, LIKE HERE, WITH CAUL FAT. CREATE A LITTLE HAMMOCK. FILL WITH THE MIXTURE. PRICK THE CORNERS WITH A SPOON: ALL AIR MUST BE REMOVED!

CAREFULLY COVER THE MEAT. WITH THE FAT, SLIDE THE DULL SIDE OF A KNIFE ALONG THE EDGES, MAKING THE TERRINES NICE AND TAUT. IT LOOKS POSH.

WE HAD SOME LEFT OVER; THEREFORE WE EVENTUALLY MADE 3 TERRINES. TWO LARGE ONES AND ONE SMALL ONE TO GIVE AWAY.

CAREFULLY WRAP WITH ALUMINUM FOIL AND PLACE THE TERRINES IN A ROASTING PAN TO COLLECT THE FAT. OTHERWISE THE OVEN WILL GET VERY DIRTY. BAKE AT 250°F FOR 2 HOURS.

AFTER 2 HOURS THEY WILL BE READY, BUT THEY WILL GO BACK INTO THE OVEN FOR A FURTHER 30 MINUTES TO BROWN, WITHOUT ALUMINUM.

LEAVE THE TERRINE TO STAND IN THE REFRIGERATOR FOR 24 HOURS BEFORE SLICING IT, BUT PREFERABLY FOR 1 WEEK, ALLOWING FOR THE FLAVORS TO FULLY DEVELOP. THE TERRINE CAN BE KEPT FOR AT LEAST 3 WEEKS.

## TIPS AND TRICKS

> DO YOU OWN A MEAT THERMOMETER? TOWARD THE END, THE TERRINES' CORE TEMPERATURE HAS TO BE 158°F.

> AS YOU NOTICED, WE ADDED THE SALT LAST, OTHERWISE THE SHALLOTS WOULD GET LUMPY.

> SALT EXTRACTS PROTEIN FROM THE MEAT AND PROTEINS ARE NECESSARY FOR BONDING. > FAT IS NECESSARY FOR THE FLAVOR AND CREAMINESS OF THE TERRINE.

> ALL THE EFFORT YOU PUT INTO IT CAN BE SEEN IN THE RESULT: YOU LITERALLY REAP WHAT YOU SOW.

*Floris*

# LET'S GET GOING

OK! I WILL GIVE YOU A FEW MORE RECIPES FOR HOMEMADE TERRINES AND PÂTÉS. A LITTLE BIT OF EVERYTHING, SO THAT YOU CAN TRY THEM. SERVE WITH YOUR OWN HOMEMADE CHUTNEYS OR PICKLED VEGETABLES.

## FALL PASTIE

6 sheets all-butter puff pastry (frozen)
5 oz mixed mushrooms
a little olive oil for frying
salt and freshly ground pepper
8 oz game fillet or steak
26 oz ground beef (coarsely ground, please!)
3 tbsp prepared mustard
5 tbsp soy sauce
5 tbsp ketchup
2 to 3 sprigs fresh rosemary, both leaves and stem, finely chopped
1 tsp. chile powder
1 tsp nutmeg
1 tsp cinnamon
1 tsp ground ginger
1 egg
bread crumbs
1 egg yolk for the crust
flour to dust the countertop
olive oil to grease

Preheat the oven to 350°F/Gas 4. Place the pastry sheets on the countertop next to each other and allow to thaw. Wipe the mushrooms clean and tear them roughly into pieces. Sauté them while stirring on very high heat in a little olive oil and season with salt and pepper. Transfer to a plate to cool. Grind the game in a food processor or ask the butcher to do it for you. Combine the ground mixture with the remaining ingredients and work into a firm ball. Add as much bread crumbs as necessary, the mixture must remain creamy, not too wet, but not too dry either. You can test it by forming a small ball of the mixture, and heating it for 2 minutes in the microwave to taste whether it is okay. You can decide whether it needs more salt. You have to season ground meat more than you think, since once fried, it loses a lot of its flavor. Create an oval ball with the mince.

Stack the pastry squares. Dust the countertop with flour. Roll out the stack into a long sheet, 2 times bigger than the meat ball.

Place the meat ball on one side of the pastry and fold the other side over it. Brush water on the edge and press firmly in place. If you are a little handy you can decorate the pastie: For example close it along the top with a frill made with your fingers.

Place the pastie on a greased baking sheet and using an apple corer or large fork, make decorative holes in the dough: They will be necessary later to allow the fat to drain. Brush the pastie with lightly beaten egg yolk.

Bake the pastie until golden brown, approx. 45 minutes. Leave to fully cool before slicing. Serve with the cranberry, walnut, and pear chutney described on page 158.

## CHICKEN LIVER PÂTÉ

*Serve with a drink and dill pickles, pearl onions, and canapés.*

2 shallots, diced
3 tbsp plus 1¼ sticks butter
1 lb chicken livers
2 cups cream
1 tbsp Cognac or brandy
sprig of thyme

Sauté the shallots in 1 tbsp of the butter until glassy. Place in the food processor bowl. Sauté the chicken livers in batches in the same pan for approx. 5 minutes. They have to stay pink on the inside! Place in the food processor. When they are all cooked, add the cream, Cognac, and 2 tbsp butter to the bowl and finely grind. Press the pâté with the round side of a spoon through a sieve into a bowl below. Transfer the pâté to a dish in which you want to serve it. In the meantime, melt the 1¼ sticks butter on low heat in a saucepan. Pour only the clear part of the melted butter over the pâté to neatly seal it. Finish with a sprig of thyme. Leave the pâté to set for at least 4 hours.

# BEEF AND PARSLEY TERRINE

2 lb pork steaks
14 oz beef steak
2 bunches of flat-leaf parsley
½ cup sweet white wine or port
2 tbsp Cognac
4 shallots, finely chopped
2 cloves garlic, finely chopped
2 tsp salt
plenty of freshly ground pepper
½ tbsp allspice
2 tbsp olive oil
1 bay leaf
some thyme sprigs

Cube all the meat. Rinse the parsley, pat dry, and chop. Pour the wine and Cognac into a bowl. Add the meat, parsley, shallots, garlic, salt, pepper, and allspice. Stir thoroughly and sprinkle with oil. Cover the meat with plastic wrap and leave to marinate in the refrigerator for 3 hours.
Preheat the oven to 300°F/Gas 2. Remove the thyme and bay from the marinade and grind all ingredients in a grinder or food processor. Press the mixture into a clay pot, smooth it out, and garnish with a bay leaf and a few thyme sprigs. Cover with a lid or aluminum foil and bake the terrine in the oven for 1 hour. Leave the terrine to cool and keep in the refrigerator for 24 hours before serving.

# SALMON AND SHRIMP TERRINE WITH FAVA BEANS AND PORTOBELLO MUSHROOMS

20 jumbo shrimp, peeled
2 slices day-old bread
¾ cup milk
21 oz salmon fillet
1 handful shelled fava beans
2 portobello mushrooms
a little oil for frying
salt and freshly ground pepper
4 eggs
14 oz white fish fillets
¾ cup cream
1 small bunch chives, finely chopped

Cut the shrimp in half lengthwise and set aside. Cut the bread into cubes and soak in the milk. Preheat the oven to 250°F/Gas ½. Cut the salmon into thin strips and set aside. Blanch the fava beans in boiling water for 3 minutes and rinse under cold water; peel. Slice the mushrooms and sauté briefly on both sides in a skillet with oil. Sprinkle with salt and pepper and set aside. Separate the egg whites from the yolks. Cut the white fish into chunks and add them to the food processor bowl. Add the drained, soaked bread, and egg yolks, and blend into a coarse puree. Pour the puree into a bowl and add the cream. Add the shrimp halves and the chives. Beat the egg whites until stiff in another bowl and carefully stir through the white fish mixture to keep it airy. Season the mixture with salt and pepper. Generously line a loaf pan with plastic wrap and allow the edges to hang over. Cover the bottom with half the salmon strips. Pour half of the white fish mousse over the salmon. Arrange the mushroom slices and fava beans on the fish. Cover with the remaining mousse. Top the mousse with the rest of the salmon. Cover the terrine with the overhanging plastic wrap and place in a larger baking pan. Fill that bowl with water halfway up the terrine and bake in the oven for 75 minutes. The terrine must feel firm when pressed; otherwise briefly return to the oven. First leave the terrine to slightly cool, then place in the refrigerator for at least 12 hours. Serve with horseradish sauce, on page 195, or green herb oil on page 166, or with a small green salad and mustard dressing.

# HAM PIE

*In this recipe I use loose or bulk sausage, available from any butcher. In Holland, I typically buy "saucisson" and remove the skin. Sausage meat is nice and fatty and well seasoned, so it gives a good, creamy flavor and texture to this pie.*

1 lb ground pork

10 oz loose sausage

7 oz ham, cubed

6 sage leaves, chopped

1 small onion, finely chopped

salt and freshly ground pepper

a few drops hot-pepper sauce

3 cups all-purpose flour and a little extra for dusting purposes

4 tbsp milk

1 stick butter and a little extra for greasing purposes

1 egg, lightly beaten

Combine the ground pork with the sausage, ham, sage, and onion in a large bowl. Season with salt and pepper and a few drops of hot-pepper sauce. Grease an 8-inch springform pan and dust with flour. Mix the remaining flour with 2 tsp salt. Combine the milk and butter in a pan with ⅔ cup water and heat until the butter melts. Add the flour and stir well into a firm ball. Remove from the pan and work into smooth dough on the countertop. Line the springform pan with parchment paper. At the top allow the paper to slightly extend beyond the pan. Roll two-thirds of the dough into a round sheet approx. 12 inches in diameter. Line the pan and leave some dough to hang over the edge. Fill the pan with the meat mixture and press down, eliminating any air bubbles. Roll out the rest of the dough into a sheet that fits on the pie and cover the pie with it. Brush some water on the edges and press into a decorative pattern, if you are able to do so. Make 3 holes in the cover, using an apple corer, for example. Trim the edges and roll out the remaining dough. Cut out 3 circles of which the inner diameter is the same as the holes you have made with the apple corer. Place the rounds on the holes, filling them. Brush the beaten egg on the dough. Bake the pie for 30 minutes in an oven preheated to 350°F/Gas 4 and then turn down the heat to 320°F/Gas 3. Bake the pie for another hour. Leave to fully cool.

Serve with coarse mustard or with the cranberry, walnut, and pear chutney from page 158.

# MARINATED SALMON IN FENNEL SEED AND PERNOD

*This recipe is for at least 25 servings, a great party dish. Making less is also possible, of course. Use a smaller piece of salmon, but preferably keep the skin on it. A side of salmon weighs approx. 3 lb. Adjust other ingredients proportionally to make a smaller quantity. Use up the salmon in the following recipe, serving 4 as an appetizer. Since you have marinated it in salt and alcohol, it will keep for a few days. Wrap well and place in the refrigerator, and then use it up in other dishes, such as the salmon tartar on page 191.*

1⅓ cups sugar
1 cup salt
2 whole sides of salmon, with skin
¾ cup fennel seeds
1 generous bunch dill, chopped
1¼ cups Pernod

Line a large baking dish with plastic wrap, allowing plenty to hang over the edges. Combine the sugar and salt. Sprinkle two handfuls of this mixture on the bottom. Place one side of salmon on the mixture, skin side down. Sprinkle with a portion of the sugar-salt mixture, fennel seeds, dill, and half the Pernod. Also sprinkle the other piece of salmon (reserve a little sugar-salt mixture) and place it on the other side of the tray. Sprinkle the top of the fish with the remaining salt mixture and cover the entire salmon tightly with the plastic wrap. Place the fish in a cool place and place a number of heavy objects on it to press it down. Cans, for example, or something similar. Leave the fish to marinate for at least 24 hours, but preferably 48 hours.
Remove the plastic wrap, scrape the salt from the salmon using a knife, and cut the salmon into thin slices.
Serve with a salad of thinly sliced fennel and lemon juice.

# SALMON TARTAR

*You will always have leftovers from the marinated salmon on the previous page. Never throw anything out!*

10 oz marinated salmon (see previous page)
1 tbsp finely chopped dill
1 small bunch arugula, mustard greens, or watercress, or a mixture thereof

*For the oil*
3 sprigs parsley
⅔ cup olive oil
a few drops of lemon juice
salt and freshly ground pepper

*Before serving*
4 tbsp horseradish sauce (see recipe on page 195)
a little coarse sea salt (Maldon, if you have it)
4 slices dark brown bread, toasted
It is fun if you own a ring mold, but it isn't necessary.

Chop the marinated raw salmon with a sharp knife and mix thoroughly, then add the dill. Heat the oil, not too hot, just warm. Put the parsley in a deep container. Finely chop the parsley using a hand blender and, while grinding, add the warm oil. Season the oil with some lemon juice, salt, and pepper.
Prepare the plates: Arrange the salmon tartar in a ring mold on the plate. Remove the ring. Garnish the tartar with a little arugula rolled in your hands into a small ball. Spread a dollop of horseradish sauce on the plate and add a swirl of the green oil around the tartar.
Sprinkle the green salad with some coarse sea salt, if desired. Serve with thinly sliced and toasted dark brown bread.

# HERRING SALAD

## WITH BEETROOT & VODKA ━━━▶

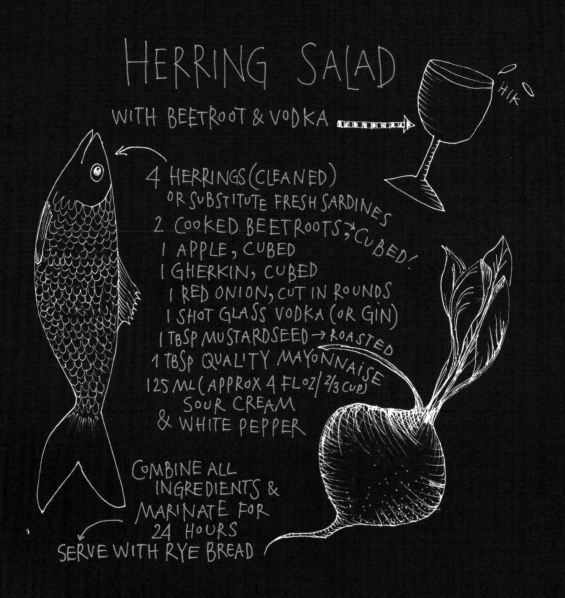

HIK

4 HERRINGS (CLEANED)
OR SUBSTITUTE FRESH SARDINES
2 COOKED BEETROOTS, CUBED!
1 APPLE, CUBED
1 GHERKIN, CUBED
1 RED ONION, CUT IN ROUNDS
1 SHOT GLASS VODKA (OR GIN)
1 TBSP MUSTARDSEED → ROASTED
1 TBSP QUALITY MAYONNAISE
125 ML (APPROX 4 FL OZ / 2/3 CUP)
SOUR CREAM
& WHITE PEPPER

COMBINE ALL
INGREDIENTS &
MARINATE FOR
24 HOURS
SERVE WITH RYE BREAD

Ets. MORE

Tél. 01.46.86.69.53

# AAN DE AMSTEL'S NOW FAMOUS PORK BELLY

*In our restaurant we make pork belly every week. It was actually supposed to be on the menu only for a short while, but, due to its huge success, it was never removed. It is a perfect "hangover cure" on a Saturday morning: Briefly bake the bacon slices in a hot oven, until the fat is crispy. Serve on bread with (fresh) horseradish sauce or fresh potato salad.*
*We use an entire pork belly, but you can also easily make it at home with a smaller bacon cut.*
*Once laid in salt and baked, you can keep the bacon in the refrigerator for up to two weeks.*
*The recipe below is for four people.*

¼ piece pork belly, without skin (ask your butcher), approx. 2 lb
1 generous handful of coarse sea salt
1 handful of fennel seeds
at least 12 bay leaves, as fresh as possible

*For the horseradish sauce*
1 piece fresh horseradish the length of your thumb (or 2 tbsp from a jar)
½ cup sour cream
juice and zest of ½ lemon
salt and freshly ground pepper

Score the fat on the pork belly with a sharp knife to make an attractive plaid pattern. Rub the entire piece with salt and fennel. This is a rough job; do not skimp on the ingredients. Press bay leaves into the grooves and inside the meat. Wrap in a clean dish towel, place in a suitable dish in the refrigerator, and cover with a heavy object. Leave to stand for 24 hours, but 2 days is even better. By processing it in this way, the meat acquires flavor, but the salt also extracts moisture from the meat, which will make the pork crispier later.
Heat the oven to 340°F/Gas 3, place the pork belly in a baking pan, and bake for at least 1 hour in the oven, or until the top is crispy and golden brown and the meat is fully cooked.
In the meantime, make the horseradish sauce: Peel the horseradish with a vegetable peeler and grate it on a fine grater. Or better still, use a food processor, as fresh horseradish is very sharp and will make your eyes tear up! Stir in the sour cream and lemon juice. (Once blended with the other ingredients the fumes will disappear.) Season the sauce with salt and freshly ground pepper. Serve with the meat.

# DUCK CONFIT

*This recipe is for 8 legs, but while you're at it and have bought such a large jar of goose fat, you might as well make more. It is not that much work and once preserved, you can enjoy it for an entire winter. Whatever you don't consume, you can put in a sealable jar. Ensure the duck is well immersed in fat, and store it in the refrigerator. The only thing is that you will probably have to borrow a large pan from a friendly local restaurant.*

8 duck legs, approx. 6 oz each
approx. 10 tbsp coarse sea salt
6–8 bay leaves
a few sprigs of fresh thyme
4 cloves garlic, crushed
8 cups goose fat (available at specialist food stores)

Put the legs in a bowl 24 hours in advance, rub them with the sea salt, bay, thyme, and garlic. Cover and put in a cool place.
Heat the goose fat in a large heavy-bottomed pan. Wipe the legs clean and slide them into the hot fat.
Leave the pan with the lid slightly open and simmer on very low heat for 2–2½ hours so that bubbles come to the surface every so often. The meat is cooked when it easily falls off the bone. Leave the legs to fully cool in the fat.
You can place those legs that you will not consume straight away in suitable clean jars and cover with the hot goose fat. Carefully seal the jars and place in the refrigerator until used.
If you would like to eat them immediately: Ladle a few spoonfuls of cooled fat into a skillet. Sauté the confit duck legs on both sides until crunchy, about 7–8 minutes. Drain on paper towels and serve immediately.
The goose fat in which you have fried the legs can be used again: Strain and leave to set. Save in the refrigerator.
It's great to use for frying potatoes. Just continue to use it until you have no more!

# POTTED SHRIMP

*Just like goose fat for duck confit, butter works as a preservative for the shrimp. Peeling them is a little bit of a chore, but you will need the shells to flavor the butter. Look at it as a relaxing job.*
*We used to like eating this in Ireland, and in our restaurant it is also often served as lunch or appetizer.*
*You can keep the potted shrimp in the refrigerator at least 10 days.*

1 lb unpeeled shrimp
2 sticks butter
2 mace blades (or pinch of ground mace)
pinch of cayenne pepper (to taste), or use paprika if you don't like it hot
pinch of nutmeg
salt and freshly ground pepper

Peel the shrimp. Initially it's a little bit trial and error, but later you will get the hang of it. First break off the head, pull up the first shell near the legs in order for the shrimp flesh to become visible. Hold between thumb and index finger. Now you can easily remove the tail. Reserve half the shells from the shrimp. Crush them briefly, with a rolling pin for example, thoroughly breaking them. Melt the butter with the shrimp shells, mace, cayenne pepper, and nutmeg. Leave the mixture to simmer on very low heat for 20 minutes and strain over a bowl. With the back of a spoon, press all the juice from the shells. Return the collected juices to the pan. Add the shrimp meat, and season with salt and pepper. The shrimp will be cooked in a jiffy in the hot butter. You can leave the heat off. Pour the mixture into small single-portion jars or bowls and ensure that the shrimp are fully covered with butter. Then leave to set in the refrigerator.
Before serving we briefly place the jars in a pan of hot water, thus slightly melting the butter and the shrimp can be easily spooned from the semi-hard butter.
We serve potted shrimp with two lemon segments, thin slices of brown toast, and a green salad with watercress, arugula, and/or butter lettuce. Sprinkle some sea salt on the salad.

# BOILED HAM WITH MUSTARD-HONEY CRUST

*This recipe is for 10 people at least, since you will obviously prepare a whole ham. Boiled ham can be kept for more than a week in the refrigerator. Always wrap neatly and with clean material.*

1 large fresh ham (can be ordered from the butcher. Ask him to leave in the bone. Here in the photo I used a suckling pig ham, but this is by no means a must!)
4 tbsp salt
2 onions, coarsely chopped
1 carrot, scraped and in chunks
4 celery ribs, in coarse chunks
¼ celeriac, peeled and cubed
3 cloves garlic, unpeeled
some thyme sprigs
3 bay leaves
2 cloves
1 tbsp juniper berries, crushed
2 tbsp honey
4 tbsp prepared spicy mustard
freshly ground pepper

Place the ham in a large pot. Pour 12 cups cold water over it, add the salt, and bring to a boil. Skim off and add the onion, carrot, celery, and celeriac. Crush the garlic and add to the broth with the thyme, bay, cloves, and juniper berries. Allow the ham to simmer for 1½ hours until fully cooked.
Remove from the broth and leave to cool for at least 2 hours on a plate.
Stir the honey through the mustard and crush a generous amount of pepper on the mixture. Spread the honey mixture on the ham and place it in an oven preheated to 350°F/Gas 4 for approx. 25 minutes or until golden brown.
Cut into slices and serve with mustard, with drinks, add a salad as an appetizer, or serve the ham with turnip greens.

# MAKE YOUR OWN DUCK HAM

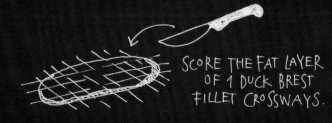

SCORE THE FAT LAYER OF 1 DUCK BREST FILLET CROSSWAYS.

FILL HALF A TRAY WITH SALT.

GRATE THE RIND OF 1 OR 2 ORANGES, SPRINKLE ON THE DUCK BREAST.

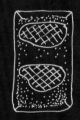

→ PLACE THE DUCK BREAST IN THE SALT & TOP WITH MORE SALT UNTIL FULLY COVERED.

COVER THE TRAY AND PLACE A HEAVY OBJECT ON IT. STORE IN A COOL PLACE.

WAIT 2 DAYS.

TA-DA! HOME MADE HAM!

FIRST RINSE THE MEAT THOROUGHLY, PAT DRY, AND CUT INTO VERY THIN SLICES USING A SHARP KNIFE.

## BE CREATIVE →

SERVE ON A SALAD, ON SOUP → ON TOP OF RISOTTO...

# PICKLED MACKEREL

*This is a good recipe as a replacement for pickled herring. That is what it most resembles, but since it's freshly prepared, it is much better than herring that has been sitting in a glass jar for weeks.*

approx. 6 mackerel fillets (ask the fishmonger to fillet 3 mackerels for you, or maybe you can do it yourself?)

1–2 red bell peppers, in thin strips

1 tbsp juniper berries, crushed

approx. 4 bay leaves

3 tbsp mustard seeds

1 tbsp fennel seeds

4 cloves

2 tsp salt

2 tbsp white peppercorns

¾ cup red wine vinegar

¾ cup water

a few sprigs of oregano

Place a nonstick pan on the heat. Place the fillets, with the skin up, in the hot pan for 10 seconds to singe. Arrange them in a nonreactive dish with the skin up. Heat all the other ingredients in a saucepan for the marinade. At the very last moment, add the oregano sprigs. Cover the fish with the hot marinade. The fish will be soaked and curl upward. Immediately cover the dish with plastic wrap and leave to cool. Place in the refrigerator to marinate for at least 1 day (and night), but preferably 2 days. Test whether the fish is cooked. If the fish is big, it often has to marinate one day longer. Serve the fish as an appetizer with potato salad or on bread with a drink.

TIP You can also do this with filleted sardines, or even with shrimp.

SPAGHETTI? NO GRAZIE NO GRAZIE

GNOCCHI

Maria helps me to keep our Amsterdam house
in a normal state.
But she also tells me every week what she has
cooked that week, what she is going to cook, and
especially how I have to cook.
Maria comes from Calabria and keeps me
enthralled with her exciting stories about her family,
their ups and downs, and especially what each
family member eats and doesn't eat.
She takes it all into account and therefore cooks at
least three dishes at home for her own
family every evening.
One without pasta, since her daughter doesn't like
it, one without rice, because her husband doesn't
like it, and a special dish for herself, with the
ingredients she loves.
And she is happy that her other
daughter is in Rome.
Otherwise she would have
to make four versions.
This is not typical only for Maria's family, it is typical
for Italy. Every Italian knows better than their
neighbor how a dish should be prepared. When
I cook, Maria stands next to me, shaking her head:
I don't do it right!

# MAKING GNOCCHI

I HONESTLY BELIEVE THAT GNOCCHI IS ONE OF THE BEST THINGS IN THE WORLD. MY NEIGHBOR, CHEF SALVATORE, MAKES THE BEST, IN MY OPINION, BUT THESE DAYS I'M PRETTY GOOD TOO.
WHICH IS WHY I WILL NOT EXPLAIN HERE HOW TO MAKE PASTA OR MAKE RISOTTO, SINCE YOU HAVE PROBABLY READ IT A MILLION TIMES. HOWEVER, I MEET A LOT OF PEOPLE WHO HAVE NO IDEA HOW TO MAKE GNOCCHI.
IT IS TRULY DELICIOUS WHEN IT IS HOMEMADE, SO PAY ATTENTION. HERE IT IS:

SCRUB POTATOES AND BOIL IN SKINS. FOR EACH 2 LB POTATOES YOU NEED: 1 EGG, 2 CUPS BREAD FLOUR (TYPE 00), AND A LITTLE SALT.

REMOVE THE SKIN WHILE THE POTATOES ARE STILL HOT. THIS IS EASIER IF YOU PRICK A FORK INTO THE POTATO.

MASH (I USE A POTATO RICER, ACTUALLY AN ESSENTIAL TOOL).

ADD THE FLOUR, BUT NOT ALL OF IT! MAYBE YOU WON'T NEED ALL OF IT. YOU CAN ALWAYS ADD SOME LATER. ALSO ADD A LITTLE SALT.

ADD A BEATEN EGG. AGAIN NOT EVERYTHING IN ONE GO; THE REST CAN BE ADDED LATER.

SWIFTLY WORK INTO A SMOOTH DOUGH. IF DESIRED, YOU CAN NOW ADD SOME FLOUR OR EGG.

THIS IS WHAT IT SHOULD LOOK LIKE.

ROLL OUT INTO A ROPE.

AND DIVIDE INTO EQUAL SECTIONS.

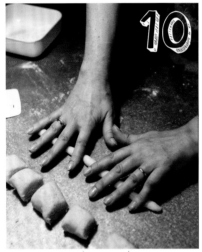

ROLL THE SECTIONS OUT INTO SMALLER "SAUSAGES."

CUT THESE SAUSAGES INTO SMALL CUSHIONS, AND LEAVE.

ROLL OVER A GNOCCHI BOARD.

OR ROLL OVER THE BACK OF A FORK.

SAVE GNOCCHI UNDER A DISH TOWEL, UNTIL USED,

OR COOK IMMEDIATELY: WHEN THEY FLOAT TO THE SURFACE, THEY ARE READY.

209

# YES! LET'S GET GOING . . .

"GNOCCHI" IS ITALIAN FOR WHAT THE ENGLISH CALL "DUMPLINGS," BUT THAT DOESN'T SOUND VERY ATTRACTIVE IN MY OPINION. HERE ARE MANY VARIATIONS ON THE BASIC RECIPE AND EVEN A TRADITIONAL RECIPE THAT IS CALLED GNOCCHI BUT IS ACTUALLY A TYPE OF BISCUIT AU GRATIN, MADE WITH POLENTA.
NOW, I ABSOLUTELY LOVE POLENTA, SO I WILL GIVE YOU THAT RECIPE AS WELL.

## GNOCCHI WITH SAGE

*A small variation on the basic recipe. This recipe uses sage, but you can use any other herb, such as parsley, basil, or rosemary. Great with rabbit stew, for example. Or with butter sauce and deep-fried sage. You know what, I will give you that recipe as well:*

1 x basic gnocchi recipe from page 208
1 bunch sage

*For the sauce*
1 bunch sage
1¼ sticks unsalted butter

Work the finely chopped sage evenly through the potato meal. Then make the gnocchi as described on the previous page.
Melt the butter for the sauce on very low heat. Carefully pour the clear part, which has risen to the top, away from the white protein components at the bottom of the pan. This is called clarifying. The proteins burn quite rapidly. Heat the clarified butter again; with a tablespoon remove any remaining whey from the pan.
Let cook on low heat until the color turns darker. You have now created a "beurre noisette." The butter will acquire a slightly nutty flavor.
Remove the stems from the sage leaves. Deep-fry them swiftly, in small portions, in the hot butter and drain on paper towels. Serve the herb gnocchi topped with a spoonful of butter sauce and sprinkled with the deep-fried sage leaves.

## WALNUT GNOCCHI

*Serve these gnocchi with lots of fried mushrooms in a cream sauce with garlic and parsley, for example.*

8 oz hot mashed potatoes
1 egg
2 tbsp walnut oil
½ cup ground walnuts
⅔ cup bread flour (type 00)
salt and freshly ground pepper
2 tbsp good-quality olive oil
2 generous tbsp butter

In a large bowl, combine the mashed potatoes with the egg, walnut oil, ground walnuts, and enough flour to make a firm ball. Add more walnut oil as needed. Season with salt and pepper. Quickly roll out into a 1-inch-thick rope. Cut it in small slices and press these slices gently on the back of a fork to create ridges. Cook in a pan with plenty of salted water and boil for

2–3 minutes until done. Rinse under cold running water and fry in a mixture of butter and good olive oil until crunchy.
Serve with fried mushrooms and a cream sauce, as desired.

## BUTTERNUT SQUASH GNOCCHI

*You can also make gnocchi from butternut squash instead of potato. They will be a nice shade of orange. Great with the butter sauce described earlier or a ragu (see recipe on page 216).*

1 butternut squash (approx. 2 lb)
salt
1 egg yolk
⅔ cup bread flour, type 00
nutmeg and freshly ground pepper
½ cup freshly grated Parmesan
2 tbsp toasted pumpkin seeds

Preheat the oven to 350°F/Gas 4. Peel the butternut squash, cut into sections, and remove the seeds and threads using a small sharp knife. Cut into slices approx. ½ inch thick. Arrange on a baking sheet lined with a sheet of parchment paper and sprinkle with salt. Bake in the middle of the oven for approx. 30 minutes until done. Press them through a potato ricer or mash until smooth with a hand blender. Using a fork, as it can get sticky, add the egg yolk and flour, and season with nutmeg, pepper, and salt. Be careful; this mixture will always be a little sticky. Do not add too much flour, as the gnocchi will become tough. You will have to become a little practiced at rolling these gnocchi: Work on a spacious surface dusted with flour and with floured hands. Quickly roll the dough into thin ropes. Cut into small cushions with a floured knife. Save on a baking sheet lightly dusted with flour until used. Bring a large pan of water to a boil. Add salt and cook in small quantities 3–4 minutes until done. Sprinkle with grated Parmesan cheese, and roasted pumpkin seeds.

IT'S PRONOUNCED "NYOKI" NOT GNOKKI OR GNOTCHI!

# GNOCCHI "QUATTRO FORMAGGI"

1 x basic gnocchi recipe from page 208
1 cup gorgonzola
1 cup fontina
⅓ cup ricotta
1 cup grated Parmesan
⅓ cup crème fraîche
2–3 tbsp milk, as needed
freshly ground pepper

Prepare the gnocchi as described on page 208. Before you cook them, melt the cheeses in the crème fraîche in a saucepan. Add some milk, if necessary.

Cover with a generous amount of freshly ground pepper. Cook the gnocchi for a few minutes until done, remove them from the water, and instantly stir them through the hot sauce. Serve immediately.

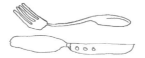

# GNOCCHI ALLA ROMANA

*Although these are called gnocchi there are no potatoes or other mashed vegetables in the recipe. They are made from polenta and then baked au gratin.*
*Delicious. Serve with fresh spicy tomato sauce.*

2 cups milk
⅔ cup polenta
nutmeg, salt, and freshly ground pepper
1 egg
approx. ½ stick butter
¾ cup grated Emmentaler (or Gruyère)
¾ cup grated Parmesan
olive oil

Heat the milk in a saucepan. When it starts to boil, trickle in the polenta, while stirring. Keep on stirring, thus preventing any lumps from forming. Season with nutmeg, salt, and pepper. Simmer for 15 minutes on very low heat. Remove from the heat and add the egg, half of the butter, and half of both cheeses.
Grease a flat low pan with a little olive oil: It can be a dish or a baking sheet, it makes no difference. Cover with the mixture. Smooth out. Leave to cool. The polenta will stiffen nicely.

Preheat the oven to 350°F/Gas 4 before serving. Cut the polenta into 1½-inch squares or cut them out with a round cookie cutter. Grease an oven dish with the remaining butter. Place the overlapping gnocchi in it and sprinkle with the remaining cheese and a few dabs of butter, if you have any left. Bake for 30 minutes and serve with tomato sauce (see page 212).

*211*

# GNOCCHI SALAD

*Hmm. I'm willing to bet that you sometimes have leftover cooked gnocchi. No problem. They can be used in a salad. Make a creamy dressing and complement the salad with crunchy vegetables.*

*Make the dressing from*
⅓ cup white wine vinegar
¼ cup sour cream
1 tsp prepared mustard
1 tsp sugar, or a little more
1 tbsp finely chopped parsley
1 clove garlic, crushed
salt and freshly ground pepper
approx. ¾ cup olive oil

*Make the salad from blanched vegetables*
green asparagus, garden peas, fava beans, or green beans

*(coarsely cut) raw vegetables*
little romaine lettuce, spinach leaf, watercress, radicchio, arugula, tomato, sliced scallions, grated zucchini, or herbs

*meat or fish*
roasted sardines, Parma ham, smoked salmon, smoked bacon, chicken

# BLACK SPAGHETTI WITH RAW TOMATO SAUCE

*I believe there are as many recipes for fresh tomato sauce as there are people in Europe. But this very simple uncooked one we like to make in the restaurant.*

*For the sauce*
8 good tasty tomatoes
zest and juice of ½ lemon
2 cloves garlic, crushed
1 red chile pepper
salt and freshly ground pepper

*For the oil*
1 small bunch of basil
½ cup olive oil, plus a little extra
salt and freshly ground pepper

*And also*
10 oz black (squid ink) spaghetti (regular spaghetti is also okay, of course, but this looks so ridiculously good)
2 balls mozzarella, torn into pieces

Puree 6 tomatoes in a blender or food processor, together with the lemon zest and juice, garlic, and chile pepper (seeds removed, if you don't go for spicy). Taste and add salt and pepper, as needed. Quarter the remaining 2 tomatoes, remove the seeds, and cut the pulp into small cubes. Stir the cubes through the sauce.

In another deep container, puree the basil with the olive oil until smooth, and add a pinch of salt. Set aside. Cook the pasta *al dente* and drain. Add a dash of olive oil to keep the pasta from sticking together.

Transfer the spaghetti immediately to four bowls. Add the tomato sauce to the pasta, sprinkle with mozzarella, and top with a trickle of basil oil.

Serve the pasta immediately; otherwise it will cool off quickly.

# TAGLIATELLE WITH ZUCCHINI AND CARROT RIBBONS, & WHITE PEPPER

*You do need a pasta machine for this recipe. If you don't own one, you could use lasagne noodles, cooked and then cut into strips. If you buy pasta use 12–14 oz.*

*For the pasta dough*
2 cups all-purpose flour
3 eggs
salt and freshly ground pepper
a little farina (Cream of Wheat)

*For the sauce*
1 cup crème fraîche
1 clove garlic, bruised but kept whole
salt and freshly ground white pepper
2 carrots, peeled
2 zucchinis
some fresh chervil, if you can get it

First make the pasta: Work all the ingredients except the farina into a firm ball in a food processor, or by hand. Leave the dough to rest in the refrigerator for one hour. Roll the dough into a nice slab and run through the pasta machine on the highest setting. Fold and repeat the process. Do this a few times until the dough starts getting smooth and supple. You can now reduce the pasta machine setting. Continue to pass the pasta through the machine until you have a long thin sheet and stop at the lowest setting but one. Sprinkle with farina and fold over and over into a rectangle. Using a sharp knife, cut the rectangle into strips. If you unfold it, you should have long strings. Keep the strips in small nests. Set aside until used, sprinkled generously with farina.

In the meantime bring the crème fraîche and garlic to a boil, generously sprinkle with salt and white pepper, turn down the heat, and simmer gently until used.

Heat two pans filled with water. Cut the carrots and zucchinis into thin slices and those slices, in turn, into thin strips. When the water boils, briefly cook the pasta in one pan and blanch the vegetable ribbons in the other pan for a few minutes. Drain the vegetables. Then drain the pasta and rinse thoroughly under cold water. Remove the garlic clove from the cream and stir in the vegetables. Return the pasta to the pan and top with the sauce.

Stir the mixture thoroughly but carefully, in order not to break the vegetables.

Serve immediately, garnish with fresh chervil, and sprinkle with salt and pepper.

# PAPARDELLE WITH SPICY LAMB RAGU AND CAPERS

3 tbsp extra-virgin olive oil

1½–2 lb leg of lamb or lamb shoulder, boned and cut into chunks

1 carrot, scraped and cubed

1 red onion, peeled and chopped

2 ribs celery, chopped

1 tbsp coriander seeds, roasted

1 tbsp fennel seeds

pinch of cumin

2 sprigs rosemary, chopped

a few sprigs of thyme, chopped

salt and freshly ground pepper

1 small can tomato puree (approx. 2 oz)

½ bottle (13 fl oz) full-bodied red wine

1 can peeled tomatoes (14 oz)

approx. 2 cups chicken broth (see page 128)

14 oz papardelle (very wide fettucine)

2 tbsp capers

dab of butter

*And also:*

chunk of Parmesan cheese for grating

Heat the oil in a heavy-bottomed pan and sear the meat in batches on all sides. Do not fry everything at the same time, as too much moisture will be released and you will end up boiling the meat. Remove the meat from the pan and set aside on a plate. In the same frying oil, sauté the carrot, onion, and celery. Add the meat, all spices and herbs, and the tomato puree. Sauté the mixture on high heat while stirring, until the tomato puree starts to smell sweet. Add the red wine and stir. Fold in the peeled tomatoes and enough broth to immerse the meat. Simmer on low heat for 1½ hours with the lid left ajar on the pan. Check occasionally whether there is enough moisture in the pan; add some hot broth if necessary. At the end, taste for salt and pepper, but remember that the capers you will add later are also salty.

Bring another pan with water to a boil. Add the pasta and boil for 10–12 minutes or until the pasta is cooked *al dente*. Drain the pasta and rinse under cold water. Add the pasta to the ragu, stir in the capers, a dab of butter, and a dash of olive oil, stir again, leave to stand for a few minutes away from the heat, and serve immediately. Top with grated Parmesan cheese.

# Risotto al limone
(LEMON RISOTTO)

2 SHALLOTS / FRENCH ONIONS
400 G (14 OZ / 2¼ CUPS) ARBORIO RICE
LARGE PAN OF CHICKEN BROTH (HOT!)
150 ML (5 FL OZ / ⅔ CUP) DRY WHITE WINE
JUICE & ZEST OF 1 LEMON
→ SALT & PEPPER TO TASTE
2 EGG YOLKS
ABOUT 100 G (4 OZ / 1 CUP PARMESAN
    CHEESE → GRATED
100 G (4 OZ / 1 STICK) BUTTER,
  PLUS A LITTLE MORE TO FINISH

AND ALSO 2 EXTRA LEMONS ←

MELT THE BUTTER IN A LARGE THICK-BOTTOMED PAN.
SAUTÉ THE SHALLOTS. ADD THE RICE AND FRY ON
HIGH HEAT WHILE STIRRING UNTIL THE RICE GRAINS
ARE GLAZED, WITH A WHITE CORE.

ADD THE WINE → FOLD IN THE LEMON JUICE. ADD THE
HOT BROTH, SPOONFUL BY SPOONFUL, UNTIL IT IS ABSORBED.
CONTINUE UNTIL THE RICE IS AL DENTE AFTER 20 MINS.
SEASON WITH SALT & PEPPER.

→FOLD IN CHEESE, UNTIL IT IS MELTED. REMOVE FROM
HEAT. STIR IN SMALL PATS OF BUTTER & EGG YOLKS.
COVER THE PAN AND TURN ON THE GRILL (BROILER).

QUARTER THE 2 EXTRA LEMONS AND GRILL (BROIL) THEM UNTIL
THEY FORM BLACK SPECKS.
ARRANGE RISOTTO AND SPRINKLE WITH LEMON ZEST.

SERVE WITH THE BURNT LEMON QUARTERS!

THEY HAVE BECOME
NICE AND SWEET.
SQUEEZE THEM
OVER YOUR PLATE.
YEY!

# RISO SALAD WITH YOUNG ZUCCHINIS, ASPARAGUS, RICOTTA, AND FLOWERS

*For the salad*

4 oz riso (rice-shaped pasta)

1 bunch green asparagus

2 small young zucchinis or 8 mini

¾ cup fresh ricotta

approx. 20 small edible flowers, available from specialist food stores or see the note below

*For the dressing*

zest and juice of 1 whole lemon

½ cup olive oil

1 tbsp honey

salt and freshly ground pepper

Cook the pasta *al dente,* approx. 10 minutes, and drain. Then rinse well under cold water to stop the cooking process. Cook the asparagus for 2 minutes and also rinse under cold water. Cut the zucchinis and asparagus into very thin slices. To do so, use a mandolin or shredder if you own one. Mix the riso with the vegetables and arrange over 4 plates. Top with the crumbled ricotta. Beat the dressing ingredients into a nice vinaigrette and pour over the salads. Scatter the flowers over the top and serve immediately.

## NOTE

Edible flowers: Geranium petals, marigold petals, nasturtium (petals and leaves), dandelion petals, daisies, hedge violets, carnation petals, rose petals, lavender, yellow iris, ground ivy, sweet woodruff, and field mushroom flowers. They can all be put in the salad. Should you have herbs in your garden or on your balcony, the flowers of green leaf herbs can also be used in the salad: Dill, chives, basil blossoms, rosemary, chamomile, chervil, arugula, spearmint, and sage.

# RISOTTO WITH RED BEET AND TALEGGIO

1½ sticks butter, cubed
2 shallots, diced
leaves of a few sprigs of fresh thyme
1¾ cups Arborio rice
6 cups dry white wine
approx. 4 cups piping-hot chicken broth (see page 128)
2 beets, cooked and diced
salt and freshly ground pepper
5 oz taleggio without rind, cubed (Italian mountain cheese with an earthy flavor, which melts easily)

Melt the ½ stick of butter in a large heavy-bottomed pan and sauté the shallots until glassy. Add the thyme and rice and fry while stirring until the rice looks glassy with a white core. Add the wine and keep on stirring. Fold in the hot broth, spoonful by spoonful, on high heat and continue to stir until absorbed. After 15 minutes, add the beet cubes. Continue until the rice is cooked *al dente* in 20 minutes. Season with salt and pepper. Stir in the cheese until fully melted, and the remaining cubed butter. Turn off the heat and place the lid on the pan. Quickly transfer the risotto to four plates and serve.

**TIP** If you are unable to find taleggio, use a cheese with a strong earthy flavor.

# ROTOLO WITH LOBSTER, WILD SPINACH & ROSEMARY BEURRE BLANC

*It takes some work, but the result is fabulous. A recipe for a lot of people, we like to make it for large dinners. Serve 1 slice as a side dish or 2 as the main course. You will easily get 12 slices from one rotolo.*

*For the pasta dough*

2 cups all-purpose flour

3 eggs

salt and freshly ground pepper

a little farina (Cream of Wheat)

*For the beurre blanc*

2 shallots, chopped

1 bay leaf

small bunch of rosemary

¾ cup white wine

½ cup crème fraîche

¾ stick chilled butter, cubed

*For the rotolo filling*

8 oz lobster tails, peeled

8 oz peeled shrimp (the larger ones taste the best)

approx. 1½ cups crème fraîche

1 egg

zest of 1 lemon

salt and freshly ground pepper

a little olive oil for frying

2 shallots, diced

1 clove garlic, crushed

2 lb wild spinach, washed

nutmeg

For the pasta, work all ingredients except the farina into a firm ball, in a food processor or by hand. Leave the wrapped dough to rest in the refrigerator for 1 hour.

Make the rotolo filling: Coarsely grind the lobster, shrimp, ½ cup crème fraîche, and egg in the food processor. Top with a little grated lemon zest and season with salt and pepper. Set aside. Heat a little olive oil in a wok or large skillet, add the shallots and garlic, and sauté the spinach in batches with the water still clinging to it, until done. Leave to drain in a colander and press as much moisture out as possible. Finely chop the spinach, stir in the rest of the crème fraîche, and season with salt, pepper, and nutmeg.

Roll out the dough into a nice sheet that fits into the pasta machine and run it through the pasta machine on its widest setting. Fold and repeat the process. Do this a few times until the dough is smooth and supple. You can now reduce the setting on the machine. Keep passing the pasta through the machine until you have a long thin sheet and stop at the second-lowest setting. Dust the sheet with farina and cut into three equal parts. Use some water to stick them together so that you have a large square mat of pasta in front of you. On the long side closest to you, place a long rope of the seafood mixture. Spread the spinach-cream mixture over the rest of the sheet. At the end leave a 1-inch border. Carefully roll, beginning with the side with the seafood mixture. Brush the clear edge with a little water and seal. Then roll the rotolo into a clean dish towel and tie with a string just like rolled meat.

Bring a flame-proof roasting pan with plenty of water and a pinch of salt to a boil. Slide in the rotolo. Cook for 20 minutes. Remove. Leave to stand and remove the string and the towel. Cut the rotolo into thick slices.

During cooking, prepare the beurre blanc: Heat the shallots with the bay, rosemary, and white wine in a saucepan. Allow liquid to evaporate on low heat and stop when you are left with approx. 4 tbsp of moisture. Strain and return the collected moisture to the pan. Add the crème fraîche. Using a whisk, stir in the butter, bit by bit. Never allow the sauce to boil, but keep it near the boiling point. When all the butter is absorbed, the sauce should have thickened considerably. Spoon some sauce on a (preheated) plate, cover with a slice of rotolo, and serve immediately.

# SMOKING FISH

HOT SMOKING IS QUICK AND GIVES A BETTER RESULT THAN SMOKING TOO LONG, WHICH IS DISGUSTING AND MAKES YOUR FOOD TASTE LIKE AN ASHTRAY. IF YOU ARE NOT SURE THE FOOD IS COOKED, YOU CAN ALWAYS REHEAT IT IN THE OVEN OR FRY IT IN THE PAN. YOU HAVE TO ACQUIRE SOME SKILL HERE, AS YOU WILL NOTICE THAT FATTER FISH VARIETIES, LARGER CUTS OF MEAT, OR FIRMER VEGETABLES HAVE TO SMOKE FOR A LONG TIME, SAY, 30 MINUTES, AND SMALL, LIGHT ITEMS ONLY A VERY SHORT TIME: SOMETIMES 5 MINUTES WILL DO IT! SMOKERS TEND TO BE EXPENSIVE, BUT YOU CAN MAKE ONE YOURSELF FOR NEXT TO NOTHING. USE WOOD CHIPS, WHICH YOU CAN BUY IN A GOOD FOOD STORE. YOU CAN ALSO USE DRIED HERBS, TEA, OR SPICES. JUST EXPERIMENT. DRIED BAY AND JUNIPER BERRY TWIGS ARE ANOTHER OPTION.

CLEAN 2 MACKEREL, OR ASK THE FISHMONGER TO DO IT FOR YOU. EITHER WAY, WASH THEM BRIEFLY AT HOME.

THEN PLACE THEM IN A BAKING PAN WITH SALTED WATER FOR 2 HOURS. I USE 3 TBSP SALT FOR APPROX 8–12 CUPS.

PAT THE FISH DRY, INCLUDING THE ABDOMINAL CAVITY (WHICH YOU CAN ALSO FILL WITH LEMON OR HERBS).

PLACE THE FOLLOWING IN A ROASTING PAN OR ON A BAKING SHEET: 3 TBSP WOOD CHIPS, 2 TBSP JUNIPER BERRIES, AND 1 TBSP FENNEL SEEDS. TEA IS ANOTHER OPTION.

FOLD A SHEET OF ALUMINUM FOIL IN HALF AND COVER THE SMOKE CHIPS AND HERBS.

COVER WITH A RACK THAT FITS ON OR INTO THE ROASTING PAN. THIS CAN BE AN OVEN RACK, A RACK FROM THE MICROWAVE, OR A TRIVET, AS LONG AS IT IS HEAT-RESISTANT.

PLACE THE FISH ON THE RACK, LIGHT THE FLAME, AND WAIT UNTIL IT STARTS SMOKING. TURN DOWN THE FIRE . . .

. . . COVER THE LOT WITH PLENTY OF ALUMINUM. ENSURE THERE ARE NO GAPS, CAREFULLY CLOSE THE EDGES. USE AN OVEN MITT IF YOUR FINGERS ARE NOT FLAME-RESISTANT.

THIS IS A FATTY FISH AND THEREFORE I SMOKE IT FOR 30 MINUTES. I WOULD SMOKE A FISH WITH LESS FAT, SUCH AS WHITE FISH, FOR ONLY 10 MINUTES AND REHEAT IT IN THE OVEN, IF NECESSARY.

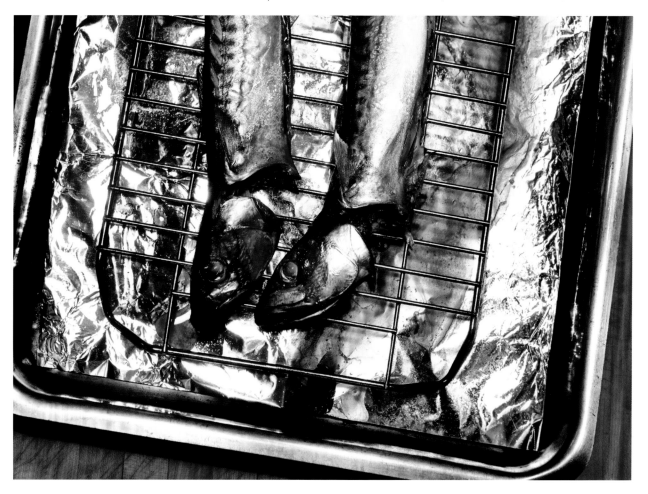

# LET'S GET GOING . . .

THE RULE TO REMEMBER IS THAT MEAT AND FISH WITH LESS FAT ARE SMOKED FOR A SHORTER TIME THAN THEIR FATTIER FAMILY MEMBERS. SMOKING FOR TOO LONG WILL RESULT IN AN UNPLEASANT BITTER TASTE. IT'S PREFERABLE THAT ANYTHING IS UNDERSMOKED RATHER THAN OVERSMOKED – YOU CAN ALWAYS FINISH IT OFF IN A PREHEATED OVEN.

## CURED AND SMOKED SALMON

*Fish that is fairly fatty lends itself better to smoking, but actually any fish can be smoked. Always cure the fish (or meat) beforehand. You can do so in a brine bath, but also by rubbing the meat with salt. You will achieve the best result if you first dry the fish before smoking it. You can do this in the refrigerator. But patting it dry with paper towels also works for the more impatient chefs.*

1 lb fresh salmon fillet, skinned
½ cup dark rum
½ cup brown sugar
approx. ¼ cup coarse sea salt
freshly ground pepper

Place the salmon in a shallow dish. Pour the rum over the salmon and leave to stand for 30 minutes. Remove the salmon from the liquid and carefully pat dry with paper towels. Discard the liquid. Combine the brown sugar, salt, and pepper. Line the bottom of a bowl or roasting pan with part of the salt-sugar mixture and place the salmon in it. Spread the rest of the mixture to fully cover the salmon. Cover the dish with plastic wrap and leave the salmon to marinate in the refrigerator for 3 to 4 hours. Place a handful of wood chips at the bottom of the smoker and get ready to smoke.

Take the salmon from the refrigerator, wipe it clean, and discard the moisture and the remaining mixture. Rinse the salmon under the water and carefully pat it clean and dry with paper towels. Smoke the salmon until done for approx. 15 minutes. The thickness will determine how long. Great with the bean salad from page 278. You can leave the salmon to cool completely and use it as sandwich filling. Delicious with the horseradish sauce from page 195.

## SMOKED TOMATO SOUP

*This is a very easy recipe and quite surprising. It often features on the menu in our restaurant. You can smoke any vegetable with high moisture content in this way. Think of zucchini, large mushrooms, eggplants, and bell peppers. I have provided a great recipe for this on page 236.*

2 lb tomatoes
2 x 14 oz cans peeled tomatoes
1 tsp paprika
1 tsp cayenne pepper
2 cloves garlic, peeled
2 cups chicken broth
salt and freshly ground pepper
2 tbsp wood chips or tea

Bring a pan with water to a boil. Using a sharp knife, score a cross in the skin at the bottom of each fresh tomato. When the water boils, add the tomatoes and blanch for ½ minute. Rinse under running water. The skin can now be easily removed. Smoke the tomatoes in a smoker for 30 minutes on low heat.

In the meantime, heat the peeled canned tomatoes in a large pan. Add the spices and garlic. Pour in the broth. Allow the soup to simmer for 30 minutes. Lastly, add the smoked tomatoes and puree the soup until smooth, using a hand blender. Taste, and add salt and pepper, as needed. Serve the soup in large bowls with a spoonful of spreadable labneh (see page 296), or a dash of olive oil.

# SPARERIBS

*At first, I was unsure about including this recipe here, since I thought it should be in the roasting section. But spareribs taste so much better if you smoke them first.*

4–6 racks of spareribs
(plan 1–1½ racks per person)

*For the sauce*
½ cup soy sauce
3 tbsp raw superfine sugar
zest and juice of 1 lime
1 bell pepper, seeds removed, finely chopped
6 cloves garlic, crushed
1 piece of fresh ginger the length of your thumb
3–4 sprigs fresh thyme, finely chopped
3 tbsp oil

Combine all the sauce ingredients and stir into a thick sauce. Use it to cover the spareribs and leave to marinate for at least 3 hours, but preferably longer. Turn on the smoker and smoke on very low heat for 20 minutes.
Cook them a further 1 hour covered with aluminum in a 350°F/Gas 4 oven. Do not forget to continue to baste them with the marinade. Remove the aluminum during the last 20 minutes.
Serve with Oof's barbecue sauce (see page 380), or the garlic sauce on the same page.
Serve with white cabbage salad with cumin (see page 261).

# SMOKED GARLIC DRESSING

*First smoke the garlic—smoke more than one bulb at the same time. Smoked garlic can be used wherever you use regular garlic, but the flavor is surprisingly different. Store smoked garlic tightly covered in the refrigerator.*

a few bulbs of good-quality garlic
2 tbsp wood chips
a few dried bay leaves

Fill the smoker with the smoke chips and bay. Place the garlic on the rack and smoke on as low a heat as possible for 30 minutes. Turn off the heat and leave the garlic in the smoker for another hour or more.

*For the dressing*
4 cloves smoked garlic
1 tbsp prepared horseradish or ½ tbsp freshly grated horseradish
4 tbsp sherry vinegar
½ cup grape seed oil or another light vegetable oil
1 tbsp fresh thyme or oregano
salt and freshly ground pepper

Flatten the garlic in order to easily remove the skins.
Add them with the horseradish and the vinegar to a blender or food processor and puree until smooth. Add the oil while blending and then the thyme. Once the dressing is thick and white, season it with salt and pepper.
This dressing is delicious on boiled potatoes, on a grilled vegetable salad, or served with red meat.

# SMOKED ROOT VEGETABLES

*Anything can be smoked, including root vegetables.*
*Contrary to meat and fish, these vegetables, which contain less moisture than tomatoes or zucchinis, for example, must be smoked longer and hotter than the other recipes so far.*
*Cut all vegetables into chunks of approximately equal size.*

231

2 carrots
2 sweet potatoes
2 waxy potatoes
2 parsnips
1 butternut squash
(all peeled and cut into chunks of the same size)
2 beets, also cut in the same size, but not peeled only washed
4 tbsp olive oil
1 tbsp thyme
salt and freshly ground pepper
3 tbsp wood chips

Mix all the vegetables in a bowl with the oil, thyme, salt, and pepper.
Arrange on the smoker rack and smoke for at least 30–40 minutes on medium heat. After 25 minutes, turn on the oven and preheat it to 350°F/Gas 4.
Bake the vegetables for a further 15 minutes, until they take on a nice color and are cooked *al dente*. Serve as a side dish with one-person chickens (see recipe on page 263).

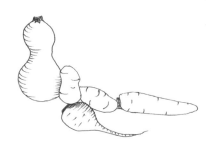

# SMOKED SHRIMP WITH LEMON & ROSEMARY SALT

*A good snack with drinks or on a table full of small dishes.*

2 lb raw jumbo shrimp
2 tbsp salt
6 cups water

*For the rosemary salt*
3 tbsp coarse sea salt
2 sprigs rosemary
zest of 2 lemons

Peel the shrimp, but leave the tails on. Stir the salt into the water. Add the shrimp and allow to soak in the brine for at least two hours.

Preheat oven to 350°F/Gas 4.

Place the shrimp on the rack in your homemade smoker (see page 228) and smoke the shrimp for 5 minutes. Remove from the smoker and cook for another 5 minutes in the regular oven. Allow to cool.

In the meantime, prepare the rosemary salt: Crush the sea salt and the rosemary leaves into a green powder in a mortar. Stir in the lemon zest.

Sprinkle on the smoked shrimp and serve as a dip with some extra salt.

**TIP** You do not need all the herb salt for this dish, so save the rest for another time. It is delicious on steak or on fried fish or chicken.

# SMOKED PORK CHOPS

2–3 tbsp salt
4 tasty pork chops, preferably organic
8 juniper berries, crushed
2 bay leaves
8 peppercorns
wood chips, a few dried bay leaves, and preferably a few dried twigs of the juniper berry bush

Dissolve the salt in water in a baking pan in which the chops fit neatly. Add the juniper berries, bay, and peppercorns, as well as the meat. Leave to soak in the brine for 2 hours or longer if you have the time.

Heat the smoker with 3 tbsp wood chips, a few bay leaves, and perhaps 8 juniper berry twigs. Pat the chops dry and smoke for approx. 8 minutes.

Heat a grill or broiler and cook the chops on high heat until crisp and golden brown. They are probably nearly cooked, and therefore do not have to be cooked for a long time.

Serve with stew or fried salsify and carrots (see page 285).

# SMOKED BELL PEPPERS

*Tasty side dish or part of many dishes on a buffet or cocktail table.*

2 yellow bell peppers
2 red bell peppers

*For the dressing*
3 tbsp balsamic vinegar
1 tsp prepared mustard
1 tbsp honey
salt and freshly ground pepper
⅔ cup olive oil

*And also*
wood chips
1 tbsp dried rosemary or Earl Grey tea
⅓ cup shaved Parmesan cheese or pecorino
small flowers of an unsprayed carthamus ☆ (from the thistle; optional, of course)

First grill the peppers by placing them on the stove burner and slowly burning them black.
If you do not own a gas stove, place them under a hot broiler. Turn over regularly; they really have to turn black!
Once scorched on all sides, transfer them to a plastic bag and tie in a knot. Leave the peppers to sweat for 30 minutes.
Remove. Using a knife, remove the skin. Rinse well under running water and pat dry. Smoke for 15 minutes in the smoker with 2 tbsp wood chips and a little dry rosemary or tea.
Make the dressing by combining the first four ingredients and then adding the oil until the dressing achieves the desired thickness.
Cut the smoked peppers into thick strips. Arrange on a dish. Sprinkle with the shaved cheese and carthamus, and top with the dressing.

☆  Carthamus is a common yellow-orange thistle, often called the saffron thistle. It is available from some florists.

# BRANDADE OF SMOKED TROUT

FLESH OF APPROX. 1 CLEANED
AND SMOKED TROUT (250 G / 9 OZ)
(SMOKE THE TROUT AS DESCRI-
BED ON PAGE 228)
5 TBSP CRÈME FRAÎCHE
1-2 TBSP HORSERADISH CREAM
DASH OF LEMON JUICE
FRESHLY GROUND PEPPER & SALT
CHERVIL TO GARNISH
250 G (9 OZ / APPROX
1¼ CUPS) MASHED POTATOES

→ BLITZ ALL THE INGREDIENTS,
EXCEPT THE CHERVIL & POTATOES, IN
THE FOOD PROCESSOR. FOLD IN THE
MASHED POTATOES → BLEND THOROUGHLY.
GARNISH WITH CHERVIL.

# SMOKED MACKEREL WITH WATERCRESS, WHITE BEANS, AND TASTY TOMATOES

*For the salad*

8 oz soaked white beans (or use 1 can cooked beans)

1 whole smoked mackerel (see page 228)

8 oz small vine tomatoes

2 bunches watercress or 2 handfuls young spinach leaves

1 small bunch parsley, washed and finely chopped

*For the dressing*

juice and zest of ½ lemon

1 shallot, finely chopped

salt and freshly ground pepper

½ cup grape seed oil or another light vegetable oil

Cook the soaked beans until done, approx. 30–40 minutes, then remove from the pan and rinse under cold water. (Or, if you use beans from a can, drain well and rinse.) Prepare the dressing by combining all the ingredients and lastly, stirring in the oil in a trickle. Fold the beans into the dressing. Set aside and allow to marinate. Carefully remove the skin from the mackerel and then the meat from the bone. Separate the fish into flakes over a large bowl. Wash and halve the tomatoes and add them. If you use watercress, trim away the tough stems. Mix the lettuce with the fish and tomato. Lastly, fold in the beans, and dressing, and garnish with parsley.

**TIP** Make a snack with the smoked fish leftovers, which my sister and I liked to make when we were children:

# CUCUMBER ROUNDS FILLED WITH SMOKED FISH

*For approx. 15 snacks*

½ smoked mackerel (or 1 can sardines)

1 tbsp butter at room temperature

2 tbsp mayonnaise (see recipe on page 380)

pinch of cayenne pepper

salt and freshly ground pepper

a few drops of lemon juice

1 whole cucumber

Mix all the ingredients, except the cucumber, in a food processor or mash them in a bowl using a fork. Season with salt, pepper, and lemon juice. Cut the cucumber in sections the length of an apple corer. Trim away the ends.
Using the apple corer, remove the seeds. You can also use a thin sharp knife, for that matter. Fill the created cavity with the fish mousse and wrap the rounds in plastic wrap. Leave to cool and set for about an hour in the refrigerator.
Cut the cucumber into thick slices with a sharp knife and enjoy!

# MILLE-FEUILLE OF SMOKED AND RAW BEET AND COMTÉ, WITH WATERCRESS, AND NUT DRESSING

4 parboiled beets

2 tbsp wood chips

2 raw beets

a small handful hazelnuts

1 bunch watercress, washed, hard stems removed, or fine spinach leaves

4 oz Comté (a cheese from the Jura, France), cubed, or use Parmesan cheese or goat cheese

leaves of 2 sprigs of fresh sage or oregano

2 tbsp hazelnut oil

*For the dressing*

4 tbsp raspberry vinegar

1 tablespoon ginger syrup or honey

8 tbsp olive oil

salt and freshly ground pepper


Smoke the beets for 20 minutes on low heat. Then cut all beets, raw and smoked, as thinly as possible on a mandolin or using a good knife. Make the dressing with the ingredients from the list and sprinkle over the beet slices.

Cover and leave to marinate for at least 1 hour until used.

Toast the nuts in a dry pan and chop coarsely.

Build the salads: Stack alternating leaves and marinated beet slices on 4 plates.

Divide the Comté among the plates and sprinkle the salads with the hazelnuts, and the sage or oregano leaves.

Trickle some hazelnut oil over each salad.

Use the leftover smoked beets the following day in a club sandwich: page 389.

Each time we stay in the Colombet family's orchard in the south of France,
Oof will first search for large rocks near the river to build a fire in our camp.
Starting a fire is of course a lot of fun, but in this case it is also vital. We cook on it and
in the evening it is our heater, since nights can get quite chilly in the country.
We stare at it together at night before we fall asleep: What will we grill on it tomorrow?

# BUILDING AN OUTDOOR GRILL

BUILDING AN OUTDOOR GRILL IS NOT DIFFICULT. FINDING A PLACE IN THE OPEN WHERE IT IS PERMITTED OFTEN IS. BE AWARE OF FIRE RESTRICTIONS. SOMETIMES THERE ARE RESTRICTIONS ON GATHERING WOOD. IF ALL ELSE FAILS, USE THE GRILLS PROVIDED IN PARKS AND CAMPGROUNDS. THE SAFEST PLACE TO USE A HOMEMADE GRILL IS NEXT TO WATER, WHETHER IT IS A RIVER OR A LARGE BUCKET OF WATER. THE WIND CAN SEND THE FLAMES IN AN UNEXPECTED DIRECTION! > OOF WILL SHOW YOU, WATCH!

DIG A HOLE. SEARCH FOR ROCKS THAT NEATLY FIT AROUND IT. BUILD A BORDER WITH TWO LAYERS OF ROCKS, WHICH MAY COME IN HANDY LATER.

CHECK WHETHER THE RACK YOU BROUGHT FITS.

GATHER WOOD AND FILL THE FIRE (YOU CAN OBVIOUSLY ALSO BRING YOUR OWN LOGS, WHICH CAN BE BOUGHT IN BAGS).

LIGHT THE FIRE. USE A PORTABLE FIRE LIGHTER; THE FIRE STARTED IMMEDIATELY.

NOW IT HAS TO BURN FOR A WHILE UNTIL THE FLAMES HAVE DIED DOWN AND THE WOOD SMOLDERS. IN THE MEANTIME, HAVE A DRINK AND WAIT.

PREPARE YOUR GEAR, IN THIS CASE 2 STEAKS, A BUNCH OF ROSEMARY, OLIVE OIL, PEPPER, AND SALT.

BRIEFLY RUB THE MEAT WITH THE OLIVE OIL AND SPRINKLE WITH PEPPER AND SALT.

THE GRILL IS SMOLDERING; THE MEAT CAN GO ON IT.

WE WANT IT HOTTER, THEREFORE OOF LOWERS THE MEAT.

REMOVE THE FIRST LAYER OF ROCKS: THAT'S MORE LIKE IT!

GRILL THE MEAT ON BOTH SIDES, DO NOT TURN IT CONSTANTLY.

JUST LEAVE IT BE.

OCCASIONALLY BRUSH WITH A ROSEMARY SPRIG DIPPED IN OLIVE OIL

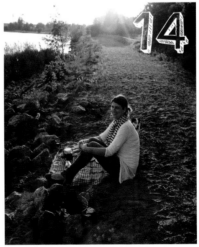

LEAVE TO REST FOR 10 MINUTES AWAY FROM THE FIRE.

YES! ONLY THEN CAN YOU CARVE THE MEAT. BON APPÉTIT!

# OK! LET'S GET GOING . . .

YOU CAN THROW MEAT OR FISH ON THE GRILL OR IN A SKILLET AS IS, WITH ONLY SALT AND PEPPER, BUT SOMETIMES A MARINADE OR "RUB" (DRY MIXTURE OF HERBS AND SPICES) IS A TASTY ADDITION AND YOU WON'T NEED ANY SAUCES.

## STICKY MARINADE

*Great for spareribs or bacon, for example.*

4 tbsp red wine vinegar
⅔ cup soy sauce
1 tbsp tomato puree
1 tsp cinnamon
1 thumb's length of peeled and grated fresh ginger
1 clove garlic, chopped
1 tbsp brown sugar

## FRESH HERB MARINADE

*Great with fish or chicken.*

1 generous handful of chopped fresh garden herbs: tarragon, chives, basil, parsley
2 shallots, diced
2 cloves garlic, coarsely chopped
2 tbsp white balsamic vinegar
pinch of salt
1 tbsp. peppercorns from the mortar
½ cup olive oil

## FENNEL SEED RUB

*Tasty on pork chops or on fish.*

5 tbsp toasted fennel seeds
4 tbsp toasted coriander seeds
2 tsp coarse sea salt
2 tsp white peppercorns
1 tbsp sugar
Coarsely grind in a mortar.

## NORTH AFRICAN RUB

*Great on lamb kebabs, lamb chops, or chicken.*

1 red onion, diced
3 cloves garlic, thinly sliced
2 tbsp cumin seeds, toasted
2 tbsp coriander seeds, toasted
1 cinnamon stick
1 tbsp caraway seeds, toasted
pinch of cayenne pepper (to taste) or
1 dried chile pepper
1 tbsp sea salt

## MEDITERRANEAN MARINADE

*Good with chicken, meat, and fish.*

1 handful fresh basil and mint
juice of 1 lemon
1 chile pepper
1 tsp coarse sea salt
2 cloves garlic
½ cup extra-virgin olive oil

Coarsely chop the herbs and crush all ingredients in a large mortar or food processor into a coarse pesto.

## SPICY SOUTH AMERICAN RUB

*Great on beef.*

zest of 2 limes
2 cloves garlic, thinly sliced
pinch of chile powder
1 tbsp paprika
1 tbsp toasted cumin seeds
2 tbsp fresh oregano, chopped
(otherwise 1 tbsp dried oregano)
1 tsp sea salt
1 tsp ground black pepper

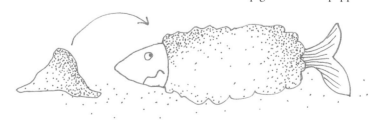

# LOBSTER WITH LIME, SCALLIONS, AND GINGER BUTTER

1 piece of ginger the length of your thumb
2 scallions
1¼ sticks butter at room temperature
fine zest of 1 lime
salt and freshly ground pepper
2 large lobsters of approx. 2 lb each, raw
extra lime

Peel the ginger and chop finely. Wash and finely chop the scallions. Beat the ginger and scallions into the softened butter using a fork, hand blender, or food processor. Further season the butter with the lime zest, salt, and pepper. Transfer the butter to a sheet of plastic wrap and roll tightly into a log. Place in the refrigerator for approx. 1 hour to set. Precook the lobsters for 3 minutes in a pan with plenty of water. Remove from the pan and allow to slightly cool. Halve them lengthwise with a sharp knife. Crack the claws with a heavy object or nut cracker. This will allow them to cook faster later and make them easier for guests to open. Place the lobster halves with the meat side up on the hot grill. Spread some butter on the meat. Briefly cook the lobsters, until the meat is no longer glassy. You can close the lid briefly on the grill in order to thoroughly cook the lobster and to allow the smoked flavor to better infuse.
Serve with slices of herb butter and lime.
Great with green asparagus with parsley gremolata (see recipe on page 286.)

# CHICKEN KEBABS WITH HONEY, PRUNES & WALNUTS

*For the marinade*

3 tbsp honey

1 tbsp *ras el hanout* (North African spice mixture), or allspice, or ½ tbsp mixed spices

2 tbsp red wine vinegar

¾ cup red wine

salt and freshly ground pepper

*And also*

8 chicken thighs, the meat cut away from the bone and then cut into equal chunks

2¼ cups prunes, pitted but left whole

½ cup walnuts

First prepare a marinade by combining all the ingredients. Arrange the chicken chunks in a pan and top with the marinade. Cover with plastic wrap and place in the refrigerator for a few hours, the longer the better. Thread the chicken chunks on skewers, alternating with the prunes. Cook the marinade and the walnuts into a syrup. Place the skewers on medium heat on the grill until done. Arrange on a dish and top with the warm marinade.
Serve with herb tabouleh and cardamom dressing (see recipe on page 282).

# CHICKEN KEBABS WITH SALAD, CROUTONS, AND YOGURT DRESSING

*For the marinade/sauce*

½ cup yogurt

2 tbsp lemon juice

1 clove garlic, crushed

2 tbsp finely chopped parsley

¼ cup olive oil

salt and freshly ground pepper

*And also*

3 chicken legs or 4 chicken thighs, boneless

2 small romaine lettuces

salt and freshly ground pepper

½ baguette

⅓ cup olive oil

Make a marinade/sauce by combining all the ingredients. Cut the chicken meat into equal chunks. Stir in half of the sauce. Place in the refrigerator to marinate for approx. 3 hours. Carefully trim away the bottom of the small romaine lettuces and quarter. Bring a pan with water to a boil. Add a pinch of salt and briefly blanch the lettuce. Cut half a baguette in equal 1-inch cubes. Season the olive oil with salt and pepper, and add the bread. Thread the chicken, bread, and lettuce alternately on skewers. Cook them on medium heat on the outdoor grill or grill pan until done. Serve with the remaining yogurt dressing. Tasty with a crispy salad sprinkled with Parmesan cheese.

253

# TROUT WITH PARSLEY & FENNEL SEED BUTTER

4 trout
¼ cup olive oil
2 cloves garlic, crushed
salt and freshly ground pepper
small bunch parsley, chopped
½ lemon, thinly sliced
1 stick butter at room temperature
1 tbsp fennel seeds, crushed in the mortar

Score the skin of the cleaned trout and rub the fish with a mixture of olive oil, 1 garlic clove, salt, pepper, and half of the chopped parsley. Fill the cavities with the lemon slices. Wrap in aluminum foil.

Make herb butter in the food processor: Combine the butter, fennel seeds, reserved parsley and garlic, salt, and pepper into a smooth mixture. Roll the butter in a sheet of plastic wrap and put in the refrigerator to harden for approx. 1 hour.

Cook the fish for approx. 10 minutes on a warm outdoor grill. Take a look after 8 minutes to check whether they are cooked! But close the aluminum quickly in order for the wrapping to retain the heat. Serve the fish topped with a slice of cold herb butter.

# WHOLE BEEF LOIN IN SPICE CRUST
# WITH ROSEMARY SALMORIGLIO
*an easy recipe serving 7*

### Create a spice mix:

USING MORTAR & PESTLE:

2 TBSP FENNEL SEEDS
2 TBSP OREGANO
2 TBSP BLACK PEPPERCORNS
2 TBSP COARSE SEA SALT

PLACE 1 WHOLE BEEF
LOIN (APPROX. 1 KG / 2 LBS)
ON A SHEET OF PLASTICWRAP

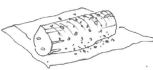

SPRINKLE WITH THE SPICES
& WRAP THOROUGHLY.
STORE FOR ABOUT 1 HOUR
IN THE FRIDGE.

SAUTÉ THE MARINATED
ROAST ON ALL SIDES.
IN A LITTLE OLIVE OIL,
THIS HAPPENS QUICKLY.
LEAVE TO REST FOR 15
MINS UNDER ALU-
MINIUM FOIL.
CUT INTO VERY THIN
SLICES & DRIZZLE
WITH THE GREEN OIL
...Ready!

### make salmoriglio:
IN A FOOD PROCESSOR → BLEND:

THE LEAVES OF 1 BUNCH
OF ROSEMARY
ZEST & JUICE OF 1 LEMON

½ TSP SEA SALT
FRESHLY GROUND PEPPER
100 ML (APPROX 3 FL OZ / ½ CUP)
GOOD-QUALITY OLIVE OIL

Chez moi
tout est subtil

CHOU~~OUTE

# LEG OF LAMB WITH NETTLES & GOAT CHEESE PESTO

*You can serve 6–8 people with a leg of lamb.*

*For the leg of lamb*
1 whole garlic bulb
1 bunch thyme
½ cup olive oil
salt and freshly ground pepper
1 leg of lamb, deboned (approx. 2 lb); or with bone (approx. 3 lb)

*For the pesto*
2 handfuls young nettle tops (or arugula if you are not such a nature person)
2 cloves garlic
½ cup olive oil
1 cup grated hard goat cheese (or pecorino)
½ cup walnuts, if desired
salt and freshly ground pepper

Coarsely chop the garlic. Strip the leaves from the thyme sprigs. Blend the garlic, thyme, oil, salt, and pepper. Also add the stripped thyme sprigs. Massage the marinade into the meat, cover, and leave the meat to marinate in the refrigerator preferably 1 night, but at least 2 hours. Allow the lamb to reach room temperature.
Preheat the oven to 350°F/Gas 4. Remove the herbs from the lamb and roast for 35–40 minutes until medium-rare. A leg of lamb with bone will have to roast a little longer, say, 40–45 minutes. Leave the meat to rest under a sheet of aluminum foil for 15 minutes.
In the meantime prepare the pesto: Pulse the ingredients in the food processor into a coarse pesto, not too fine. Taste and add salt and pepper, as needed.
Cut the lamb into thin slices. Serve with nettle pesto and boiled young potatoes.
Great with lukewarm green vegetable salad (see recipe on page 171).

# MACKEREL FILLETS WITH BAY, GARLIC, AND BELL PEPPERS

14 fresh bay leaves, cut into pieces
1 red bell pepper, seeds removed
2 cloves garlic
½ red chile
¼ cup olive oil
coarse sea salt
4 mackerel fillets, cleaned

In the food processor, make a coarse paste with the bay leaves, bell pepper, garlic, and red chile. Add as much oil as needed for the mixture to stick together. Season with salt.

Score the skin side of the fish fillets a few times and cover with some of the paste. Grease a baking sheet. Place the fish with the filled side up and cook under a hot broiler for approx. 8 minutes.

Also possible on the outdoor grill: Cover the other side of the fillets so that the skin side cooks on the hot grill. Thoroughly oil the skin and do not turn the fish. Bake until done just a smidge away from the highest fire.

Serve with white cabbage salad with cumin.

# WHITE CABBAGE SALAD WITH CUMIN

*A remarkably simple but fun salad for all seasons.*

*For the salad*
¼ head white cabbage, very thinly sliced, using a mandolin or the food processor
1 bunch watercress, leaves only, or arugula, or dandelion leaves (used here)
1 large bunch mint, leaves only
2 tbsp cumin seeds, roasted

*For the dressing*
1 clove garlic
1 tbsp cumin seeds, roasted
juice of 1 lemon
salt and freshly ground pepper
⅔ cup grape seed oil or other light vegetable oil

Combine all the ingredients for the salad. Add the first four ingredients for the dressing to a deep container and puree until smooth. Pour in enough oil to create a creamy dressing. Pour over the salad and leave to stand so the flavors infuse.

# ONE-PERSON CHICKEN WITH SAGE, GARLIC, AND MUSHROOMS

*Along the Canal St. Martin, behind our house in Paris, a group of people, primarily students, often eat together at the end of the day as late as the summer weather allows. It is quite a bit cheaper than eating out and at least as much fun. The best urban picnic site ever.*

3 whole garlic bulbs
1 bunch fresh sage, finely chopped
a few sprigs of thyme
salt and freshly ground pepper
olive oil
4 cockerels or poussins (spring chickens)
2 lb fresh forest mushrooms: portobello, chanterelles, chestnut mushrooms, giant mushrooms, oyster mushrooms, all cleaned

Halve the three garlic bulbs. The bottom halves will cling together nicely. Save them, peel the loose cloves, and chop them finely. Fill the chickens with part of the mixture of chopped garlic, sage, thyme, salt, and pepper. Rub them with olive oil, salt, and pepper, and place on a baking sheet. Distribute the halved garlic bulbs between them and a few of the mushrooms. Arrange the remaining mushrooms on another baking sheet, top with the remaining garlic, thyme, and sage mixture. Drizzle with some olive oil and sprinkle with salt and pepper. Preheat the oven to 350°F/Gas 4. Place the chickens in it and roast for approx. 45 minutes or until done. Add the mushrooms in the last 10 minutes.
Briefly leave the birds to rest after roasting.
Take them with mushrooms, garlic, and all on a picnic or serve with the squash au gratin from page 281 (handy, it can also go into the oven), and fried wild spinach.

# MULLET WITH CHERMOULA

*Plan on 2 small mullets per serving.*

8 mullets, cleaned and scaled (ask the fishmonger)

*For the chermoula* (Hassane told us you say "Tsar-millah")
a few strands saffron
3 tomatoes, quartered, seeds removed, pulp cubed
3 roasted bell peppers, cubed
1 small bunch cilantro
1 small bunch mint sprigs
1 small bunch parsley (preferably flat-leaf)
juice of 1 lemon
2 tsp toasted cumin seeds, coarsely crushed in a mortar
salt and freshly ground pepper
olive oil

Preheat the oven to 350°F/Gas 4.
Prepare the chermoula: Soak the saffron in 3 tbsp warm water. Combine all other ingredients. Lastly, stir in the saffron threads with the moisture and season the chermoula with salt and pepper.
Place the mullets in a greased roasting pan, cover with half of the chermoula, and place in the hot oven for approx. 7 minutes. Once the fish is cooked, pour the other half of the sauce over it, and serve with bread and a green salad.

# LAMB CHOPS IN A CRUST OF LEMON, MINT, AND PISTACHIO NUTS

4 oz capers
4 tbsp grated lemon zest
2 cloves garlic, crushed
4 tbsp chopped mint
½ cup pistachio nuts, chopped
4 tbsp olive oil or more
4 lamb chops
olive oil for frying

Coarsely chop the capers. Mix with lemon zest, garlic, mint, and chopped nuts. Add the olive oil and blend into a smooth dressing. Pour into shallow bowl. Pat the lamb chops dry and score the fat, thus preventing the chop curling up on the grill. Place them in the mixture you have made in the bowl and leave to marinate for 1 hour. Remove. Ensure that all chops are well covered with the marinade. Cook on an outdoor grill or in a skillet on both sides on high heat until medium-rare. Serve with mint sauce.

## MINT SAUCE

3 shallots, diced
1 small bunch of mint sprigs, washed and finely chopped
1 tbsp cold butter plus ½ stick extra, in pats
3 tbsp white wine vinegar
1 tbsp honey
salt and freshly ground pepper

Sauté the shallots with half of the chopped mint in the 1 tbsp butter until the shallots turn glassy. Add the vinegar and then the honey. Bring the mixture to a boil and allow the acid from the vinegar to slightly evaporate. Remove from the heat and beat in the extra pats of cold butter until the sauce thickens. Season with salt and pepper.

*Yvette ,*
*Charles & Marie*

# GRILLED FENNEL SALAD

2 bulbs fennel

juice of 2 lemons

½ cup good-quality olive oil

⅓ cup pistachio nuts, halved

1 bunch fresh watercress, cleaned

1 small bunch dill, coarsely chopped

1 handful other type of lettuce, cleaned: here I used dandelion leaves, but arugula or mesclun are other options

1¼ cups soft goat cheese

salt and freshly ground pepper

Remove the tough outer layers from the fennel and the tops, and slice them from top to bottom, as thinly as possible. Cook them on an outdoor grill, or oven rack to broil. Transfer to a large dish. Pour a portion of the lemon juice and oil over the fennel, to allow the flavors to infuse. Toast the nuts briefly in a hot dry pan until they release their aroma. Trim away the hard stems from the watercress bunch, and thoroughly wash and dry the leaves. Mix them and the dill with the other lettuce. Arrange the salad on the plate with the fennel. Then top with the crumbled goat cheese. Trickle some lemon juice and oil on the plate and sprinkle with the pistachio nuts. Season the salad with salt and pepper.

# LUKEWARM SALAD WITH POTATOES, GREEN BEANS, AND GIANT BEANS

26 oz fine waxy potatoes, such as Roseval potatoes

8 oz green beans, cleaned

14 oz can giant beans (large haricot beans) (though soaking overnight and then cooking yourself always tastes better!)

*For the dressing*

1 small bunch parsley, washed and chopped

1 small bunch tarragon, washed and chopped

2 tbsp pine nuts

1 clove garlic, crushed

4 tbsp extra-virgin olive oil

juice of ½ lemon

salt and freshly ground pepper

⅓ cup freshly grated Parmesan cheese

Scrub the potatoes, cut them into approx. 1 inch cubes, and boil until done in salted water. Cook the green beans for approx. 3 minutes. Drain and rinse briefly under cold water. Drain the giant beans and also rinse under cold water. Coarsely grind the ingredients for the dressing in a mortar or food processor. Stir into the salad and serve immediately.

GRILLED FENNEL Salad
YUM

# FLATBREAD WITH CHICKPEAS AND SAGE

1¼ cups lukewarm water
1 package yeast (2¼ tsp)
4 cups all-purpose flour and a little extra
14 oz can chickpeas, drained and rinsed
a few sprigs sage, chopped
salt and freshly ground pepper

Stir the yeast into the lukewarm water and briefly allow to dissolve. Combine the flour and chickpeas in a food processor or in a large bowl and mix well. The chickpeas have to burst open! Combine the sage, salt, and pepper, and add the water. Work thoroughly, at least some 10 minutes, into a smooth dough. If necessary, add flour if it is too sticky. Dust a bowl with a little flour and place the dough ball in it. Cover with plastic wrap. Put in a draught-free place and leave the dough to rise for at least 1 hour. Dust the work surface and remove the risen flour ball from the bowl. Knock down the dough again and divide the ball into equal portions the size of apricots. Sprinkle with flour and keep until used, at least 1 hour, on a serving tray dusted with flour. Place a flat pan or shallow skillet on the heat. Roll the small dough balls into thin elongated pieces and cook in the pan until they puff up. Turn halfway through until they are cooked.

**TIP** You can also cook them on the outdoor grill! Cook them toward the end, when the fire has slightly subsided.

# PIZZA BIANCA WITH FLATBREAD

*For 10–12 small pizzas as a side dish or 24 mini pizzas: Great when served with drinks.*

2⅔ cups mixed mushrooms
3 tbsp olive oil, plus a little extra
a few twigs fresh thyme (reserve some for garnish)
1 clove garlic, chopped
salt and freshly ground pepper
1 quantity of dough, as described above
7 oz taleggio (Italian mountain cheese with an earthy flavor, which melts easily; otherwise use raclette cheese or mozzarella)
24 drops truffle or hazelnut oil

Slice the mushrooms. Heat a skillet with olive oil and briefly sauté the mushrooms with a little thyme. Toward the end add the garlic, and season with salt and pepper. If desired, save some thyme for the garnish. Set aside to slightly cool. Line a baking sheet with parchment paper and butter well. Make the dough as described above and create pizzas in the size of your choice. Then cover them with mushrooms and taleggio. Cook in an oven preheated to 340°F/Gas 4 for approx. 15 minutes until golden brown. Leave to slightly cool and sprinkle with a little truffle oil.
Delicious as a meal served with a beet salad (see page 172).

# BUTTERNUT SQUASH & POTATO SALAD FROM THE OVEN, WITH FRESH SAGE

2 butternut squash
4 waxy potatoes, with skin
⅔ cup olive oil
1 clove garlic, crushed
2 tsp ground paprika
1 bunch fresh sage, chopped (save some leaves for the garnish)
salt and freshly ground pepper

Preheat the oven to 350°F/Gas 4. Cut one of the butternut squash in two and scoop out the seeds and pulp, leaving a shell. Peel the remaining squash using a peeler. Halve and discard the seeds. Cube all the butternut pulp. Cut the potatoes to the same size. Make a dressing with the olive oil, garlic, paprika, sage, salt, and pepper.
Mix with the squash and potato cubes. Line a baking sheet with parchment paper. Spread the cubes on it and bake for 30 minutes until *al dente* and golden brown. Turn occasionally. Lastly, add the scooped-out squash shells to the oven and bake a further 10 minutes. Before serving, transfer the potato and squash cubes back to the hollowed butternuts.
Garnish with a few fresh sage leaves.
Great with leg of lamb (see recipe on page 258) or the smoked chops on page 235.

# CARROT SALAD WITH CUMIN

3 carrots, peeled
1 clove garlic, crushed
1 tbsp cumin seeds
4 tbsp olive oil
2 tbsp red wine vinegar
pinch of cayenne pepper
a few leaves cilantro to garnish
salt

Grate the carrots coarsely on a mandolin or in the food processor. Make a dressing with the remaining ingredients and blend them with the carrot salad. Keep the salad in the refrigerator until ready to serve. Prior to serving garnish with a few cilantro leaves. Good with Arab lamb burgers on page 384, or with chicken kebabs on page 253.

# RÖSTI FRITTERS WITH ROSEMARY

6 waxy, medium potatoes
leaves of 6 twigs rosemary
sea salt
some light oil for frying

Cut the potatoes into a very fine julienne (very thin strips) in the food processor, or use a good mandolin, or grater. Thoroughly pat them dry. Add the rosemary and a little salt to the grated potatoes. Heat a thin coat of oil in a skillet and fry 3 heaps of potato mixture in the oil at a time. Do not stir or touch! When the edges turn golden yellow, turn and fry on the other side. Allow to drain on paper towels. Can be easily made in advance: Heat the fritters for 6 minutes prior to serving in an oven preheated to 350°F/Gas 4.

# SUNCHOKES AU GRATIN

3 lb sunchokes
salt and freshly ground pepper
¾ cup thick cream
1¼ cups crème fraîche
pat of butter to grease an oven dish
2½ cups grated Gruyère

Peel the sunchokes. Bring a pan with water to a boil and add salt. Cook the sunchokes 5–7 minutes until nearly done. Swiftly rinse and cut into slices as thin as possible. This is easiest on a mandolin, but a sharp knife also works.
Beat the cream with the crème fraîche and season with salt and pepper.
Butter an oven dish and preheat the oven to 350°F/Gas 4.
Place a third of the sunchoke slices in the oven dish, sprinkle with a portion of the Gruyère, and top with a portion of the cream. Continue until all the ingredients are used. Finish with the cheese and place the dish in the oven.
Bake the gratin for approx. 30 minutes, or until golden brown.

# FRESH BEAN SALAD WITH RADISH AND CAESAR DRESSING

salt

7 oz green beans, cleaned and broken in half

7 oz sugarsnap peas, cleaned

1⅓ cups shelled fava beans, preferably fresh, but otherwise frozen

1 bunch radishes

1 small bunch flat-leaf parsley, coarsely chopped

*For the dressing*

1 clove garlic, crushed

2 generous tbsp mayonnaise

2 generous tbsp sour cream

½ cup freshly grated Parmesan cheese

1 canned anchovy fillet

juice of ½ lemon

salt and freshly ground pepper


First, prepare a large bowl filled with water and ice cubes. Then heat a pan with water and a pinch of salt and bring to a boil. Briefly blanch the beans, starting with the green beans, as these need the most time.

Once the beans are cooked *al dente*, remove them with a slotted spoon and submerge in the ice water.

When they are ice-cold remove from the ice water and leave to drain. Peel the fava beans. In the meantime, wash and clean the radishes. Quarter them and add them to the beans. Also stir in the parsley.

Make the dressing by thoroughly blending the ingredients. Taste for salt: Due to the anchovy fillet and cheese it may very well be salty enough.

Blend the dressing with the bean salad. A great salad with the chicken kebabs on page 253.

# SQUASH AU GRATIN

1 butternut squash approx. 2 lb)

2 small squash

4 tbsp olive oil

pinch of cayenne pepper

pinch of paprika

pinch of nutmeg

salt

4 eggs

1 cup crème fraîche

1½ cups grated cheese (Emmentaler tastes good)

Peel the butternut squash, remove the seeds, and cut the pulp into approx. 1-inch cubes. Cut off the cap of the small squash. Scoop them out, first the seeds and then the pulp. Leave approx. ½ inch pulp inside the skin. Also cut the scooped-out pulp into chunks. Mix all squash cubes with olive oil, cayenne pepper, paprika, nutmeg, and salt.

Arrange on an oiled baking sheet and cook for 30 minutes or until the edges start turning black, in an oven preheated to 350°F/Gas 4. Leave the squash cubes to cool and then puree.

Beat the eggs with crème fraîche, stir in the squash puree, then the cheese. Fill the mini squash.

Preheat the oven to 350°F/Gas 4. Place the mini squash in it. Lay the caps next to them.

Roast for approx. 40 minutes or until done.

Cut them into wedges, peel. Serve with red meat or with one-person chicken (see page 263).

# HERB TABOULEH WITH CARDAMOM DRESSING

2⅔ cups couscous, red quinoa, or bulgur

2 cups mixed nuts (hazelnuts, walnuts, pine nuts, etc.)

4 bunches different green herbs (cilantro, parsley, basil, and mint are my favorites)

½ cup raisins

*For the dressing*

1 tbsp seeds from cardamom pods, otherwise ½ tbsp cardamom powder

2 tbsp honey

1 clove garlic, crushed

juice of 2 lemons

salt and freshly ground pepper

1⅔ cups olive oil

Follow the directions on the packaging for the couscous, which will typically recommend using one and a half parts boiling water to one part couscous. Pour over the couscous in three steps. Allow to soak briefly each time and fluff with a fork in order for the grains to separate. Transfer to a large bowl; the couscous will swell considerably. (If using quinoa or bulgur, soak well until soft or follow directions on the packets.)

Toast the nuts in a dry pan until they begin to color. Taste whether the couscous is cooked. Wash the herbs and chop them. Stir them through the couscous with the nuts and raisins.

Prepare the mayonnaise: Crush the cardamom into powder in a mortar. Combine with the other ingredients and toward the end stir the oil in a thin trickle through the dressing until it thickens.

Stir the dressing through the couscous and keep in a covered bowl until served.

(You can easily make this side dish a day in advance, but do put it in the refrigerator overnight).

# ZUCCHINI PROVENÇAL STYLE

*This is not even a recipe, but once prepared in this way, you will never want to eat zucchinis any other way. Norbert and Valerie always make this for us when we build the fire together in their back garden in the south of France. The secret is primarily in the high-quality olive oil.*

Wrap whole, medium-sized zucchinis in aluminum foil. Place them in the hot fire, as you do when you roast potatoes. They will be cooked after 20 minutes. Do not forget to turn occasionally if you do not cook them in, but on top of, the fire. Remove from the fire, open the aluminum, and transfer the zucchini to your plate. Cut in half lengthwise. Top the cooked zucchini with good-quality olive oil and sprinkle with sea salt and pepper. Eat with a spoon!

# FRIED SALSIFY AND CARROT AU GRATIN WITH GORGONZOLA

285

1½ lb salsify (substitute parsnip or turnip)

½ cup milk

3 carrots

salt and freshly ground pepper

⅔ cup thick cream

5 oz gorgonzola

1 clove garlic, crushed

1 sprig rosemary

2 tbsp olive oil

¼ cup slivered almonds


Brush the salsify clean under cold running water. Peel them using a peeler (wear rubber gloves when peeling the salsify, as they release a sap which will give you orange hands, which is why this vegetable is also sometimes referred to as "cook's sorrow") and cut them into 2-inch sections. Rinse and immediately place in a bowl with 2 cups water mixed with the milk; reserve.

Preheat the oven to 350°F/Gas 4.

Peel the carrots and cut them into sections like the salsify. Bring the milk-water mixture with the vegetables and a pinch of salt to a boil and cook the vegetables for 8 minutes until nearly done. In the meantime, heat the cream with half of the gorgonzola in a saucepan, add the garlic, pepper, and rosemary, and leave to simmer on low heat until used.

Using a skimmer, remove the vegetables from the cooking liquid and place them in a baking dish greased with olive oil. Top with the sauce. Crumble the remaining gorgonzola on the vegetables and sprinkle with almonds. Bake au gratin until golden brown for approx. 20 minutes. Serve with beef loin (for example, see recipe on page 256), and mashed potatoes.

ON THE SIDE

# GREEN ASPARAGUS WITH PARSLEY GREMOLATA

*For the gremolata*
1 generous bunch flat-leaf parsley
zest of 1 lemon
juice of nearly 1 whole lemon
2 cloves garlic, crushed
2 tbsp olive oil
salt and freshly ground pepper

16 green asparagus (most of the time this is 1 bundle, if you have thin asparagus)

Combine all the ingredients for the gremolata in a food processor into a sort of "pesto." Bring a pan with liberally salted water to a boil. Peel the woody bottom of the asparagus stems. Blanch for 3 minutes; they must stay green and crunchy. Rinse under cold water. Until serving, place the asparagus in a bowl with the gremolata, to allow them to marinate. Eat cold or lukewarm.

# GREEN BEANS WITH WALNUTS

*For the dressing*
½ cup walnut oil
1 shallot, diced
3 tbsp red wine vinegar
salt and freshly ground pepper

14 oz green beans
½ cup walnuts

Make the dressing by beating the oil in a thin trickle through the other ingredients.
Bring a large pan with salted water to a boil. Blanch the beans for approx. 5 minutes, until cooked *al dente*.
Drain in a colander over the sink. Toast the nuts briefly in a dry frying pan.
Place the beans in a serving dish, top with the dressing, and sprinkle with walnuts.

# LONG LEEK PIE

4 sheets all-butter puff pastry

3 leeks

¾ cup white wine

pat of butter

a few thyme sprigs

salt and freshly ground pepper

½ cup aged goat cheese, grated or crumbled

1 egg white, loosely beaten

Stack the puff pastry sheets and roll them out lengthwise into a long and narrow strip. Using the back of a knife, score a rectangle about 1 inch around the inside of the pastry edge, like a picture frame.

Cut the leeks into three sections and remove the dark green leaf and the bottom. Wash carefully, then simmer until cooked in the white wine, butter, thyme, salt, and pepper for approx. 20 minutes. Remove from the liquid and pat dry. Place them neatly next to each other within the rectangle you have created in the puff pastry.

Top with goat cheese and brush the outer edges with lightly beaten egg white.

Bake the pie in an oven preheated to 400°F/Gas 6 for approx. 25 minutes. The edge will rise considerably.

Delicious with leg of lamb (see page 258) or with fennel salad as on page 270.

My sister and I often used to make cheese together.
We hung the cloth with the curds on a branch of the lilac tree in the garden and couldn't wait until it was ready.
We ate the young cheese on toast with tomatoes, actually much like cottage cheese.
As children we did not have the patience to leave the cheese to age for very long.
But you do, as I do too now.

# MAKING CHEESE

ODDLY ENOUGH, TO MAKE CHEESE YOU DON'T NEED MUCH EQUIPMENT AND IT IS ACTUALLY ONLY ABOUT AS MUCH WORK AS MAKING TEA.

YOU CAN DECIDE WHEN YOU THINK THE CHEESE IS "READY." EACH STAGE OF THE CHEESE MAKING HAS A DIFFERENT FLAVOR AND ANOTHER TEXTURE. BY ADDING SALT TO THE CHEESE, YOU WILL SLIGHTLY EXTEND ITS SHELF LIFE, SAY, ONE WEEK. HERE IS A STEP-BY-STEP GUIDE FOR A COW'S MILK CHEESE; BY STEP 5 I WILL HAVE MADE RICOTTA, BUT I WILL CONTINUE TO MAKE A CHEESE THAT IS MOST LIKE COW'S CHEESE. EXPERIMENT WITH GOAT'S MILK OR SHEEP'S MILK.

WITH THIS RECIPE YOU CAN MAKE A CHEESE WEIGHING APPROXIMATELY 8 OZ.

YOU WILL NEED: 4 CUPS ORGANIC MILK, 4 CUPS ORGANIC BUTTERMILK, A FEW DROPS OF LEMON JUICE, AND I TSP SALT (TO TASTE).

292

PREPARE
ONE 14 OZ CAN, OF WHICH THE INSIDE IS LACQUERED WHITE (AGAINST RUST, WHICH OFTEN OCCURS IN CANS), ONE OTHER CAN OR WEIGHT THAT SNUGLY FITS INTO IT, ONE PIECE OF CHEESECLOTH OR FINE FABRIC, ONE LONG PIECE OF ELASTIC, ONE SMALL PLATE.
USING A CAN OPENER, CUT THE TOP AND BOTTOM OFF THE CAN AND SAVE ONE LID FOR LATER.

HEAT THE TWO MILKS IN A LARGE PAN. ADD THE LEMON JUICE.

WHEN THE MILK IS NEAR BOILING, IT WILL SEPARATE INTO WHEY AND CURD. CONTINUE TO STIR FOR I MINUTE.

STRAIN AND STIR UNTIL ALL WHEY HAS DRAINED.

YOU HAVE JUST MADE RICOTTA! THAT'S HOW FAST IT IS.

ADD SALT AND STIR.

NOW YOU HAVE LIGHTLY SALTED FRESH CHEESE. HIGH TIME TO MAKE ACTUAL CHEESE . . .

PLACE THE CLOTH IN THE CAN AND POUR IN THE CURDS.

PULL UP THE CORNERS, ALLOWING THE YOUNG CHEESE TO SINK IN.

IF NECESSARY, CUT THE CLOTH TO SIZE AND COVER WITH THE LID.

COVER WITH ANOTHER CAN AND PLACE THEM BOTH ON A PLATE. TIGHTLY WRAP THE ELASTIC AROUND BOTH CANS. AFTER A WHILE YOU CAN TIGHTEN THE ELASTIC. PLACE IN THE REFRIGERATOR FOR 12 HOURS.

TA-DA! YOU'VE MADE AN ACTUAL CHEESE! YOU CAN NOW ROLL IT THROUGH HERBS, IF YOU SO DESIRE, OR EAT IT AS IS, WITH A TOMATO ON TOAST, FOR EXAMPLE. YOU CAN ALSO RETURN THE CHEESE IN A TRAY WITH WATER AND SALT TO THE FRIDGE – 1 TSP SALT FOR 2 CUPS WATER. THIS IS CALLED "PICKLING." THE CHEESE WILL DEVELOP MORE FLAVOR AND ALSO AN ENTIRELY DIFFERENT STRUCTURE. DO THIS FOR THREE DAYS AT THE MOST.

# TRUE CHEESE BOARD

*From now on, you can make it yourself!*

Front left, you will see the same cheese as the cheese on the right, which is sprinkled with sea salt and rosemary.
Only the first cheese has spent three days in a brine bath, giving it an entirely different structure and flavor. In terms of flavor it is fairly similar to mozzarella.
I have mixed cracked black pepper and roasted mustard seeds through the tall cheese at the back. By roasting mustard seeds, not only does the color get darker, but the flavor changes to that of nuts, which obviously goes well with cheese.
Experiment with the shape of your cheeses. This will result in a nicely varied board.

**TIP**    Serve with, for example:
Lavash crackers (see page 110)
Crostini (see page 110)
Fig butter (see page 113)
Cranberry, walnut, and pear chutney (see page 158)
Apple-date chutney (see page 159)
Confit de vin (see page 17)

# LET'S GET GOING . . .

MAKING CHEESE ALSO MEANS A WHOLE LOT MORE: JUST THINK OF HANGOP, A SIMPLE CHEESE, WHICH YOU CAN EAT SWEET, BUT WHICH IS ALSO TASTY SAVORY, ON TOAST, FOR EXAMPLE.
AND THIS TOO HAS VARIATIONS: LEBANESE LABNEH IS ALSO A YOGURT CHEESE, WHICH YOU CAN EASILY MAKE YOURSELF.
THE LONGER YOU LEAVE THE CHEESE, THE FIRMER IT GETS.

## HERB CHEESES

*These are variations on the cheese I made on the previous page.*

Before straining the cheese, stir a handful of chopped thyme, chives, nettles, or parsley through it.

Add 2 tbsp briefly roasted coriander seeds to the curds.

Add 2 tbsp herbes de Provence to the curds.

Add 2 chopped jalapeño peppers, or harissa to the curds.

Add 1 tbsp crushed black pepper and 1 tbsp roasted mustard seeds to the curds.

Finish the cheese as described on page 293. Serve topped with spicy olive oil and a little sea salt, paprika, or cayenne pepper.

?FROMAASH? THAT'S FRENCH FOR CHEESE

## HANGOP

*Hangop is the simplest cheese you can make yourself, without the use of coagulants or other additives. You cannot buy it in the store, but it is so simple that you just have to try it. Hangop is eaten as a dessert, but if you have a little left over, it is also great for breakfast!*

4 cups yogurt
1 cup thick cream
seeds from a vanilla bean
zest of 1 lemon
¾ cup confectioners' sugar

Place a clean dish towel in a strainer. Place the strainer on a bucket. Pour the yogurt into it and cover with plastic wrap. Set aside for one night in the basement or in a cold place in the house. The following day, whip the cream, vanilla, lemon zest, and sugar. Carefully fold the yogurt into the whipped cream and serve the hangop with red fruit.

## SPREADABLE LABNEH

*Labneh is a yogurt cheese from Lebanon. It is very similar to hangop, but it is always salted and eaten as a savory dish. Have it as a cheese spread on bread, on soup or salads, or on toasts with a drink.*

½–1 tsp salt, to taste
1 clove garlic, crushed (optional)
4 cups whole (full-fat) yogurt

Mix the salt and garlic through the yogurt. Place a clean dish towel on a colander or strainer. Pour the yogurt on it and tie the towel with a string or elastic band. Hang over the sink or over a bucket. Or cover with plastic wrap and hang in the strainer over a bucket. Let it hang for 12–24 hours. Regularly wring the towel; the aim is for as much moisture (whey) as possible to drain from the yogurt. You will be left with a spreadable cheese. Serve sprinkled with fresh garden herbs, or sesame seeds and a little olive oil. Complement with crispy bread.

MILK

# SEASONED LABNEH BALLS IN OLIVE OIL

*This is a variation on the recipe for spreadable labneh on the previous page.*
*If you leave the yogurt to hang longer, the labneh becomes drier and you can roll it into balls.*

*For approximately 25 balls*
2 tsp salt
1 tsp black pepper
1 clove garlic, crushed (optional)
8 cups preferably Greek or Turkish yogurt, but any regular whole (full-fat) yogurt will do
2 cups olive oil (or more, if necessary)
a few bay leaves, some red chile flakes, or something else you like, perhaps cardamom pods
1 jar dried oregano approx. ¼ cup)
1 jar dried thyme approx. ¼ cup)

Mix the salt, pepper, and garlic through the yogurt. Place a clean dish towel on a colander or strainer and pour in the seasoned yogurt. Cover with plastic wrap and put in a cool place, or pull the corners together and tie the dish towel with a thick elastic band or string as tightly as possible around the yogurt, thus increasing the pressure.
Make a loop in the string and hang the filled towel over a bucket or over the sink.
It is handy to turn a stool upside down, hang the towel on the cross, and place a bucket under it.
Or you can hang the towel from a tree outside, if the weather isn't too hot. You'll come up with something.
Hang the towel for at least 3 days in a cool place. Every day try to tighten the towel a little more (as much moisture as possible has to be extracted).
Place half of the olive oil, the bay leaves, and other spices in an attractive, tall glass container, preserving jar, or clean vase.
Mix the dried oregano and thyme on a plate. With clean hands, create small balls, the size of a walnut, with the drained yogurt, and carefully roll through the herbs. Slide them into the oil one by one and top up the container with olive oil in order for the balls to "float."
Eat them as a snack with a drink or serve after a meal as part of a cheeseboard.

# BUTTERMILK HANGOP WITH CARAMEL SAUCE

*A very old-fashioned Dutch recipe, and truly delicious. You will need more buttermilk than for yogurt hangop, just because buttermilk is thinner and therefore more of it will drain away. Buttermilk hangop has a totally different structure from yogurt hangop; it looks more like custard. This dish used to be eaten topped with crumbled bread crust, but this is no longer the case. I replace it with crunchy almond cookies, but gingersnaps also fit the bill.*

*For the hangop*
4 cups buttermilk
3 tbsp brown sugar
1 tsp cinnamon
4 crunchy cookies (amaretti, gingersnaps)
1 tbsp toasted almonds

*For the caramel sauce*
1 cup sugar
½ cup water
½ stick butter
¾ cup thick cream

Wet a clean dish towel and place it in a strainer or colander. Hang the strainer over a large bucket and pour in the buttermilk. Cover with plastic wrap or a lid and leave to stand for at least 2 nights. Then transfer the cheese to a large bowl and beat in the brown sugar and cinnamon using a whisk or hand blender.

Prepare the caramel sauce: Heat the sugar and water in a saucepan. Reduce to a syrup and remove from the heat; stir in the butter. Be careful, as it can splatter considerably. Continue to stir and return to low heat until the desired caramel color is achieved. Remove from the heat and fold in the cream. Leave the sauce to slightly cool until used.

Transfer the hangop to a plate and cover with a little caramel sauce. Top with the crumbled cookies and sprinkle with the toasted almonds.

# GOAT YOGURT HANGOP WITH THYME AND OLIVES

4 cups goat yogurt
½ cup thick cream
leaves of a few sprigs of fresh thyme
pinch of crumbled dried chile pepper (or chile flakes)
approx. 15 Taggiasche (or other tasty) olives, pitted and halved
pinch of sea salt

Place a strainer on a bucket in a cool place. Place a clean dish towel in the strainer and pour in the yogurt.
Cover and leave to stand for 1 night.
The following day, whip the cream, add the thyme, crumbled chile pepper, and olives, and season with salt. Scrape the drained yogurt from the towel and carefully fold it into the whipped cream. Place in the refrigerator in order to allow the flavors to thoroughly infuse.
Serve with crusty bread and a drink, for example.

On the way back from Brittas Bay Beach to Dublin when I was a child, my friends and I sang this song so long
and so loud in the car that our parents sometimes gave in and eventually we were treated to an actual ice cream.
As a child I didn't like ice cream at all but it was a good song!
As an adult, I married Oof, who is just crazy about ice cream. He often makes ice cream,
just because he likes it so much, and he feeds me all kinds of flavors he came up with himself.
I ended up loving ice cream as well and now we often make it together, even more often than I would like.
Even when it's cold outside!

# MAKING ICE CREAM

MAKING ICE CREAM IS EASY WITHOUT A MACHINE. EVEN IF YOU NEED TO MAKE A LOT, AN ICE CREAM LOG SUCH AS THIS ONE IS A SOLUTION. I WILL MAKE A VERY SIMPLE ONE HERE. IT IS UP TO YOU TO DO SOMETHING WITH IT, FOR EXAMPLE, YOU CAN ADD NUTS, RASPBERRIES, OR CHOCOLATE SHAVINGS.
YOU DON'T OBVIOUSLY HAVE TO MAKE A MOCHA FLAVOR AS I DEMONSTRATE HERE.
IN THE FOLLOWING PAGES, I WILL GIVE YOU SOME VARIATIONS. YOU CAN ALSO USE HALF MILK/HALF CREAM, FOR EXAMPLE, IF YOU DON'T WANT YOUR ICE CREAM TO BE TOO RICH. BUT OH WELL, I DO LIKE IT CREAMY.
>>> BY THE WAY, DO NOT ADD ALCOHOL IF CHILDREN WILL BE EATING IT, BUT THAT GOES WITHOUT SAYING.

308

PREPARE: 6 EGG YOLKS, 1 CUP SUGAR, 1 CUP STRONG COFFEE, 3 TBSP. COFFEE LIQUEUR, 2 CUPS CREAM, AND CHOCOLATE CHUNKS.

BEAT THE YOLKS AND SUGAR INTO A WHITE FOAM.

ADD THE COFFEE AND A THIRD OF THE CREAM.
STIR WELL INTO A SMOOTH SAUCE.

POUR THE SAUCE INTO A SAUCEPAN ...

AND BRING TO A BOIL WHILE STIRRING.

UNTIL THE SAUCE THICKENS AND STICKS TO THE SPOON, LIKE SO.

LEAVE THE CUSTARD TO COOL, I PUT IT IN THE OPEN WINDOW.

IN THE MEANTIME WHIP THE REST OF THE CREAM.

FOLD IN THE COOLED CUSTARD AND THE LIQUEUR (OPTIONAL!).

LINE A MOLD WITH PLASTIC WRAP.

POUR IN THE MIXTURE AND COVER.

FREEZE FOR AT LEAST 5 HOURS.

MEANWHILE MELT A LITTLE CHOCOLATE IN A DOUBLE BOILER.

POUR INTO AN ICING BAG, CUT THE TIP, AND DECORATE IT ALONE.

...OR ALL TOGETHER.

# BRRR...LET'S GET GOING

WARNING! IN THESE RECIPES THE EGGS ARE PROCESSED RAW, WHICH MEANS THAT YOU HAVE TO BE CAREFUL IF YOU PLAN ON SERVING YOUR ICE CREAM TO THE ELDERLY, THE SICK, OR SMALL CHILDREN. THESE GROUPS TYPICALLY HAVE LOWER RESISTANCE AND COULD, IN THEORY, BECOME ILL.
"SEMIFREDDO" IS THE ITALIAN WORD FOR HALF-FROZEN.

## PISTACHIO WAFERS WITH MARMALADE SEMIFREDDO

*For approximately 12 people*

3 oranges
⅓ cup sugar
2 tsp vanilla sugar
4 oz marmalade
2 cups thick cream
1 cup crème fraîche
5 egg yolks
pinch of salt
approx. 24 pistachio wafers (see recipe on page 363)

Grate the skin of 2 oranges and squeeze all 3 oranges. Bring the juice with half of the sugar and vanilla sugar to a boil and cook for at least 10 minutes until reduced by one quarter. Stir in the marmalade and leave to cool. Bring the cream, the crème fraîche, orange zest, and reserved sugar to a boil and lower the heat. Stir until the sugar has dissolved. Beat the egg yolks in a bowl. Pour in half of the hot cream and continue to stir. Pour the egg-cream mixture back into the pan with the remaining cream and stir until the mixture thickens. The cream has to be thick enough to stick to the back of a spoon. Add the cream to the orange syrup. Add the salt, stir and place in the freezer for at least 4 hours.

Place a scoop of semifreddo on a wafer. Top with another wafer, creating a "sandwich." Serve immediately or wrap them one by one in plastic wrap and keep in the freezer until used.

## YOGURT SEMIFREDDO WITH CRANBERRY CRUNCH

*For 1 cake pan or 10–12 people*

*For the crunch*
½ cup brown sugar
⅓ cup all-purpose flour
1 stick butter
⅔ cup dried cranberries (reserve some for the garnish)
½ cup rolled oats

*For the semifreddo*
⅔ cup sugar
3 egg yolks
1 vanilla bean, seeds scraped
¾ cup milk
¾ cup thick cream
¾ cup yogurt

First make the crunch. Preheat the oven to 350°F/Gas 4.
Combine all the ingredients in a food processor and blitz into a crumbly dough. Spread over a baking sheet lined with parchment paper and press into a flat cake. Bake for 20–25 minutes until crisp and golden brown. Leave to fully cool.
Cover a cake pan with plastic wrap and allow the edges to hang over the pan. Beat the sugar with the egg yolks into a very stiff white foam. Bring the vanilla bean, together with the seeds, and milk to a boil. Simmer for 10 minutes. Remove the vanilla bean and blend the milk with the egg yolks while stirring, return the mixture to the pan, and continue to stir until it thickens. It has to be as thick as thin custard. Remove the pan from the heat. Leave the custard to slightly cool.
Beat the cream until stiff. Carefully fold the cream and yogurt into the custard and pour half of it into the cake pan. Crumble the cranberry crunch using a rolling pin. Sprinkle the crumbs on the semifreddo mixture in the pan, and top with the remaining semifreddo mixture. Reserve some of the crumbs for the garnish. Cover the semifreddo with the overhanging plastic wrap. Place the mold in the freezer to harden overnight.
Before serving, carefully lift the ice cream out of the mold. Unwrap and slice. Arrange on small plates and sprinkle with the reserved cranberry crunch and a few dried cranberries.

# THREE-COLOR SEMIFREDDO WITH CHOCOLATE AND MINT

*For 1 cake pan or 10–12 people*

4 cups milk
2¾ cups thick cream
1 vanilla bean, seeds scraped
8 egg yolks
¾ cup superfine sugar
4 oz semisweet chocolate, in chunks
5 oz milk chocolate, in chunks
5 oz white chocolate, in chunks
a few sprigs fresh mint, very finely chopped
⅓ cup chopped pistachio nuts for garnish

Heat the milk, half of the cream, and the vanilla (seeds and bean) until very hot (do not boil) and allow to infuse for approx. 10 minutes. Beat the egg yolks with the sugar until white and foamy. While stirring, add one spoonful of the hot milk-cream mixture to the egg mixture and then pour the egg mixture, while stirring, into the hot milk. Continue to cook and stir until the custard thickens and sticks to the back of a tablespoon. Take the pan from the heat and remove the vanilla bean. Do not allow the custard to boil. In the meantime, melt each chocolate over a double boiler, one by one, in 3 bowls. Leave them and the custard to slightly cool. Whip the remaining cream until stiff. Divide into 3 portions. Also divide the custard into 3 portions.
Stir the 3 chocolates through the three custards. Stir the chopped mint through the white chocolate mixture. Fold the portions of whipped cream through each chocolate mixture. Line a cake pan with plastic wrap. Add the milk chocolate mixture. Cover and immediately place in the freezer. Place the other two bowls in the refrigerator. After an hour or two, when the milk chocolate ice cream has slightly frozen, add the white chocolate mixture. After a further 2 hours, pour in the last layer and completely cover the semifreddo in order for it to fully freeze. Serve in slices sprinkled with chopped pistachio nuts.

# SAFFRON SEMIFREDDO WITH CITRUS COMPOTE

*For this semifreddo you don't have to make custard. I thought that I would give you another variation. The ice cream will be quite light with this recipe.*
*For 1 cake pan or 10–12 people*

a few strands of saffron
4 eggs, separated
⅓ cup sugar
2 cups thick cream
salt

*For the grapefruit compote*
2 lb grapefruit
¾ cup water
⅔ cup sugar
1 tbsp lemon juice
½ vanilla bean
3 tbsp liqueur, Verveine (lemon verbena), for example

Place the saffron threads in an eggshell with warm water and allow to soak briefly. Line a cake pan leaving excess plastic wrap hanging over the edges, as it will have to cover the ice cream later. Beat the egg yolks with the sugar into a creamy mixture. Add the saffron and stir. Beat the cream until nearly stiff. Whisk the egg whites until stiff in another bowl with a pinch of salt. Fold the egg yolks into the whipped cream and then carefully add the cream mixture to the egg whites. Gently pour the mixture into the mold and fold the plastic wrap over it. Place in the freezer.

Prepare the compote: Place a grapefruit on a cutting board. Using a sharp knife, cut away, from top to bottom, the peel and the white underneath. Move to the next section until the entire grapefruit is peeled.
Over a bowl, remove the pulp from the sections; the juice will be collected in the bowl. Repeat for all of the grapefruit. In a saucepan heat the water, sugar, and lemon juice.
With a sharp knife, remove the seeds from the vanilla bean and add to the mixture. Also add the empty bean, which you will later remove. Bring the mixture to a boil. Lower the heat and continue to cook until you have a syrup (about 7 minutes). Add the grapefruit sections and the liqueur and leave the compote to cool until used. Prior to serving, remove the ice cream from the mold. Unwrap, slice, and serve with the compote.

# EARL GREY TEA AND MINT SORBET

*Serves 4 people as a dessert, but at least 8 people as sorbet to cleanse your palate during a large dinner party as they do in posh circles . . .*

3 cups water
4 tea bags Earl Grey tea
small bunch fresh mint
1 cup sugar
juice of 1 lemon

You'll also need a bottle of Champagne if serving during a dinner party.

Bring 2½ cups of the water to a boil, transfer to a large bowl, add the tea bags, and allow to infuse for 7 minutes. Remove the tea bags and squeeze them thoroughly above the bowl. Wash the mint and add the sprigs (stalks and leaves intact) to the tea. Bring the remaining water and sugar to a boil in a saucepan and stir until the sugar has dissolved. Add the syrup and the lemon juice to the tea, and leave the mixture to fully cool. Once it is lukewarm, place in the refrigerator to fully chill. Remove the mint sprigs. Churn into a sorbet in an ice-cream maker or place the mixture in the freezer and fluff it up every hour with a fork. The sorbet will be ready after approximately 4 hours, depending on your freezer.

For a palate cleanser, fill half a glass with Champagne and drop a small scoop of sorbet into the glass. Serve immediately and provide a small spoon.

# pineapplegranita
## with passion fruit

1 PINEAPPLE
2 TBSP (APPROX. 1/8 CUP) CASTER SUGAR
JUICE OF 1/2 LEMON
75 ML (2 1/2 FL OZ / 1/3 CUP) WATER
4 PASSIONFRUIT

PEEL THE PINEAPPLE AND REMOVE THE "EYES".
CUT THE FRUIT INTO FOUR SECTIONS AND REMOVE
THE CORE. CUT THE FRUIT INTO CHUNKS AND
PUREE INTO A PULP IN THE FOOD PROCESSOR.

HEAT THE SUGAR, LEMON JUICE AND WATER
INTO A SYRUP IN A SAUCEPAN. ADD THE PINE-
APPLE PULP → STIR WELL!

LET IT COOL DOWN AND PLACE IN THE FREEZER.
BEAT UP EVERY HOUR USING A FORK. AFTER
ABOUT 4-5 HOURS YOU WILL HAVE MADE
GRANITA! SERVE IN AN ATTRACTIVE
TALL GLASS COVERED WITH PASSION FRUIT.

> GRANITA IS SIMILAR TO SORBET, BUT SINCE
> LESS SUGAR IS USED → THE ICE CRYSTALS
> ARE LARGER.

# RASPBERRY SORBET

4 cups raspberries (these days easily available in your supermarket's frozen food section!)
⅔ cup superfine sugar
½ cup water

Purée the raspberries in a blender. If you do not like small seeds, press the pulp through a strainer.
Heat the sugar and water in a saucepan, stir until the sugar has dissolved. Pour the syrup onto the raspberry pulp and leave to fully cool.
Churn the sorbet in an ice-cream maker for approximately 30 minutes or freeze the mixture in the freezer.
If using the freezer, fluff up the sorbet every hour and it will be ready in approximately 4 hours.

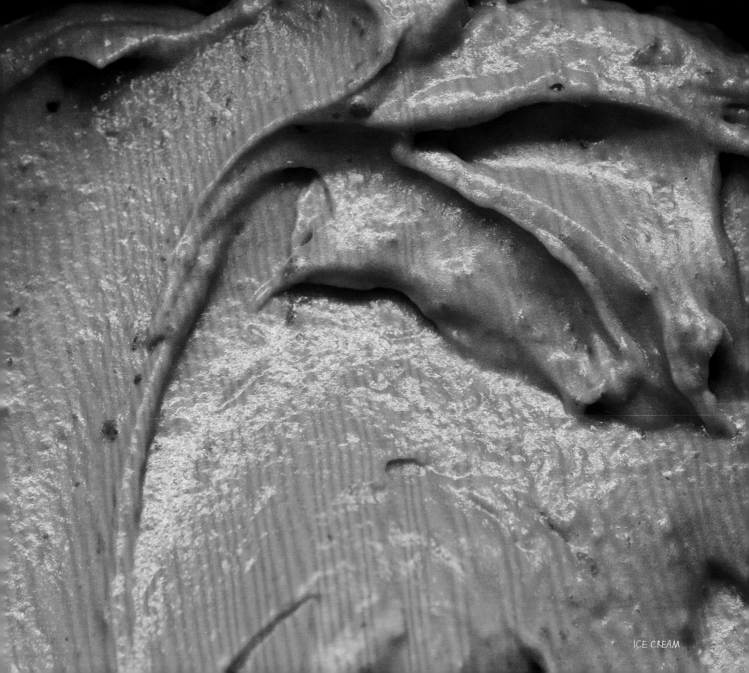

# GREEN TEA ICE CREAM

2 tbsp green tea powder (or use 2 green tea bags)
2–3 tbsp boiling water
1¼ cups milk
1 vanilla bean, seeds scraped
2 egg yolks
⅓ cup superfine sugar
1¼ cups thick cream

Leave the tea powder or tea bags to soak in the water for 10 minutes.
Heat the milk until very hot but do not boil. Leave it to infuse with the vanilla bean and the seeds for 10 minutes. Beat the egg yolks with the the superfine sugar until white and foamy. Strain the milk mixture into it and stir well. Also add the steeped tea. Return the mixture to the pan and stir over low heat until thicker, like a crème anglaise or thin custard.
Leave to fully cool.
Beat the cream until stiff and fold into the cold custard.
Transfer the cream mixture to an ice-cream maker and churn for approximately 20 minutes.
If you do not have an ice-cream maker, you can do this: Place the ice cream in the freezer and briefly fluff up every hour with a fork into nice firm ice cream. It will be ready in approximately 4 hours.

☆ The time for churning depends on the ice-cream maker; follow your appliance manufacturer's instructions.

# APPLE SORBET WITH APPLE CRISPS

*For the sorbet*
2 cups organic apple juice
3 Granny Smith apples, peeled and cubed
juice of ½ lemon
⅓ cup sugar

*For the crisps*
1 apple, Royal Gala or Elstar, for example

Bring all the sorbet ingredients to a boil in a saucepan. Cook for 10 minutes on low heat and then puree into a smooth sauce using a hand blender. Leave to fully cool.

Pour the sauce into an ice-cream maker and churn for approx. 30 minutes. If you don't have an ice-cream maker, you can place the container in the freezer. Fluff up every hour with a fork. The ice cream will be ready in approx. 4 hours.

For the crisps, preheat a fan-forced/convection oven to 140°F. Cut the apple into slices horizontally with a sharp knife. Arrange the slices on a sheet of parchment paper on a baking sheet. Dry them in the oven for approx. 3 hours. Turn halfway through.

Before serving, stack the ice cream, alternating with the crisps, and secure with a skewer, just to be on the safe side.

# BLOOD ORANGE SORBET

*For the sorbet*
juice of 3 lb blood oranges, or approx. 2 cups juice
zest of 2 blood oranges
⅔ cup water
1 cup sugar

*For the compote*
2 lb blood oranges, pink grapefruit, and oranges
¾ cup water
1 cup sugar
juice of ½ lemon
½ vanilla bean
1 tbsp liqueur, cranberry or bay, for example (see recipe on page 99)

For the sorbet, heat the juice and zest, water, and sugar until very hot, while stirring, until the sugar has dissolved. Do not boil or it will get bitter!

Remove the syrup from the heat and pour into a container that fits into the freezer. Leave the syrup to cool on the countertop and then place in the freezer. After 30 minutes, scrape along the edges with a spoon in order to release the ice crystals and stir well. Repeat this every hour until the right consistency is achieved, which will take 4 to 5 hours, depending on your freezer.

You can also churn the sorbet in an ice-cream maker, if you own one. In this case, you will make the sorbet in approx. 30 minutes. In the meantime prepare the compote: Put an orange on the cutting board. Using a sharp knife, peel away the orange and white peel, from top to bottom. Proceed until the entire orange is peeled.

Cut away the pulp between the sections over a bowl; the released juice will therefore be collected in the bowl. Repeat for all oranges and grapefruit.

In a saucepan, heat the water, sugar, and lemon juice, and the collected juice. Using a sharp knife, scrape the vanilla seeds from the bean and add them to the mixture. Also add the empty bean, and remove it later. Bring the mixture to a boil. Then lower the heat and simmer until you have a syrup. This will take approx. 7 minutes. Add the orange sections and liqueur and leave the compote to cool until used.

To serve, place a scoop of sorbet in a tall glass and add the compote.

# YOGURT ICE CREAM WITH VANILLA, WALNUTS, AND DATES

*For the ice cream*
½ cup superfine sugar
1 tbsp cornstarch
pinch of salt
2 eggs
2 cups milk
2 vanilla beans, seeds scraped
1½ cups whole yogurt

*To garnish*
a handful of dates and walnuts
maple syrup or pancake syrup

Beat the sugar, cornstarch, salt, and eggs in a large bowl into a smooth mixture. Heat the milk, and the vanilla seeds and beans, and leave to steep for 10 minutes. Strain the hot milk over the egg mixture, while stirring. Return everything to the pan and heat, while stirring, until it thickens into a nice custard. Leave the custard to cool and stir in the yogurt. Place in the refrigerator to fully cool. Pour into an ice-cream maker and churn into an airy light ice cream. If you don't own an ice-cream maker, have no fear, place the ice cream in the freezer and briefly fluff it up every hour with a fork. The ice cream will be ready in approx. 4 hours. Serve with halved, pitted dates, and a few walnuts. Top with maple syrup.

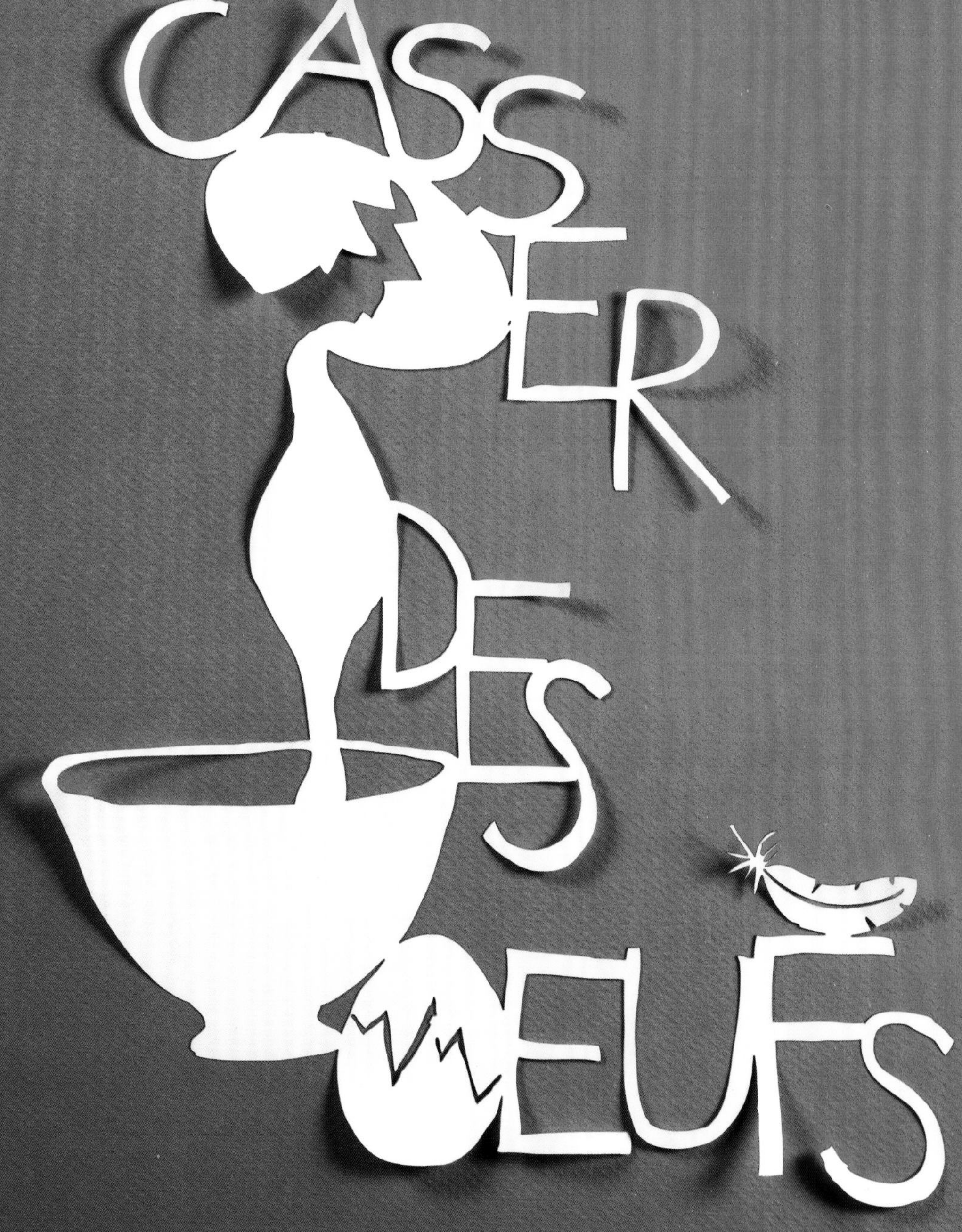
CASSER
DES
OEUFS

# MAKING ZABAGLIONE

YOU WILL NEED A LITTLE PATIENCE TO MAKE ZABAGLIONE, BUT MAKE IT AND EVERYONE WILL LOVE YOU FOR IT. SERVE AS IS, IN A SMALL BOWL, OR WITH LADYFINGERS FOR DUNKING. THE ART OF THIS DESSERT IS TO KNOW WHEN TO STOP BEATING. IT HAS TO BE NICE AND THICK, BUT IF IT GETS TOO HOT, THE EGG WILL TURN INTO LUMPS IN YOUR DESSERT AND YOU WILL HAVE TO START AGAIN. BUT IT WON'T COME TO THAT, SINCE YOU WILL JUST FOLLOW THE STEP-BY-STEP PLAN:

PREPARE YOUR INGREDIENTS: PER PERSON USE: 1 EGG YOLK, 1 TBSP SUGAR, AND 4-5 TBSP MARSALA.

PUT THE YOLKS IN A BOWL, WHICH WILL LATER FIT ON A PAN OF BOILING WATER. ADD THE SUGAR.

PATIENTLY WHIP INTO AIRY WHITE FOAM.

POUR IN THE MARSALA, WHILE STIRRING.

PLACE THE BOWL OVER A PAN OF SOFTLY BOILING WATER, ENSURE THAT THE WATER DOES NOT TOUCH THE BOWL, AND CONTINUE TO BEAT . . .

UNTIL AIRY AND THICK. IMMEDIATELY POUR INTO GLASSES OR SMALL BOWLS. >>>

# LET'S GET GOING . . .

EGGS SERVE ALL SORTS OF PURPOSES. IT ONLY GETS COMPLICATED WHEN YOU START HEATING THEM: IF THEY GET TOO HOT, ANY SAUCE OR CREAM THICKENED WITH EGG TURNS INTO SCRAMBLED EGGS. THE ART THEREFORE CONSISTS OF KEEPING THE MIXTURE NEAR THE BOILING POINT. ONCE YOU GET SOME PRACTICE, YOU WILL MAKE THE MOST DELICIOUS DESSERTS. JUST TAKE A LOOK:

## VIN SANTO ZABAGLIONE WITH PINK GRAPEFRUIT

3 pink grapefruit
3 tbsp sugar
2 eggs
4 tbsp vin santo (Italian dessert wine) or another sweet dessert wine

Place a grapefruit on a cutting board. Using a sharp knife, peel the yellow peel and also the white pith from top to bottom. Proceed until the entire grapefruit is peeled. Over a bowl, remove the pulp between the sections; the juice will be collected in the bowl. Repeat for all grapefruit and stir a tablespoon of sugar through the juice with the grapefruit sections. Set aside. Beat the eggs, the remaining sugar, and wine with a mixer into a foamy mass in a double boiler, in approximately 5 minutes. Arrange the fruits in 4 attractive glasses, cover with the zabaglione and serve immediately!

## CUSTARD

2 cups milk
½ cup crème fraîche
1 vanilla bean, seeds scraped, or 1 tsp vanilla extract
4 egg yolks
⅓ cup sugar
1 tbsp cornstarch

Heat the milk with the crème fraîche, the vanilla seeds, and the bean until hot (do not boil) and leave to simmer on low heat for 15 minutes. Then remove the vanilla bean. Beat the egg yolks with the sugar and cornstarch into a foam, and while stirring, add the hot milk. Return the mixture to the pan. Heat slowly on low heat while stirring, until the mixture thickens. Remove from the heat and leave to cool until used. The custard will further thicken. If you want to serve the custard warm, keep it over a double boiler. Place a sheet of plastic wrap directly down on the custard to prevent a skin from forming.

## CRÈME ANGLAISE

*This sauce is quite similar to custard, but no cornstarch is added here for thickening purposes. Crème anglaise is typically used as a sauce and custard is served as a dish on its own. Once you have become handy, you can opt to use other flavorings instead of vanilla. See the recipe on the next page.*

2 cups milk
2 vanilla beans, seeds scraped
5 egg yolks
⅓ cup sugar

Heat the milk with the vanilla seeds and the beans until hot (do not boil) and leave to simmer on low heat for 15 minutes. Then remove the vanilla beans. Beat the egg yolks with the sugar into a foam, and while stirring, add the hot milk. Return the mixture to the pan. Heat slowly on low heat while stirring, until the mixture thickens. Crème anglaise has to be as thick as a cream of asparagus soup. Remove from the heat and leave to cool until used. The sauce will slightly thicken. If you want to serve the sauce warm, keep it over a double boiler. Place a sheet of plastic wrap directly down on the mixture to prevent a skin from forming.

# CHOCOLATE FONDANT CAKE

*For one cake*
*(enough for at least 12 people)*

1¼ sticks butter
8 oz amaretti (light Italian almond cookies, or another crisp cookie)
4 oz semisweet chocolate, in chunks
2½ cups thick cream
2 tbsp sugar
⅓ cup Amaretto or Frangelico liqueur
cocoa powder for sprinkling

Line a cake pan, approximately 9 inches in diameter, with plastic wrap, allowing the excess to hang over the rim. Melt the butter. Crush the cookies in a food processor or mortar. Mix the butter with the cookie crumbs and press the mixture evenly on the bottom of the pan. Melt the chocolate in the microwave or in a double boiler. Leave to slightly cool. Beat the cream and sugar until stiff. Carefully stir the melted chocolate into the whipped cream and add the liqueur. Fill the pan with the chocolate mixture and smooth out the top with a spatula. Cover the cake with the excess plastic wrap and place in the refrigerator to chill for at least 4 hours Before serving, lift the cake out of the dish, remove the plastic wrap, and sprinkle with cocoa powder. Serve small wedges with crème anglaise with lemongrass.

# CRÈME ANGLAISE WITH LEMONGRASS

2 cups milk
1 vanilla bean, seeds scraped
3 lemongrass stems, white part only, crushed
5 egg yolks
⅓ cup sugar

See recipe for crème anglaise. Remove the lemongrass stems when you remove the vanilla beans from the hot milk.

# CHAMPAGNE CREAM

*This light cream can be used as a filling for many pastries, often combined with fresh fruit. Instead of Champagne you could also use espresso to make a mocha cream, which is also delicious.*

½ cup thick cream
⅔ cup Champagne (more ordinary bubbles will also do)
⅓ cup sugar
3 egg yolks and 1 whole egg
1 tbsp cornstarch
juice of ½ lemon

Beat the cream until stiff and set aside in the refrigerator. Beat the Champagne, sugar, egg yolks, egg, cornstarch, and lemon juice with a mixer in a double boiler into a firm white cream. Leave to briefly cool. Carefully fold in the whipped cream.

# SPONGE CAKE

*A basic recipe for many desserts. Great, for example, with whipped cream and jam between two layers and sprinkled with powdered sugar. It is a light cake, as it contains no butter, but you do have to practice. I personally have had a few failures in the past. Therefore strictly adhere to the recipe. REALLY do not open the oven, not even on the sly . . .*

329

4 eggs
½ cup superfine sugar
pinch of salt
½ cup all-purpose flour, sifted
¼ cup cornstarch, sifted
butter and flour for the cake pan

Thoroughly butter an 8- or 9-inch round cake pan. Cut a circle the size of the bottom of the cake pan out of parchment paper, line the pan with it, and butter it. Dust the greased pan with flour and tap the excess flour off the pan.
Preheat the oven to 340°F/Gas 3. Beat the eggs with the sugar and salt in a food processor (or take a very long time using a hand blender . . .) into a very foamy white mass. While stirring, fold the flour and cornstarch the batter. Try to keep as much air as possible in the batter but also spread the flour evenly through it. Pour the batter into the cake pan. Bake the cake in the oven for approximately 40 minutes. Do NOT open the oven during the first 30 minutes. Once the cake has cooled off, you can split it, fill it, and further finish it.

.

# VANILLA FRITTERS WITH ZABAGLIONE

*This recipe is for those who know Oof well and want to make him happy, for it is his favorite dessert.*

*For approximately 25 fritters*
½ stick butter
1 cup white wine or water
1 tbsp sugar
approx. 4 tsp vanilla sugar
zest of 1 lemon
pinch of salt
1⅔ cups all-purpose flour
4 eggs, separated

*And also*
generous oil for deep-frying
confectioners' sugar
1 x zabaglione recipe (see page 326)

Melt the butter with the wine in a saucepan, add the sugar, vanilla sugar, lemon zest, and salt.
Remove the pan from the heat and stir in the flour with a wooden spoon. Return the pan briefly to the heat and stir into a smooth batter. Remove the pan from the heat again and, using a hand blender, beat in the egg yolks one by one.
Beat the egg whites with a pinch of salt in another bowl until stiff and carefully spoon the foam into the batter. Heat the oil in a deep pan.
Grease two coffee spoons with oil and scoop small balls from the batter, which you immediately slide into the hot oil. Fry the fritters for a few minutes until golden brown and cooked. Turn halfway through. Always fry small quantities.
Allow to drain on paper towels.
Serve the fritters on a large tray and dust with confectioners' sugar or superfine sugar.
Serve with the zabaglione in a bowl as a dip.

# RASPBERRY CLAFOUTIS

*For 6 small glasses or 1 large baking pan*

3 eggs

1 cup milk

½ cup sugar

seeds from 1 small vanilla bean or 2 tsp vanilla sugar

pinch of salt

½ cup all-purpose flour

½ stick butter, plus extra for greasing purposes

¼ cup kirsch, rum, or a delicious homemade liqueur (see pages 98 and 99)

2 cups raspberries

confectioners' sugar for dusting

Generously butter 6 ovenproof glasses. Beat the eggs with the milk, sugar, vanilla, salt, and flour into a smooth mixture. Melt the remaining butter and fold it in. Add the liqueur.

Pour the batter into the glasses and top with the raspberries.

Bake in an oven preheated to 350°F/Gas 4 for approx. 15 minutes or until the clafoutis turns a golden brown.

Leave to slightly cool and sprinkle with confectioners' sugar.

 Serve warm with raspberry sorbet (see recipe on page 315).

TIP If you make the recipe for children and you do not want to use alcohol, replace the liqueur with orange juice.

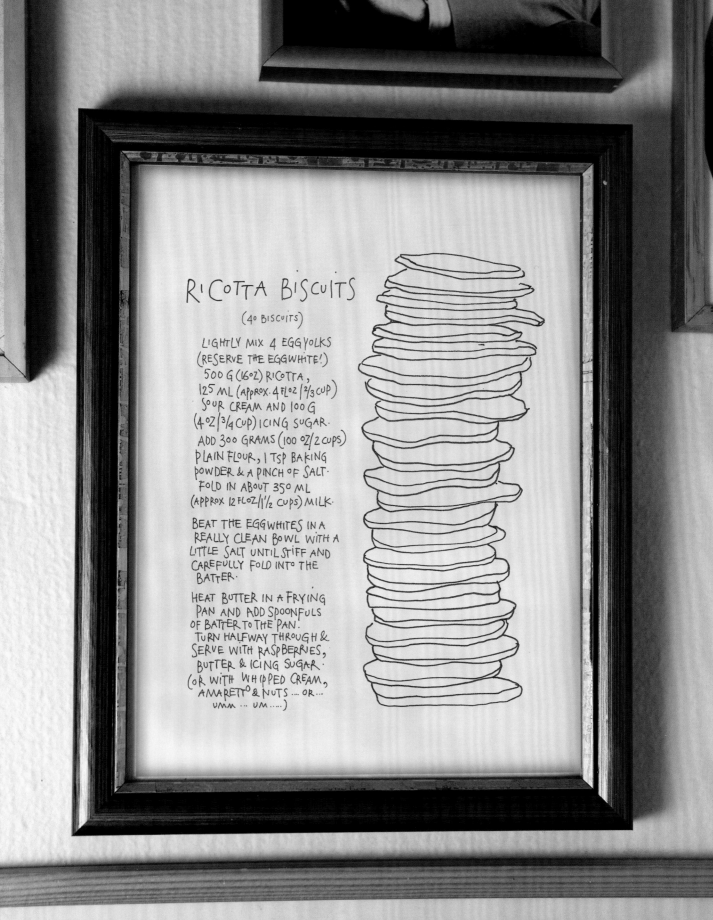

# RICOTTA BISCUITS

(40 BISCUITS)

LIGHTLY MIX 4 EGG YOLKS
(RESERVE THE EGGWHITE!)
500 G (16 OZ) RICOTTA,
125 ML (APPROX. 4 FL OZ / 2/3 CUP)
SOUR CREAM AND 100 G
(4 OZ / 3/4 CUP) ICING SUGAR.
ADD 300 GRAMS (100 OZ / 2 CUPS)
PLAIN FLOUR, 1 TSP BAKING
POWDER & A PINCH OF SALT.
FOLD IN ABOUT 350 ML
(APPROX 12 FL OZ / 1 1/2 CUPS) MILK.

BEAT THE EGGWHITES IN A
REALLY CLEAN BOWL WITH A
LITTLE SALT UNTIL STIFF AND
CAREFULLY FOLD INTO THE
BATTER.

HEAT BUTTER IN A FRYING
PAN AND ADD SPOONFULS
OF BATTER TO THE PAN.
TURN HALFWAY THROUGH &
SERVE WITH RASPBERRIES,
BUTTER & ICING SUGAR.
(OR WITH WHIPPED CREAM,
AMARETTO & NUTS .... OR ...
UMM ... UM .....)

Joris

# PINK MINI TRIFLES

*For 4 glasses*

8 slices butter cake (here I used madeleines—small French cakes shaped like long fingers, ladyfingers)

⅔ cup medium or cream sherry

1 x custard recipe (see page 328)

2 cups red fruit (strawberries, or raspberries, or both)

¼ cup sugar

With a small glass, cut out rounds in the cake and sprinkle each round with a teaspoon of sherry. Make sure that you have twice as many cake rounds as glasses. Prepare the custard. Stir in half of the fruit. Leave to cool. Place a slice of cake in each glass. Cover with a spoonful of cream-fruit mixture and top with a second slice of cake. Cover with another spoonful of cream-fruit mixture. Seal all glasses with plastic wrap and place them in the refrigerator for at least 2 hours to set. In the food processor, puree the other half of the fruit with the sugar, and strain. Collect the coulis (sauce) in a bowl and pour it into a decanter. Before serving add a dash of coulis to each trifle, covering the top of each glass with an even layer.

# PEAR AND GINGER TIRAMISÙ WITH GRATED CHOCOLATE

*For 4 glasses*

1 pear

generous dash of ginger syrup

8 ladyfingers (Italian sponge cake fingers)

dash of Marsala wine

1 cup strong coffee

3 eggs

½ cup sugar

1 cup mascarpone

2 pieces preserved ginger

2 oz chocolate (preferably semisweet) from the refrigerator, grated

Peel the pear, quarter it, and remove the cores. In a saucepan, bring enough water to a boil to cover the pear and add a generous dash of ginger syrup. Keep close to the boiling point and poach the pear for 20 minutes. Leave the pear to cool in the cooking fluid and then slice.

Very carefully split the ladyfingers in half. Blend the Marsala with the coffee. Arrange 4 ladyfinger halves upright along the inside of 4 glasses. Pour a little coffee into each glass and gently swirl the glasses in order for all the sponge cake to absorb the coffee. Separate the eggs. Beat the yolks with half of the sugar until the mixture turns light yellow. Beat in the mascarpone into a smooth mixture. Beat the egg whites until stiff. Add the remaining sugar and continue to beat into stiff peaks. Carefully fold the egg whites into the mascarpone mixture. Finely chop the ginger and add. Place the pears in the glasses between the ladyfingers. Top with a generous dollop of cream until the glasses are filled. Leave to chill in the refrigerator for at least 90 minutes. Serve sprinkled with the grated chocolate.

# FRENCH TOAST WITH CINNAMON BREAD AND RASPBERRY SORBET

*For the French toast*
4 eggs
¾ cup milk
2 tbsp raw superfine sugar
1 tbsp cinnamon
zest of 1 lemon
12 slices cinnamon bread
½ stick butter

*And also*
6 scoops raspberry sorbet (see recipe on page 315)
confectioners' sugar to garnish
and little stars (optional)

Beat the eggs in a deep dish with the milk, sugar, cinnamon, and lemon zest. Place the bread in the egg mixture and allow it to briefly soak. Melt the butter in a skillet. Place the bread in it and fry on both sides until golden brown. Serve two French toasts per person with a scoop of raspberry sorbet on a plate and sprinkle with confectioners' sugar.
If desired, add little stars for that extra dramatic effect.

# PAVLOVAS WITH FRUIT (FOR MY MOTHER)

*Mom, this recipe makes 12 meringues, the size of large beverage coasters, as for your birthday. (You can also make 20 smaller ones, but, be careful, they will increase in size in the oven.)*

*For the meringues*
6 egg whites
1 tbsp cornstarch, sifted
1 scant tbsp white wine vinegar
2 tsp vanilla sugar
pinch of salt
1¾ cups superfine sugar
¼ cup boiling water

*In addition you will also need*
a lot of fresh fruit: 1 pint strawberries, 2 bananas, 2 trays mixed berries, fresh pineapple (in short, whatever's available)
a few sprigs of mint
dash of liqueur (whatever you have in the kitchen)
⅔ cup thick cream
2 cups sour cream
confectioners' sugar

Preheat the oven to 400°F/Gas 6. Line a baking sheet with parchment paper and set aside.

Beat the egg whites in a large and very clean bowl. While beating, pour in the sifted cornstarch, the white wine vinegar, the vanilla sugar, and salt. When the egg whites get foamy, slowly add the sugar, little by little, in order for it to be fully absorbed. Then add the boiling water, tablespoon by tablespoon, until the mixture is stiff and glossy.

Fill an icing bag with the egg whites and pipe small turrets, or using a tablespoon create small heaps on the baking sheet lined with parchment paper.

Bake the meringues for 10 minutes in the hot oven, lower the temperature to 190°F, and bake for a further hour.

Try not to open the oven, as they may collapse.

Turn off the oven and leave them to dry for at least 1 hour or preferably overnight in the warm oven.

All this can be done 1 day in advance.

Wash the fruit and cut it smaller if you find it necessary. Cut the mint into strips and blend in with the fruit. Also stir a dash of liqueur through the fruit salad. Whip the cream with a dash of liqueur and possibly some sugar to taste, but I don't believe it's necessary. Fold the whipped cream into the sour cream.

Place a meringue on each plate. Top with a generous dollop of cream. Cover with the fruit salad. Sprinkle with confectioners' sugar and serve immediately.

**TIP** You can color the meringues with food colorings. Always use just a tiny amount, since the color is quite strong!

# PANETTONE & CUSTARD PUDDING

*You're probably familiar with bread pudding. An English dessert—but also good for breakfast, you know! The very similar "bread and butter pudding" is made with day-old or leftover bread. It is rich but once you taste it you'll find it difficult to stop. In our restaurant we make a variation on this old recipe by using Italian panettone instead of regular bread, making it slightly lighter. A dessert for 4–6 people.*

¾ cup pitted and soaked prunes

4 tbsp Amaretto (Italian sweet almond-flavored liqueur)

8 oz panettone (Italian sweet brioche-like bread, easily available around Easter; otherwise use sponge cake)

½ stick butter

1⅔ cups milk

seeds from 1 vanilla bean or 2 tsp vanilla sugar

⅓ cup sugar

2 eggs

1 egg yolk

confectioners' sugar to garnish

You will also need: Two baking dishes, one smaller and another larger.

Heat the oven to 350°F/Gas 4.

In the smaller baking dish, cover the prunes with the Amaretto. Slice the panettone. Butter the slices and put them under a hot broiler until golden brown. Overlap the bread slices on top of the prunes in the dish.

Heat the milk with the vanilla and sugar in a saucepan until very hot (do not boil). Beat the eggs with the yolks and pour the hot milk into the eggs, while stirring. Pour the egg mixture onto the panettone in the oven dish. Place the dish in a larger dish or baking pan in the oven and fill the larger dish with hot water until it reaches the rim of the smaller one.

Bake the panettone-custard pudding in the oven for 25 minutes until golden brown and before serving, sprinkle with confectioners' sugar. Serve hot!

# DOUGHNUTS WITH COCONUT-LEMON FILLING

*For approx. 6 doughnuts*

½ x recipe for sponge cake batter on page 329

*For the filling*

4 egg yolks (reserve the egg whites!)

½ cup sugar

⅓ cup cornstarch

1⅔ cups coconut milk (whole can)

5 tsp butter, chilled

zest of ½ lemon

*For the meringue*

4 egg whites

pinch of salt

1 cup superfine sugar

First prepare the filling: In a bowl beat the egg yolks with the sugar and cornstarch until foamy using a hand blender.

Heat the coconut milk in a saucepan. Stir a full tablespoon of hot coconut milk through the egg batter and then add all of the coconut milk. Return the coconut mixture to the pan and bring to a boil, while stirring. The cream will thicken. Beat the chilled butter swiftly through the cream. Add the lemon zest and immediately remove the pan from the heat.

Pour the cream into an icing bag or clean mixing bowl and allow to fully cool.

Prepare the sponge cake batter, as described on page 329.

Grease a cake pan and line the bottom with parchment paper. Pour the batter into the pan and spread to approx. ½ inch thick. Bake the cake until done in approx. 15–20 minutes. Leave to cool.

Cut out circles with a glass. Plan 2 circles per person.

Beat the egg whites until stiff; add a dash of salt. Add the superfine sugar, spoonful by spoonful, and beat into stiff white peaks. Cover half of the cake rounds with two generous tablespoons of lemon filling. Top with a cake round.

Generously spread the beaten egg white on the doughnuts, on all sides. Use a spoon to slightly swirl the foam, thus creating peaks. Line a baking sheet with parchment paper.

Using a spatula, carefully arrange the doughnuts on the baking pan and place in a fan-forced/convection oven with the broiler preheated to 340°F/Gas 4 for a further 5 minutes in order to color them. Serve quite quickly.

# BABA À LA LIQUEUR DE LAURIER

*For 4 servings*

346

*For the babas*

1 package yeast (2¼ tsp)

1 tbsp sugar

¼ cup lukewarm milk

⅔ cup all-purpose flour

1 egg, loosely beaten

pinch of salt

3 tbsp butter, at room temperature

*For the syrup*

2 cups water

⅔ cup sugar

1 generous glass bay liqueur (see recipe on page 99; I use at least ⅔ cup, but less is okay)

*And also*

⅔ cup thick cream

Grease 4 small round baking pans, preferably in the shape of a mug.

In a large bowl, leave the yeast, sugar, and lukewarm milk to stand for 5 minutes until it starts to foam.

Using a hand blender with dough hooks, beat in one third of the flour into a smooth batter. Leave to rise, covered with plastic wrap, for 20 minutes in a warm place.

Lightly beat the egg with a pinch of salt in a bowl. Stir the remaining flour in two parts through the yeast mixture and finish with the beaten egg. Beat in the butter, spoonful by spoonful. Only add the new spoonful when the previous one is fully absorbed. Beat the batter for at least 5 minutes.

Distribute the batter among the buttered pans. They should be approximately half full. Place on a baking sheet and allow to rise for a further 15 minutes or until the batter has risen to the edge of the pan.

Preheat the oven to 340°F/Gas 4.

Place the babas in the oven and bake for approx. 15 minutes until golden brown. Leave to cool for 5 minutes, lift them from the pans, and leave to fully cool on a rack.

In the meantime, prepare the syrup: Heat the water in a saucepan. Add the sugar and stir until it has dissolved. Leave the sugar syrup to cool. Stir in the liqueur.

Before serving, whip the cream. Place a baba in a soup plate. Cut lengthwise, generously top with the liqueur syrup, and serve with unsweetened whipped cream.

# MIXED BERRIES AND CHAMPAGNE DELIGHT

*Great, this recipe combines all sorts of recipes, which I have already described earlier.*
*You will have to go back and forth through the book, but you will be glad you went to the trouble!*

½ x recipe for Champagne cream (see page 329)
½ x basic recipe for sponge cake (see page 329)
3 tbsp blackberry or raspberry jam (see page 12 or 16)
1–2 tbsp blackberry and thyme syrup, to taste
4 oz marzipan (see recipe on page 356)
pinch or drop of pink food coloring
a lot of confectioners' sugar
2 cups mixed berries
and you will need a toothpick

First prepare the Champagne cream. Make the cake batter according to the recipe and pour into a square cake pan, if you have one, but a round one will obviously also do the job. Bake the cake and leave to cool. Lightly beat the jam with the blackberry syrup. Spread the jam on the cake and cover with the Champagne cream. Color the marzipan with the pink coloring and work through until evenly colored. Roll into a rope. Dust a rolling pin with confectioners' sugar and roll the marzipan out on a countertop, also dusted with confectioners' sugar. Again dust with confectioners' sugar when it starts getting sticky. Using a ravioli cutter (with a zigzag knife), or a regular sharp knife, cut a rectangular strip that is twice as high as the cake and generously fits around it. Wrap the cake with the marzipan trim, secure with a toothpick, and fill the top with fresh fruit. Dust with confectioners' sugar.

# PARISIAN APPLE TARTLETS

*For 6 individual tartlet bases*
2 cups all-purpose flour
1¼ sticks chilled butter
½ cup sugar
1 egg
1 tsp cinnamon
pinch of salt

*For the filling*
3 tart cooking apples with red skin
⅓ cup superfine sugar
2 tbsp all-purpose flour
2 eggs
¾ cup thick cream
seeds from 1 vanilla bean
mix of 1 tbsp granulated sugar & ½ tbsp cinnamon
⅔ cup apricot jam
2–3 tbsp Calvados
6 tbsp crème fraîche

Combine the tartlet base ingredients swiftly into an even dough. This is easiest in a food processor.
Use a few drops of ice-cold water if necessary.
Leave the dough to rest in the refrigerator for 1 hour. Then roll out the dough on a countertop dusted with flour and use to cover 6 well-buttered individual pie dishes. Prick the bottoms with a fork.
Preheat the oven to 350°F/Gas 4.
Blind bake the tartlet bases for 10 minutes (if you are making a large pie, say, 9-inch diameter, bake a little longer, i.e. 15–20 minutes).
Quarter the apples, remove the cores, but not the attractive peel. Cut the sections into very thin slices. Stir the sugar through the flour. Stir in the eggs into a nice paste. Heat the cream, vanilla, and bean, bring to the boil and then remove from the heat. Remove the bean, and add the hot cream to the flour-egg paste, while stirring.
Pour that cream into the prebaked pie crusts and cover with the overlapping apple slices.
Sprinkle with the cinnamon-sugar mix.
Bake the tartlets in the preheated oven for 15–20 minutes (a larger version will be done in approx. 25 minutes).
Leave to slightly cool.
Heat the apricot jam in a pan. Dilute with a tbsp of Calvados or water. Press the jam through a strainer over a bowl and spread the collected apricot jelly on the tartlets.
Serve the tartlets with a tablespoon of unsweetened good quality crème fraîche.

DU CHOCOLAT POUR TOUS !

# MAKING CHOCOLATES

WHEN MAKING CHOCOLATES, YOU, FIRST AND FOREMOST, NEED SOME SKILL. MELTING CHOCOLATE IS JUST NOT THAT EASY AND YOU HAVE TO ACQUIRE SOME EXPERIENCE. STIRRING TOO MUCH IS BAD, SINCE THE CHOCOLATE WILL BECOME GRAINY. HEATING IT TOO MUCH IS ALSO BAD, SINCE IT WILL ALSO BECOME DRY AND GRAINY. UNDER ALL CIRCUMSTANCES, THE FOLLOWING APPLIES: IF AT FIRST YOU DON'T SUCCEED, TRY AND TRY AGAIN. AND BE PREPARED FOR SOME FAILURES. FOR YOUR FIRST CHOCOLATES, STOCK UP ON SOME EXTRA CHOCOLATE. THEN YOU CAN MAKE ANOTHER BATCH, NO WORRIES! THE BEST TEMPERATURE FOR CHOCOLATE IS 104°F, HENCE A LITTLE WARMER THAN BODY TEMPERATURE. JUST CHECK WITH YOUR FINGER.

FOR THE FILLING (GANACHE) YOU NEED TWICE AS MUCH CHOCOLATE AS CREAM: 1/2 CUP CREAM AND 7 OZ CHOCOLATE (70% COCOA).

HEAT THE CREAM IN A HEAVY-BOTTOMED SAUCEPAN. YOU CAN ADD FLAVORING SUCH AS CINNAMON, LIQUEUR, OR NOTHING!

MELT 2 TBSP BUTTER IN THE HOT CREAM.

FINELY CHOP THE CHOCOLATE AND ADD IT TO THE CREAM. TURN OFF THE HEAT AND LEAVE TO MELT.

STIR THE MIXTURE CAREFULLY INTO A GLOSSY SMOOTH MASS.

POUR THE GANACHE INTO A TRAY LINED WITH PLASTIC WRAP AND PLACE IN THE REFRIGERATOR FOR AT LEAST 2 HOURS.

TRANSFER TO WAX PAPER.

CUT INTO EQUAL SQUARES.

MELT 7 OZ CHOCOLATE OVER A DOUBLE BOILER.

355

USING A CARVING FORK, QUICKLY DIP THE GANACHE IN THE CHOCOLATE . . .

AND LEAVE THE CHOCOLATES TO DRY ON PARCHMENT PAPER.

CREATE AN ICING BAG WITH WAXED PAPER.

FILL IT WITH 4 OZ MELTED WHITE OR MILK CHOCOLATE.

THIS IS HOW YOU DECORATE THE CHOCOLATES PROFESSIONALLY!

LEAVE TO DRY AND NEATLY TRIM. SERVE WITH COFFEE!

# LET'S GO...

MAKING CHOCOLATES IS FUN, ISN'T IT? THERE ARE, OF COURSE, HUNDREDS OF VARIATIONS, BUT WITH A FEW BASIC RECIPES, I HOPE THAT YOU WILL START EXPERIMENTING. I LIKE TO LOOK IN THE DISPLAY WINDOWS OF PATISSERIES AND CHOCOLATIERS FOR INSPIRATION. BUT MAYBE YOU ARE A CREATIVE GENIUS!

## ROSEMARY AND SEA SALT CHOCOLATES

*You can also replace the rosemary in this recipe with chile pepper, thyme, or strong black or green tea.*

*For the filling*
½ cup thick cream
1 sprig rosemary
pinch of salt
1 tbsp red wine vinegar
4 oz semisweet chocolate
5 tsp butter

*For the couverture*
semisweet chocolate
5 tsp butter
1 tbsp salt flakes or coarse sea salt

Heat the cream, rosemary, and salt until very hot. Leave to infuse for about 30 minutes; do not boil the cream and try not to stir it. Strain the cream; add the wine vinegar and the chocolate. Set aside in order for the chocolate to melt due to the heat of the hot cream. Carefully continue to stir for a few minutes. Beat in the butter using a whisk. Leave to slightly cool and transfer the filling to an icing bag. Pipe the filling in the shape of little balls on waxed paper. Leave to set in the refrigerator. Melt the semisweet chocolate and butter over a double boiler. Dip the fillings into the chocolate and swiftly return them to the waxed paper. Sprinkle with a few salt flakes and leave to fully set.

## MARZIPAN

*Making marzipan is very easy. And once you have made a considerable quantity you will find that you can do all sorts of things with it. You can cover it with chocolate, for example. Instead of water you can also use liqueur or add coloring agents. It freezes easily, so make a lot of it!*

1½ cups blanched almonds
2 cups confectioners' sugar
2–3 tbsp water or orange blossom water

Finely grind the almonds in a food processor. (Or use ready ground almond meal.)
Sift the confectioners' sugar over them and add a few drops of water or other liquid. Work the marzipan by hand into a supple and smooth dough. Wrap the dough in plastic wrap and allow to rest in the refrigerator for a few hours.
You can easily roll out the marzipan if you keep the rolling pin and the counter-top dusted with confectioners' sugar.

## FILLED DATES

*It is great fun to make these Moroccan sweets with your homemade marzipan.*

⅓ cup shelled pistachios
4 oz marzipan, made with orange blossom water
1 tbsp extra orange blossom water
confectioners' sugar
20 large dates (but regular ones are also fine)

Chop two-thirds of the pistachio nuts. Work the marzipan with the chopped nuts and a little orange blossom water. Roll into 20 balls with your hands dusted with confectioners' sugar. Carefully pit the dates and fill them with the marzipan balls. Press a whole pistachio nut on each date and serve them, preferably in one of those beautiful tiny paper cups, if you can lay your hands on them.

## ALMOND CHOCOLATES

1 stick butter
4 oz semisweet chocolate (at least 70% cocoa)
1⅓ cups confectioners' sugar
1¼ cups almond meal
2 tbsp mascarpone
3 tbsp liqueur, to taste
approx. 25 whole blanched almonds
4 oz milk chocolate

Melt the butter and the semisweet chocolate in a double boiler. Carefully stir in the confectioners' sugar, almond meal, mascarpone, and the liqueur. Remove from the heat and leave to set. Form into oval balls and press them onto the countertop so that they stay put. Top with a whole almond. Melt the milk chocolate in a double boiler and dip the chocolates halfway into it. Leave to dry on a rack or on waxed paper.

## CINNAMON STICKS

½ cup thick cream
7 oz semisweet chocolate (at least 70% cocoa)
5 tsp butter at room temperature
1 tsp cinnamon plus 2 tbsp extra
1 tsp ground ginger
2 tbsp superfine sugar

Heat the cream until very hot and turn off the heat. Grate the chocolate and add it to the warm cream with the butter, 1 tsp cinnamon, and ground ginger. Let the chocolate melt and occasionally stir gently. Leave to set until nearly hard.
Beat using a mixer and transfer to an icing bag with a large round tip. Pipe sticks, 1 inch long, on waxed paper. Leave to slightly stiffen in the fridge. Stir the remaining cinnamon into the sugar and roll the sticks in this.

## CRUNCHY CHOCOLATES

2 tbsp golden syrup (available in gourmet food stores) but honey also works well
5 tsp butter
½ cup superfine sugar
1¾ cups puffed rice cereal
1 tbsp cocoa powder
4 oz milk or semisweet chocolate

Heat the honey and the butter in a saucepan. Stir in the superfine sugar, puffed rice, and cocoa. Grease a rectangular shallow baking sheet. Add the mixture. Slightly press and even out with the back of a spoon or spatula. Leave to cool and transfer to a board. Heat the chocolate in a double boiler. Pour over the cake on the board and even out using the spatula. Leave to set in the refrigerator and cut into cubes.

## IRISH FUDGE

*If you do not like alcohol, replace it with the same quantity of milk.*

2 cups sugar
approx. 4 tsp vanilla sugar
1 stick butter
1 cup thick cream
¼ cup Irish whiskey

Line a square brownie baking pan with waxed paper. Combine all the ingredients in a saucepan. Bring the mixture to a boil on low heat and simmer for 30 minutes. Test the fudge for consistency by putting a droplet into cold water. If you are able to form it into a ball, it is ready! Leave the fudge to cool for a few minutes.
Stir occasionally until it thickens into a slightly crumbly consistency. Pour into the baking pan; leave to fully cool and dry for 6 hours. Use the paper to lift it out and cut into cubes. Leave a little space between each one so that they to continue to dry.

## COW PATS

*Yeah, funny name! But that's what I used to call them. They are actually peanut-raisin rock cookies. You can replace the peanuts with cashew nuts or almonds.*

12 oz milk or semisweet chocolate
½ stick butter
⅔ cup raisins
¾ cup peanuts

Heat the chocolate and the butter in a double boiler. Stir in the raisins and peanuts. Drop spoonfuls of the mixture on a large sheet of waxed paper. Leave to dry and set in the refrigerator.
If you are in a decorative mood, you can melt a little white chocolate and with the help of a spoon run a thin trickle of white chocolate on the rocks. They will no longer look like cow pats, but perhaps that's for the best.

357

# ROSEMARY SHORTBREAD

*I didn't like shortbread as a child. I only started liking it later, especially if it is a little savory, as the recipe here, with rosemary. Cut them small: They taste better and are posher with coffee than those ridiculously large pieces I received as a child.*

1¼ sticks butter
¼ cup superfine sugar
1 tbsp honey
1⅔ cups self-rising flour
2 tbsp finely chopped rosemary
pinch of salt
extra rosemary sprigs to garnish

Preheat the oven to 340°F/Gas 3. Grease a springform pan or pie dish approx. 9 inches in diameter.
Beat the butter and the sugar and honey into a creamy mass. Stir in the flour, with the rosemary and salt. Do not beat too long; it just has to be well blended. Knock down a few times on a countertop dusted with flour until it turns into a smooth dough ball.
Press the dough into the pan and even it out. Cut the raw "pie" into small wedges or fingers with the dull edge of a knife. Prick holes in the dough with a fork and garnish each wedge with a small sprig of rosemary.
Bake the shortbread in the oven for 15–20 minutes until light brown. Leave to cool in the pan for 10 minutes and then carefully remove it. You can now break it along the scored lines and serve.

# ALMOND TUILES

*In this recipe I say that you have to let them cool on a rolling pin, but if you carefully press them on a bottle cap, you will create small cups, which you can fill! With vanilla cream, for example, and red fruit.*

For at least 20 tuiles
2 egg whites
a teeny pinch of salt
3 tbsp confectioners' sugar
2 tbsp all-purpose flour
3 tbsp softened butter
3 tbsp slivered almonds

Beat the egg whites, salt, and confectioners' sugar until stiff. Stir in the flour and the butter. With the help of a spoon, drop dollops of batter on a baking sheet lined with parchment paper. Sprinkle with the almonds and bake the tuiles in an oven preheated to 350°F/Gas 4 for 5 minutes until golden brown. Always bake small quantities. While still very warm, remove the tuiles from the baking sheet and place them on something round, such as a rolling pin or a small bottle. Leave them to cool, resulting in nicely curled tuiles.

# ALMOND-CINNAMON COOKIES

For a full cookie jar
½ cup superfine sugar plus extra
1¾ sticks butter
2 cups all-purpose flour
1 egg
zest of 1 lemon
1 tbsp cinnamon or mixed spices
⅔ cup slivered almonds
pinch of salt

*To garnish*
candied cherries, whole almonds, whole walnuts, etc.

Combine all the ingredients in a food processor and grind. Roll into ropes with a diameter of approx. 1 inch and roll them through the extra sugar. Wrap them in plastic wrap and place them in the refrigerator for 1 hour to firm.
Preheat the oven to 350°F/Gas 4. Cut the rolls into slices, and garnish with a nut or cherry, or whatever you have.
Bake in the oven for 12 minutes until light brown. Leave to cool before serving.

# COCO ROCHERS

*Sophie, our French pastry chef, taught me how to make these fantastic French cookies. You can make them as large as you wish. I love them small, almost like chocolates.*

*This recipe is for approx. 20 cookies.*
1⅓ cups shredded coconut
½ cup sugar
2 egg whites

*And also*
3 oz white chocolate, in chunks
1 tbsp shredded coconut
3 oz semisweet chocolate, in chunks

Beat the coconut, sugar, and egg whites swiftly into a thick batter. Roll into balls the size of a golf ball and with thumb and index finger press a top, thus creating a "hill." Preheat the oven to 340°F/Gas 3. Place the hills on a sheet of paper parchment on a baking sheet and bake for approx. 12 minutes until light brown. Leave to fully cool. Melt the white chocolate in a double boiler and dip the tops of half the cookies into the chocolate. Sprinkle with coconut and leave to set until the coffee is ready. Repeat with the semisweet chocolate and remaining cookies.

# CHOCOLATE COOKIES

*For at least 30 cookies*
1 cup all-purpose flour
½ stick butter, chilled
⅓ cup sugar
2 tbsp cocoa powder
2 tbsp shaved semisweet chocolate

Work all the ingredients together into a smooth dough. Add a few drops of cold water, if it is too dry. Allow the dough to rest for at least an hour. Roll out on a flour-dusted countertop. Cut out small rectangles or use a cutter. Place them on a cookie sheet lined with parchment paper. Preheat the oven to 350°F/Gas 4. Bake until done in approx. 10 minutes. Leave them to cool before serving, allowing the chocolate to set.

# PISTACHIO WAFERS

*For 15–20 wafers*
5 oz semisweet chocolate
⅔ cup pistachio nuts, skins removed
¼ cup raisins

Slowly melt the chocolate in a double boiler. Stir as little as possible. Pour spoonfuls of melted chocolate onto waxed paper and press them into round wafers with the back of the spoon. Press the pistachio nuts and raisins into the middle of the wafers and leave to fully harden. Peel them from the paper and serve!

# HAZELNUT & LEMON CANTUCCINI

*For approx. 24 slices*

pinch of salt
1⅔ cups self-rising flour
2 eggs, beaten
½ cup sugar
2 tsp vanilla sugar
zest of 2 lemons
¼ cup sunflower oil
¼ cup milk
¾ cup hazelnuts, coarsely chopped

Preheat the oven to 340°F/Gas 4. Line a large baking pan with parchment paper. Stir the salt into the flour. Beat two-thirds of the beaten eggs in a bowl using a hand blender (you will need the reserved one-third later to spread on the cookies). While stirring, add the sugar and vanilla sugar, as well as the lemon zest and oil. Sift the flour over a bowl and stir. Add the milk, adding a little more if it appears necessary. Lastly, quickly mix in the chopped nuts. Cut the dough in half, and roll both halves into two equal ropes. Slightly separate them on the baking pan and coat them with the reserved egg. Bake the cookie ropes for 25–30 minutes or until golden brown. Leave to slightly cool on a rack and cut each into 12 equal slices with a sharp knife. Return to the baking pan and bake for a further 10 minutes on each side until golden brown. Leave to fully cool on a rack.

# CANDIED CHOCOLATE ORANGE CURLS

*For approx. 40 curls*

3 oranges
1¾ cups sugar plus extra
5 oz milk or semisweet chocolate

Squeeze the oranges. Reserve the juice. Remove all of the white pulp and cut the peel into thin strips. Bring the peels, the juice, and a glass of water to a boil, transfer the peels to paper towels and leave to drain.
Bring the sugar and 2½ cups water to a boil and simmer the peels in the sugar syrup for 1½ hours.
Add more liquid if it boils dry. Remove the peels from the thickened syrup. Strain.
Sprinkle a little sugar on a plate and coat the peels one by one with the sugar. Leave to dry on waxed paper.
Melt the chocolate in a double boiler and dip half of the orange curls in it. Leave them to dry again.
Keep in the refrigerator.

# Orange Marmalade Drops

Preheat to 375°

Sift :

   2/3 cup sugar

Beat until soft :

   1/3 cup butter

Add sugar gradually. Blend these ingredients till light & creamy. Beat in :

   1 egg

   6 tablespoons orange marmalade

Sift :

   1½ cups flour

  & resift with :

   1¼ tsp. baking powder

                   if cookies too dry — add more marmal.' if too moist — add flour & grated lemon rind.

Stir sifted ingred. into butter mix. Drop batter from teaspoon, well apart on greased sheet. Bake cookies for 8 minutes (or so).

# rose tea
# Marshmallows

FOR THIS RECIPE YOU WILL REALLY NEED A FOOD PROCESSOR WITH A WHISK OR A HAND BLENDER AND LOTS OF PATIENCE.

TO FILL A BAKING SHEET YOU WILL NEED:

- 3 LEAVES / OR 2 1/4 TSP GELATIN / POWDERED GELATIN
- 250 ML (8 FL OZ / 1 CUP) ROSE PETAL TEA (... OR REGULAR TEA OF COURSE!)
- 500 GRAMS (16 OZ / 2 1/4 CUPS) GRANULATED SUGAR
- 150 GRAMS (5 OZ / JUST UNDER 1/2 CUP) GOLDEN SYRUP (THICK SUGAR SYRUP)
- PINCH OF SALT
- DROP OF PINK FOOD COLORING

**1** SOAK THE GELATIN LEAVES IN COLD WATER (OR DISSOLVE THE POWDERED GELATIN IN A TBSP. OF WARM WATER)

**2** BRING THE TEA, SUGAR SYRUP, AND SALT TO A BOIL. SIMMER FOR ABOUT 7 MINS UNTIL IT FORMS A THICK SYRUP.

**3** SQUEEZE THE GELATIN LEAVES, PLACE THEM IN THE FOOD PROCESSOR, AND BLITZ ON MEDIUM SPEED OR ADD THE DISSOLVED GELATIN MIXTURE TO THE FOOD PROCESSOR.

**4** POUR A THIN TRICKLE OF HOT SYRUP ONTO THE MIXTURE. IF IT TURNS WHITER, THE PROSESSORS' SPEED CAN BE INCREASED. → KEEP ON BLITZING INTO THIKC WHITE FOAM & UNTIL THE BOWL FEELS LUKEWARM. → THIS TAKES 15 MINUTES! ADD THE COLORING.

**5** GREASE A SHEET OF PARCHMENT PAPER. PLACE ON A SERVING TRAY AND SPREAD THE MIXTURE ON IT: 2 CM OR 3/4 INCH THICK. ←

**6** LEAVE TO DRY FOR 8–12 HOURS. CUT INTO SQUARES OR CUT OUT SHAPES.

THIS IS HOW EASY IT IS ⇐

CREMA DE CACAHUETE
ERDNUSSMUS
PASTA D'ARACHI
عجينة فول سوداني
DAKATIN
PATE D'ARACHIDE
PEANUT BUTTER

# CHEWY WHOLE-WHEAT COOKIES WITH CHOCOLATE

*For approx. 40 cookies*

1½ sticks butter at room temperature

1⅛ cups superfine sugar

1 egg

⅔ cup whole-wheat flour

2 tsp vanilla sugar

¾ cup toasted walnuts or pecans, ground

½ tsp baking powder

pinch of salt

½ tsp cinnamon

2 cups rolled oats

7 oz chocolate, grated or chopped into small chunks

Preheat the oven to 350°F/Gas 4.

Beat the butter and the superfine sugar until creamy, stir in the egg. Combine all the dry ingredients and half the grated chocolate and stir everything in the mixing bowl into a nice dough. Grease a cookie sheet or line it with parchment paper. With clean hands, roll the dough into balls the size of a walnut and arrange on the cookie sheet, not too close to each other. Bake in the oven until golden brown in 12–15 minutes.

Leave to fully cool.

Melt the remaining chocolate in a double boiler. Leave to slightly cool and pour into an icing bag. Pipe thin trickles of chocolate onto the cookies. If you don't own an icing bag, you can use a spoon. Leave to dry again and serve!

# NUTTY WINTER COOKIES

*For approx. 45 cookies*

1 stick butter and a little extra for greasing purposes

1⅓ cups superfine sugar

3 tbsp peanut butter

2 eggs

2 tsp vanilla sugar

1⅛ cups all-purpose flour

1½ cups oat flakes (organic store) or rolled oats

1 tsp baking powder

pinch of salt

1 tsp cinnamon

⅓ cup walnuts, chopped

⅓ cup raisins

Beat the butter, superfine sugar, and peanut butter until creamy. Stir in the eggs, one by one, and then the vanilla sugar. Sift the flour over another bowl and blend with the oat flakes, baking powder, salt, and cinnamon. Fold into the butter mixture. Finish with the nuts and raisins. Knock down swiftly into a smooth dough and wrap in plastic wrap. Leave to rest in the refrigerator for 1 hour. Preheat the oven to 350°F/Gas 4. Line a cookie sheet with parchment paper and coat with a little melted butter. Using two tablespoons, create oval balls from the dough, the size of a walnut, and place them on the cookie sheet, approx. 2 inches apart. Bake the cookies for approx. 12 minutes; they will still feel soft, but that's how it has to be! Leave them to slightly cool on the cookie sheet and then using a spatula transfer them to a rack to further cool. Keep in an airtight sealed cookie jar.

# CHOCOLATE & CARAMEL TRUFFLES

4 oz semisweet chocolate

⅓ cup sugar

2 tbsp water

½ stick butter

⅔ cup thick cream

1¼ cups cocoa powder

and attractive chocolate or paper cups

Melt the chocolate in the microwave or in a double boiler. Leave to briefly cool. Melt the sugar in the water in a heavy-bottomed pan. Gently swirl the pan in order for the sugar to color evenly. Remove from the heat when the caramel turns amber. Careful! *Caramel is extremely hot!* Stir in the butter in pats until melted. Pour in the cream. This may splatter, so keep your distance. Stir into a smooth sauce on low heat. Add the caramel to the chocolate and leave the mixture to fully cool. Place in the refrigerator to further cool for at least 3 hours. Now you can create curls with a tablespoon from the hardened chocolate. Drop them into a bowl with cocoa powder and roll them with the help of two other spoons, so that all sides are covered with cocoa. Place the truffles immediately back in the refrigerator to firm again.

Serve in chocolate cups. Or paper cups.

# LAPSANG TRUFFLES

⅓ cup crème fraîche

⅓ cup thick cream

½ stick butter

1 generous tbsp lapsang souchong tea leaves (Chinese black tea with a smoky flavor)

7 oz semisweet chocolate, chopped

5 oz semisweet chocolate sprinkles

Bring the crème fraîche, cream, and butter to a boil in a heavy-bottomed saucepan. Stir in the tea.

Melt the chocolate in a double boiler. Pour the cream through a fine strainer over the chocolate and stir carefully until the chocolate has an even color. Leave to cool in the refrigerator.

Go do something else in the meantime . . .

When the chocolate has become firm, roll into balls with the help of two tablespoons. Roll them through the sprinkles. Always keep in the refrigerator until ready to serve.

# NUT-CARAMEL BAR WITH DRIED FIGS

*For approximately 12 bars*

1⅓ cups blanched almonds

1⅓ cups walnuts or pecans

1⅓ cups sunflower seeds, pumpkin seeds, or pine nuts, or a mixture of them all

7 oz dried figs, finely chopped

juice and zest of ½ orange

sunflower oil for greasing purposes

1⅓ cups superfine sugar

3 tbsp maple syrup

½ stick butter

pinch of salt

Preheat the oven to 340°F/Gas 4. Arrange the nuts over a sheet of parchment paper on a cookie sheet and bake for approx. 15 minutes until golden brown and crisp, turning halfway through. Transfer the nuts to a bowl and stir in the figs and orange zest. Line a shallow rectangular baking sheet with waxed paper. Brush the waxed paper with a thin layer of oil. Heat the sugar, syrup, and orange juice in a heavy-bottomed saucepan until the sugar has dissolved. Stir gently with a wooden spoon, but beware of splatters, since it will get very hot. Lastly, stir in the butter and salt. The sauce will become thicker. Fold in the nuts and stir well. Pour the mixture onto the greased paper and spread evenly.

After approx. 15 minutes, score the slab into bars with the back of a knife when it is nearly cool.

Leave to fully cool.

Break the slab along the score lines.

You can keep the bars for some time in a sealed box separated by sheets of waxed paper.

# MAKING MUSTARD

YOU PROBABLY NEVER THOUGHT THAT MAKING MUSTARD WAS THIS EASY. I WILL GIVE YOU THE RECIPE FOR BASIC MUSTARD.
ONCE YOU HAVE MADE IT, YOU WILL NO DOUBT COME UP WITH NEW INGREDIENTS: TARRAGON VINEGAR, TOASTED MUSTARD SEEDS
FOR A NUTTY FLAVOR, NUTMEG, CLOVES, CARAWAY SEEDS, OR WITH GARLIC, CHILE PEPPERS, OR HONEY INSTEAD OF SUGAR.
BE CAREFUL WITH THE SUGAR: IT CAN CHANGE THE TASTE DRAMATICALLY. SOME PEOPLE LIKE A LOT OF SUGAR, OTHERS DO NOT
LIKE IT AT ALL.

FOR 1 JAR YOU WILL NEED: 4 OZ MUSTARD SEEDS, 3/4 CUP WHITE WINE VINEGAR, 1 TSP TURMERIC, 1/4 CUP SUGAR, SALT, PEPPER.

FOR A SMOOTHER EFFECT, YOU CAN SOAK THE MUSTARD SEEDS OVERNIGHT IN THE VINEGAR, BUT THIS IS NOT ABSOLUTELY NECESSARY.

PLACE THE MUSTARD SEEDS AND THE VINEGAR IN A FOOD PROCESSOR.

ADD THE SPICES AND THE SUGAR.

BLITZ FOR APPROX. 6 MINUTES UNTIL IT'S A NEARLY SMOOTH MUSTARD. YOU CAN TAKE LONGER FOR A SMOOTHER MUSTARD IF YOU SO DESIRE.

TRANSFER THE MUSTARD TO A JAR, CLOSE THE LID, AND PLACE IN REFRIGERATOR UNTIL USED. IT WILL GET BETTER WITH TIME.

# LET'S GET GOING . . .

MAKE ALL THESE SAUCES A DAY IN ADVANCE, SO THAT THEY ARE READY IN THE REFRIGERATOR AFTER A NIGHT ON THE TOWN.

## KETCHUP

*For approx. 4 jars*

5½ lb tomatoes
1 red bell pepper
2 medium onions, finely chopped
1 clove garlic, crushed
½ cup vinegar
⅓ cup sugar
pinch of salt
2 tsp grated ginger
2 tsp paprika
2 tsp nutmeg
pinch of cayenne pepper
1 tbsp coriander seeds
1 clove
freshly ground pepper

Wash the tomatoes and cut into chunks. Wash the bell pepper and cut the pulp into chunks; remove the seeds. Combine the tomato, bell pepper, onions, garlic, and a little water in a pan and simmer for approx. 1 hour. Stir occasionally to prevent burning. If necessary add a little water. Puree the sauce until smooth, away from the heat, using a hand blender. Return to the heat and add the vinegar, sugar, and all spices. Leave the sauce to simmer for a further 1½ hours or until sufficiently thickened. Taste and add salt and pepper, as needed. Pour the hot sauce into sterile jars. (See instructions under jam making on page 12). Seal the jars with a suitable lid and turn upside down until cooled. The ketchup has a shelf life of 1 year. Once opened, the jar must be kept in the refrigerator.

## MUSTARD MAYONNAISE

1 egg yolk
salt and freshly ground pepper
1 tbsp lemon juice or vinegar
2 tbsp prepared coarse or fine mustard (to taste)
¾ cup sunflower oil or as much as needed

Ensure that all ingredients are at room temperature. Beat the egg yolk lightly in a bowl with the salt, pepper, lemon juice, and mustard. While stirring with a mixer, blend the sunflower oil with the egg mixture, first drop by drop and then in a thin trickle, into a thick creamy mayonnaise. Great with chips, of course!
*Oh! Be careful, this mayonnaise must be refrigerated and consumed within a few days since it contains raw egg.*

## OOF'S BARBECUE SAUCE

*Oof makes a divine, very American barbecue sauce, which I spoon up straight from the pan onto bread.*

2 cups ketchup
½ can dark beer
½ cup red wine vinegar
¼ cup raw superfine sugar
2 tbsp Worcestershire sauce
salt, to taste
1 clove garlic, finely chopped
pinch of cayenne pepper
1 stick butter
1–2 tbsp chopped jalapeño peppers

Cook all the ingredients in a saucepan on low heat into a thick sauce. Leave to cool or serve warm, either way.

## TOOMEH: LEBANESE GARLIC SAUCE

1 potato, peeled and boiled
2–4 cloves garlic (or more!)
salt and freshly ground pepper
2 tbsp mayonnaise (see recipe above)
2 tbsp thick yogurt
1 tbsp lemon juice, or more, to taste

Mash the potato. Crush the garlic with a pinch of salt into a paste. Add to potato and stir well with pepper. Stir in mayonnaise, yogurt, and lemon juice.

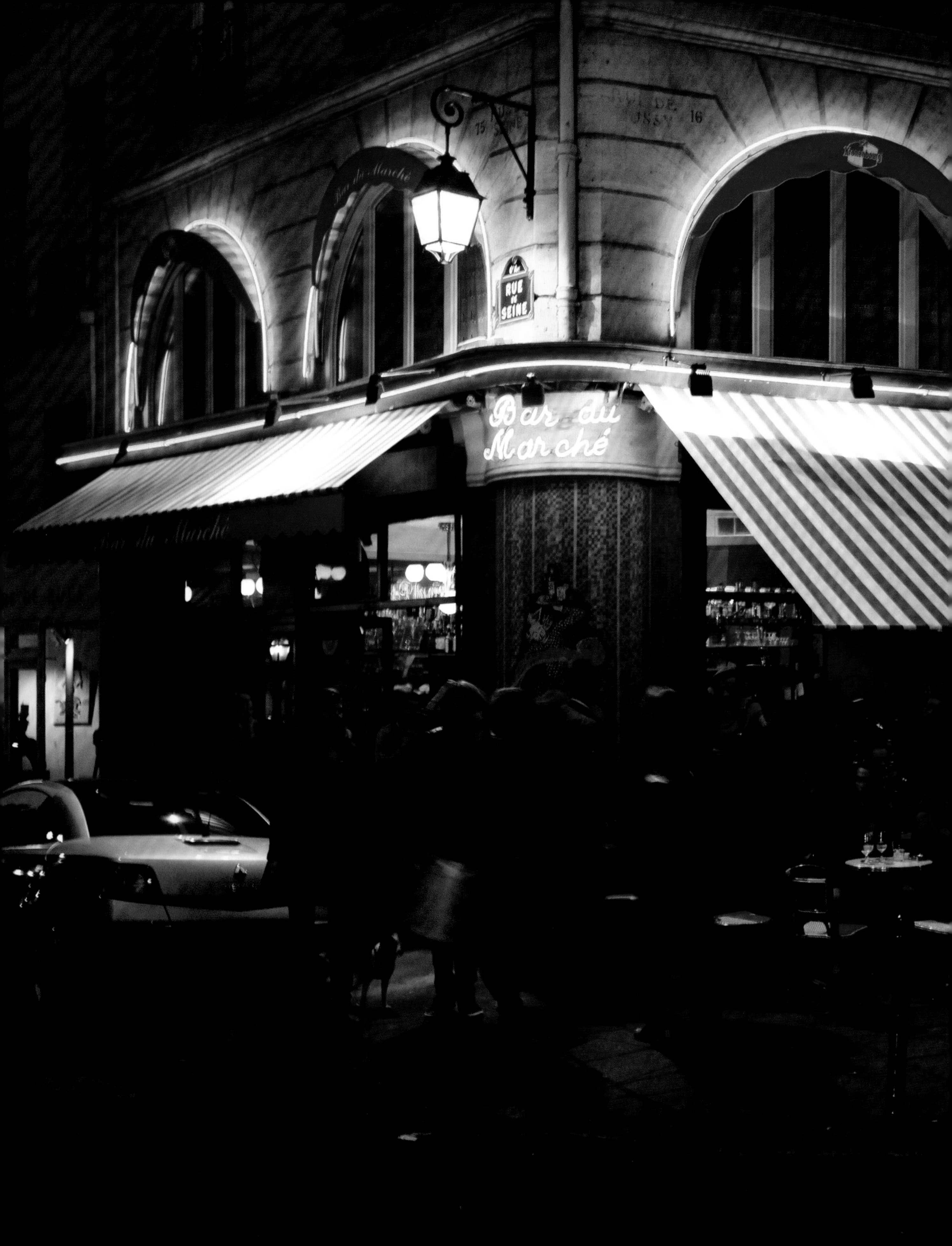
Bar du Marché
RUE DE SEINE
Bar du Marché
Bar du Marché

# ARAB LAMB BURGER

21 oz ground lamb, from leg of lamb, preferably home-ground in the food processor

⅓ cup bulgur, soaked in ¾ cup boiling water until tender

1 onion, finely chopped

2 cloves garlic, finely chopped

1 tsp cinnamon

½ tsp allspice

1 tsp paprika

4 tbsp finely chopped fresh cilantro

zest of ½ lemon

2 generous tbsp pine nuts, briefly toasted in a dry pan

salt and freshly ground pepper

*And also*

4 flatbreads with chickpeas and sage from the grill (see page 273) or just 4 good pitas

green salad and carrot salad (see page 274)

toomeh, Lebanese garlic sauce (see page 380 or another sauce on that page)

Work all the ingredients for the burger into a firm ball. Separate into 4 or 6 equal parts and roll each part into a ball. Press flat into a burger. Heat a broiler until burning hot. Broil a few minutes until golden brown, turning halfway through, until done. I like it if the inside is still a little pink.

Cut the flatbreads halfway to create pouches. Fill them with the burgers and a little green and carrot salad. Serve with toomeh.

*Toomeh (page 380), flatbread with chickpeas (page 273), carrot salad with cumin (page 274), and Arab lamb burger.*

# OMELETTE WITH SAUSAGE, CUMIN, POTATOES, AND SPINACH

8 oz sausages (go for tasty Italian or French sausages)
a little olive oil for frying
10 oz spinach, washed
1 small onion, diced
1 large waxy potato, washed but not peeled, thinly sliced
6 eggs
½ cup thick cream
1 tbsp cumin seeds, briefly toasted in a dry pan
salt and freshly ground pepper
1 ball buffalo mozzarella

Remove the skin from the sausages and crumble the meat into the hot olive oil in a nonstick skillet.
Sauté the meat while stirring until done and drain on paper towels. Cook the spinach in the pan on high heat. Fold the cooked spinach at the bottom of the pan over the uncooked leaves at the top. Transfer to a colander in the sink to drain. Heat a dash of oil in the skillet. Add the onion and potato slices. Cook half covered with a lid for approx. 10 minutes on medium heat. Turn occasionally. Remove the lid and turn up the heat, allowing the potatoes to become crispy on the edges. Preheat the broiler. Beat the eggs with the cream, cumin seeds, salt, and pepper and pour over the mixture in the pan. (You can also use a pie dish lined with buttered parchment paper, and place the sautéed onion and potatoes on the bottom.) Carefully shake the pan (or pie dish) back and forth in order for the egg to spread evenly. Spread the spinach and sausage on the omelette. Cover with mozzarella chunks. Put the omelette under the broiler in the oven and cook until done for approx. 7 minutes. Serve in wedges with plenty of thick toasted bread.

# CLUB SANDWICH WITH CHEESE, BACON, SMOKED BEET, & CELERY SALAD

*For this recipe, I assume that you still have some smoked beet left over; otherwise you can find the recipe on page 243, or you can use precooked beets.*

*For the celeriac salad*
½ small celeriac or ¼ large one
juice of 1 lemon
½ cup crème fraîche
1 tbsp mayonnaise (see page 380)
salt and freshly ground pepper

*And also*
2 smoked beets (see page 243) or 2 regular boiled ones
16 bread slices, preferably whole wheat
8 slices bacon or thinly sliced pork belly (see page 195)
a pat of butter
mayonnaise as a spread
a few nice lettuce leaves, arugula, or regular butter lettuce
8 slices tasty farmhouse cheese

First prepare the salad: Peel the celeriac and grate on a fine setting. This is easiest with the grater in the food processor. Trickle lemon juice over it in order to prevent discoloration and then stir the crème fraîche and mayonnaise through the grated celeriac. Season the salad with salt and pepper and keep in the refrigerator until used. Rub the peel away from the beets and slice.
Toast the bread slices in a toaster or broiler.
Fry the bacon in a pat of butter in a nonstick pan until crispy.
Spread mayonnaise on all bread slices. Cover the bottom 4 slices with lettuce and cheese. Top with a generous tablespoon of celeriac salad. Cover with the next bread slice, topped with lettuce, bacon, and beet. Cover with another bread slice with lettuce, cheese, and salad, and add the last bread slice. Secure sandwich with two toothpicks and cut diagonally in half.

Charles

# Bloody Mary

STICK A
CELERY STALK
IN IT!

A FEW DROPS
OF LEMON JUICE

3 PARTS
TOMATO JUICE

1 PART VODKA

TABASCO

THE ORIGINAL & GENUINE
LEA
&
PERRINS
SOS WORCESTERSHIRE

FLAVOR YOUR DRINK WITH
TABASCO &
WORCESTERSHIRE SAUCE!

# STICKY CINNAMON SCROLLS

*Right! A little bit of a hangover also requires something sweet, of course. These are ready in a little over 30 minutes, really no time at all. And usually everything will be in the pantry, so you don't have to leave the house. An ideal breakfast.*

*For approximately 8 scrolls*

2⅓ cups self-rising flour (or all-purpose flour and 2–3 tsp baking powder)
pinch of salt
½ stick butter, chilled
⅔–¾ cup buttermilk (or regular milk)

*And also*
large chunk of spreadable butter
sugar
cinnamon
raisins
nuts—walnuts, pecans, peanuts, whatever you have in the cupboard, coarsely chopped
1 egg, lightly beaten

Preheat the oven to 350°F/Gas 4.
In a bowl, mix the flour with a little salt and the butter until the dough looks like coarse sand. Slowly add the buttermilk into a supple dough.
Roll the dough ball out into a very thin slab (say, ⅛ inch thick) on the countertop dusted with flour.
Liberally spread butter on the dough. Sprinkle with sugar, cinnamon, raisins, and chopped nuts.
Roll the slab lengthwise into a long rope.
Butter a baking sheet or cover with parchment paper. Cut the roll into equal small rolls and place them upright against each other on the sheet. They don't have to fit tightly. Brush with the lightly beaten egg and bake the scrolls for approx. 25 minutes until golden brown and cooked on the inside.
Serve with chilled butter. Also delicious with whipped cream or unsweetened crème fraîche.

# BUTTERMILK FLAPJACKS WITH BACON

*For 16–20 flapjacks*
¾ cup all-purpose flour
¾ cup buckwheat flour
1 tsp baking powder
2 tbsp sugar
2–3 cups buttermilk
1 egg
2 tsp vanilla sugar
butter for frying
5 oz bacon rashers

Combine all the ingredients except the bacon and butter into a nice batter.
Melt the butter in a nonstick shallow skillet. Fry 2 slices of bacon on both sides until light brown. Pour a spoonful of batter onto each slice; fry on medium heat until holes form in the flapjacks. Turn and allow the other side to color.
Serve with homemade apple syrup jam.

# APPLE SYRUP JAM

*For 4–5 jars*

4½ lb sweet-sour apples for cooking
1⅓ cups raw superfine sugar

Wash the apples and chop the whole apples. Bring these chunks to a boil in a bit of water. Simmer for approx. 30 minutes, until the apples break open. Puree the mixture with a hand blender. Drain the apple sauce in a strainer over another pan while stirring occasionally. This will take at least 1 hour.
Bring the collected apple puree to a boil on high heat, and reduce by approximately three quarters. Stir occasionally.
Add the sugar while stirring. Continue to stir until it has fully dissolved and reduce further.
Pour the apple syrup jam into thoroughly cleaned jars, seal, and set aside, upside down, for 5 minutes.
Leave to fully cool. The syrup will get thicker once it is cold.

DO
NOT
FORGET
THE
DOG

# CHICKEN BISCUITS

*For 20–30 biscuits, depending on the size of your dog.*
*Make small biscuits for a small dog and larger ones for a great lump of a dog.*

7 oz boiled chicken (or leftovers from yesterday)
⅓ cup chicken broth (homemade, hence salt-free)
1 tbsp butter at room temperature
⅔ cup whole-wheat flour
⅓ cup cornstarch

Preheat the oven to 340°F/Gas 4. Grind the chicken with the broth and the butter in a food processor. Add the flour and cornstarch. Work the dough into a firm ball. Roll into a thin sheet on a flour-dusted countertop. Cut out shapes or cut into cubes. Bake until golden brown for 20 minutes. Leave to cool and keep in an airtight jar.

# LIVER CHEWIES

⅔ cup wheat germ (organic store)
8 oz chicken or beef livers
1⅛ cups whole-wheat flour
3 eggs

Blend the ingredients in a food processor until smooth. Grease a brownie baking pan with a little oil and cut a sheet of parchment paper the size of the bottom. Butter thoroughly. Press the mixture into the pan. Bake the biscuit for 20 minutes in an oven preheated to 340°F/Gas 4. Leave to cool and transfer to a board. Leave to fully cool, then cut into small cubes using a large knife. Keep in the refrigerator or freezer.

# DOGGY BISCUITS

⅔ cup hot water or salt-free homemade broth (beef cubes often contain too much salt!)
2 tbsp olive oil
1 egg
1 clove garlic, crushed
2⅔ cups all-purpose flour

Combine all the ingredients into a firm dough in a bowl. Roll into a thin sheet approximately ⅛ inch thick on a flour-dusted countertop. Cut the dough into strips or cut out shapes using a cookie cutter. Preheat the oven to 400°F/Gas 6 and bake the doggy biscuits for approx. 30 minutes until golden brown. Keep in a sealable jar.

*Biscuits in the shape of dogs: doggy biscuits; biscuits that spell MARIE: chicken biscuits; the small diamond-shaped biscuits are the liver chewies.*

*Jessica*

*Joy*

*Valentijn*

*Horas*

# SUNDAY BRUNCH

FOR APPROX. 6 SERVINGS

VEAL BROTH
GARNISH WITH A LOT OF CHOPPED CHERVIL, SEE RECIPE ON PAGE 128
*
EGGS BENEDICT
KEEP THE HOLLANDAISE SAUCE WARM IN A VACUUM FLASK OR IN A DOUBLE BOILER.
SEE RECIPE ON PAGE 39.
OR
SALMON AND SHRIMP TERRINE
WITH FAVA BEANS AND PORTOBELLO MUSHROOMS, SEE PAGE 185
WITH IRISH BROWN SODA BREAD TOAST, SEE RECIPE ON PAGE 29
OR
OEUF COCOTTES
WITH FILLING OF YOUR CHOICE, SEE PAGE 36
*
BERRIES AND CHAMPAGNE DELIGHT, SEE RECIPE ON PAGE 349

# BIRTHDAY BREAKFAST

FOR 2

STICKY CINNAMON SCROLLS
MAKE HALF OF THE RECIPE ON PAGE 392
*
FRENCH TOAST WITH CINNAMON BREAD
SEE PAGE 338
MAKE TWO, SERVE WITH RASPBERRY SORBET, OR RASPBERRY JAM, SEE RECIPES ON PAGES 315 AND 16
*
PAVLOVAS WITH FRUIT
AND LIGHT A CANDLE, OF COURSE!
SEE RECIPE ON PAGE 341.

# LUNCHES

## EXQUISITE 3-COURSE LUNCH
## EASILY PREPARED IN ADVANCE

FOAMY GARDEN PEA SOUP WITH BASIL AND AVOCADO CREAM (SERVE COLD!)
SEE RECIPE ON PAGE 15

\*

POTTED SHRIMP
SEE RECIPE ON PAGE 198

\*

PARISIAN APPLE TARTLETS
SEE RECIPE ON PAGE 350. TURN ON THE OVEN WHEN YOU SERVE THE MAIN COURSE.
THE TARTLETS CAN BE HEATED WHILE YOU MAKE COFFEE

## LUNCH BUFFET
## FOR APPROX. 10 SERVINGS

TABOULEH WITH POMEGRANATE
DOUBLE THE RECIPE ON PAGE 48

\*

LONG LEEK PIE
PREPARE THE RECIPE ON PAGE 289 TWICE OR PREPARE ONE LARGE ONE ON A BAKING SHEET

\*

PICKLED MACKEREL
DOUBLE THE RECIPE ON PAGE 205

\*

GREEN ASPARAGUS WITH PARSLEY GREMOLATA
DOUBLE THE RECIPE ON PAGE 286

\*

ZUCCHINI FLAPJACKS WITH BASIL CREAM
TRIPLE THE RECIPE ON PAGE 54

\*

TERRINE DE CAMPAGNE
SEE RECIPE ON PAGE 180

\*

FRESH BEAN SALAD WITH RADISH AND CAESAR DRESSING
SEE RECIPE ON PAGE 278

# HIGH TEA

FOR A FUN GROUP OF PEOPLE, SERVING 12–20

\*

CHOCOLATE-GINGER FUDGE CAKE WITH PECAN NUTS AND CINNAMON CREAM
SEE RECIPE ON PAGE 87

\*

PEAR-HAZELNUT CAKE
SEE RECIPE ON PAGE 83

\*

IRISH TEA BRACK
SEE RECIPE ON PAGE 84

\*

GINGERBREAD MUFFINS
SEE RECIPE ON PAGE 81

\*

ROSEMARY SHORTBREAD
SEE RECIPE ON PAGE 359

\*

PAVLOVAS WITH FRUIT
SEE RECIPE ON PAGE 341

\*

BISCUITS
SEE RECIPE ON PAGE 30

\*

WITH JAM: APRICOT-ALMOND JAM
SEE RECIPE ON PAGE 16

\*

TASTY MINI MUFFINS
SEE RECIPE ON PAGE 25

\*

SAVORY PIES
BAKE SMALL ONES, IF YOU HAVE SMALL BAKING PANS, OR TWO LARGE ONES CUT INTO SMALL CHUNKS
ALL RECIPES ON PAGE 60

\*

ZUCCHINI FLAPJACKS WITH BASIL CREAM
SEE RECIPE ON PAGE 54

\*

SERVE WITH TEA:
ELDERBERRY BLOSSOM TEA, FOR EXAMPLE, OR FRESH ICED TEA
RECIPES ON PAGE 77 AND 77
BUT ALSO CHILL SOME WHITE WINE OR CHAMPAGNE

# COLD EVENING BUFFET

FOR GROUPS OF 20-30, CAN EASILY BE PREPARED IN ADVANCE

\*

## MARINATED SALMON IN FENNEL SEED AND PERNOD
RECIPE ON PAGE 188

\*

## WHOLE BEEF LOIN IN HERB CRUST WITH ROSEMARY SALMORIGLIO
MAKE 2 AND CUT AS THINLY AS POSSIBLE, SEE RECIPE ON PAGE 256

\*

## FRITTATA WITH MINT, SPINACH, AND PECORINO
MAKE THE RECIPE 2-3 TIMES, IN AS LARGE A DISH AS POSSIBLE, AND CUT INTO SMALL CUBES
SEE RECIPE ON PAGE 46

\*

## HAM PIE
MAKE TWO, SEE RECIPE ON PAGE 187

\*

## APPLE-DATE CHUTNEY SERVED WITH PASTIES
SEE RECIPES ON PAGES 159 AND 184

\*

## SALAD WITH LENTILS, APPLE, AND CILANTRO
TRIPLE THE RECIPE ON PAGE 69

\*

## LUKEWARM SALAD WITH POTATOES, GREEN BEANS, AND GIANT BEANS
TRIPLE THE RECIPE ON PAGE 270

\*

## GREEN ASPARAGUS WITH PARSLEY GREMOLATA
TRIPLE THE RECIPE ON PAGE 286

\*

## HOMEMADE FOCACCIA
BAKE AT LEAST TWO AND CUT INTO SMALL CHUNKS, SEE RECIPE ON PAGE 22
SERVE WITH A HIGH-QUALITY OLIVE OIL

# DRINKS WITH SNACKS

FOR A GROUP OF 12-20

*

POMEGRANATE PROSECCO
AND DELICIOUS WELCOME DRINK, RECIPE ON PAGE 102

*

SMOKED SHRIMP WITH LEMON & ROSEMARY SALT
RECIPE ON PAGE 232

CROSTINI AND HERRING SALAD WITH BEET AND VODKA
RECIPES ON PAGE 110 AND 192

*

LAVASH CRACKERS WITH FAVA BEAN MINT DIP
RECIPES ON PAGE 110 AND 113

*

POLENTA MUFFINS FILLED WITH SALMON IN CHAMPAGNE AND SQUASH PICKLES
RECIPE ON PAGE 120

*

DOLMAS FILLED WITH WILD RICE
RECIPE ON PAGE 175

*

LAMB BALLS WITH SESAME AND CILANTRO SALSA
RECIPE ON PAGE 122

*

CROSTINI WITH CHICKEN LIVER PÂTÉ
RECIPES ON PAGE 110 AND 184
SERVE WITH:
PICKLED CUCUMBER
RECIPE ON PAGE 158

*

DRUNKEN AVOCADO SOUP SHOTS
DOUBLE THE RECIPE ON PAGE 119

*

SEASONED LABNEH BALLS IN OLIVE OIL
MAKE THE RECIPE ON PAGE 298
SERVE WITH HOMEMADE FOCACCIA, SEE PAGE 22

SET UP A DRINKS BUFFET:
ALSO PROVIDE YOUR OWN HOMEMADE DRINKS, ENABLING PEOPLE TO MIX THEIR OWN DRINKS
SUCH AS NUT WINE, VERMOUTH, GINGER ALE (RECIPES PAGES 98 & 99).
AND A LARGE PITCHER OF LEMONADE (PAGE 100) OR RHUBARB ICED TEA (PAGE 78) FOR DESIGNATED DRIVERS OR CHILDREN.
FILL A CRATE WITH ICE CUBES AND ALL YOUR DRINKS: BEER, WHITE WINE, ETC.
THIS PROVIDES YOU WITH BOTH ICE CUBES AND COOLED DRINKS.

# ON THE GRILL

\*

BOTH CHICKEN KEBABS
IN THE RECIPES ON PAGE 253

\*

LOBSTER WITH LIME, SCALLIONS, AND GINGER BUTTER

RECIPE ON PAGE 250

\*

BEEF LOIN IN HERB CRUST WITH ROSEMARY SALMORIGLIO
CUT THE MEAT INTO THIN SLICES AND THREAD THEM ON METAL SKEWERS
THEY ONLY HAVE TO BE COOKED FOR A COUPLE OF MINUTES ON EACH SIDE

RECIPE ON PAGE 256

\*

ARAB LAMB BURGERS

RECIPE ON PAGE 384

\*

SPARERIBS

RECIPE ON PAGE 231

\*

SMOKED PORK CHOPS
FIRST PICKLED, THEN SMOKED, AND THEN FINISHED ON THE GRILL

RECIPE ON PAGE 235

FLATBREAD WITH CHICKPEAS AND SAGE

MAKE DOUBLE THE RECIPE ON PAGE 273

\*

ALL SAUCES

ON PAGE 380

\*

TABOULEH WITH QUINOA, CORN, SCALLION, AND GOAT CHEESE
DOUBLE THE RECIPE ON PAGE 59

\*

ZUCCHINI PROVENÇAL STYLE
PREPARE AS MANY ZUCCHINIS AS THERE ARE GUESTS, RECIPE ON PAGE 282

\*

CARROT SALAD WITH CUMIN
TRIPLE THE RECIPE ON PAGE 274

410

# DINNER FOR 12

*

SMOKED TOMATO SOUP WITH LABNEH
DOUBLE THE TOMATO SOUP RECIPE ON PAGE 230
SERVE WITH A SPOONFUL OF SPREADABLE LABNEH ON PAGE 296
SERVE WITH COUNTRY BREAD WITH HAZELNUTS AND ROASTED CUMIN
RECIPE ON PAGE 22

*

ROTOLO WITH LOBSTER, WILD SPINACH & ROSEMARY BEURRE BLANC
SERVE EVERYONE ONE SLICE OF THE RECIPE ON PAGE 224

*

LEG OF LAMB WITH NETTLES AND GOAT CHEESE PESTO
PREPARE 2 LEGS OF LAMB FOR 12 PEOPLE, DOUBLE THE RECIPE ON PAGE 258

*

GREEN BEANS WITH WALNUTS
DOUBLE THE RECIPE ON PAGE 286

*

RÖSTI FRITTERS WITH ROSEMARY
MAKE DOUBLE THE RECIPE ON PAGE 277

*

CHEESE BOARD
RECIPE ON PAGE 295

*

SAFFRON SEMIFREDDO WITH CITRUS COMPOTE
RECIPE ON PAGE 311

*

COFFEE AND TEA WITH COCO ROCHERS,
ALMOND TUILES, AND PISTACHIO WAFERS
RECIPES ON PAGES 362 AND 363

# DINNER FOR TWO

*

MILLE-FEUILLES OF SMOKED AND RAW BEET WITH COMTÉ
WATERCRESS AND NUT DRESSING
HALVE THE RECIPE ON PAGE 243

*

WARM CUCUMBER SOUP WITH DEEP-FRIED PARSLEY
HALVE THE RECIPE ON PAGE 137

*

TROUT WITH PARSLEY AND FENNEL SEED BUTTER
DOES NOT HAVE TO BE ON THE GRILL, CAN ALSO BE COOKED IN THE OVEN, HALVE THE RECIPE ON PAGE 254

*

GRILLED FENNEL SALAD
HALVE THE RECIPE ON PAGE 270

*

SPINACH AND GOAT CHEESE BUTTER BUNS WITH PISTACHIO NUTS
MAKE THE ENTIRE RECIPE ON PAGE 25 AND PLACE THE REST IN THE FREEZER

*

RASPBERRY SORBET
RECIPE ON PAGE 315

*

COFFEE AND FILLED DATES
SEE RECIPE ON PAGE 356

# MÉNAGE À TROIS

*

SALMON TARTAR
PLAN ON 4 OZ OF SALMON PER PERSON, RECIPE ON PAGE 191

*

ONE-PERSON CHICKEN WITH SAGE, GARLIC, AND MUSHROOMS
PREPARE ALL FOUR, IT WILL BE EATEN, OTHERWISE LEFTOVERS THE FOLLOWING DAY, RECIPE ON PAGE 263

*

GREEN ASPARAGUS WITH GREMOLATA
HALVE THE RECIPE ON PAGE 286

*

RÖSTI POTATOES WITH ROSEMARY
MAKE THE ENTIRE RECIPE ON PAGE 277 AND PLACE THE REST IN THE FREEZER

*

VANILLA FRITTERS WITH ZABAGLIONE
RECIPE ON PAGE 330

*

COFFEE AND A LOT OF CHOCOLATES
RECIPES ON PAGE 362 AND 363

*

# WHAT TO COOK FOR A FUNERAL

THIS MAY SOUND STRANGE,
BUT I KNOW FROM EXPERIENCE HOW IMPORTANT FOOD IS AFTER A FUNERAL, OR IN THE WEEK SURROUNDING A DEATH.
THE SURVIVING FAMILY OFTEN DO NOT FEEL LIKE COOKING OR EATING OR HAVE NO TIME, BUT IN THE MEANTIME THE HOUSE
IS FULL OF INTERESTED PARTIES.
AS A GOOD NEIGHBOR OR FRIEND, IT IS YOUR TURN TO BRING A MEAL.

THE FOLLOWING ARE A NUMBER OF RECOMMENDATIONS:
*
SWEET POTATO SOUP WITH BUTTERED CASHEWS
TRIPLE THE RECIPE ON PAGE 143
*
ITALIAN BREAD SOUP
TRIPLE THE RECIPE ON PAGE 144
*
CHUNKY CHOWDER
TRIPLE THE RECIPE ON PAGE 134
*
GNOCCHI ALLA ROMANA
TRIPLE THE RECIPE ON PAGE 211
SERVE WITH TOMATO SAUCE
TRIPLE THE RECIPE ON PAGE 212
*
FALL PASTIE
MAKE THE ENTIRE RECIPE ON PAGE 184
SERVE WITH CRANBERRY, WALNUT, AND PEAR
RECIPE ON PAGE 158
*
LENTIL SALAD
RECIPE ON PAGE 166
WITH SLICES OF FRIED SAUSAGE
*
BOILED HAM
RECIPE ON PAGE 201
WITH A LITTLE MUSTARD, SALAD, AND RYE BREAD
*

BAKE CAKES FOR VISITORS:
BANANA RUM CAKE
RECIPE ON PAGE 84
*
ORANGE POLENTA CAKE
RECIPE ON PAGE 93
*
MAKE A LARGE POT OF SAGE & LEMON TEA, WHICH CALMS THE NERVES
RECIPE ON PAGE 76

# TABLE OF CONTENTS

*419*

# INDEX OF DISHES

*421*

422

# INDEX OF INGREDIENTS

429

*Joris*

DANK JE WEL, MERCI, THANK YOU:
OOF, JORIS, DENISE, MARIETTE, VICTOR, SOPHIE, TON, EMILIE, LIESKE, JAAP, SOPHIE, CLAARTJE, JESSICA,
MEREL, VALENTIJN, HORAS, KELLY, LAURA, ALEX, HASSANE, JOY, MONA, MAS, JESSY, MICHELLE, CHARLES,
GEORGE, JAQUELINE, MAURICE, CHRISTOPHE, NORBERT, VALERIE, MATHIS, MAGALI, NICOLAS, MAXANCE &
DE VERDERE HELE FAMILIE COLOMBET, FLORIS, FINETTE, LOLA, JULIA, PAT, JOANNA, MONIQUE, EMMANUEL,
CAROLA, CARRIE, PIETER, XAVIER, LAURENS, RENSKE, MARTIJN, NICK, ERIK, ROELAND, DAVID, PIA, ROMAIN,
ANNETTE, LAURENS, MARTIN, INGE, BARTINA, ANNE, HENNIE > TANJA
& MARIE

*Kelly, Sophie & Yvette*